# Favorite Recipes®
## of Home Economics Teachers

# MEATS

## Including Poultry & Seafood

© Favorite Recipes Press/Nashville EMS MCMLXXXI
Post Office Box 77, Nashville, Tennessee 37202

Library of Congress Cataloging in Publication Data
Main entry under title:
Favorite recipes from home economics teachers.
    Includes index.
    1. Cookery (Meat)  2. Cookery (Sea food)  I. Title:
Meats, including poultry and seafood.
TX749.F337      641.6'6        81-5383
ISNB 0-87197-134-8           AACR2

# Dear Homemaker:

The meat makes the meal! You've probably heard that since you were a child "helping" Mom in the kitchen. And through the years, no doubt you've collected dozens of favorite recipes that use meat in every possible way. But occasionally, all of us run out of ideas. That's why you're sure to enjoy this new cookbook so much!

It's filled—front to back—with hundreds of creative recipes from simple, down-home fare to specialties you'll want to save for your favorite guests. In addition, there are two bonus sections on *Poultry* and *Seafood* you'll enjoy just as much. What's more, each recipe is a personal favorite of a Home Economics Teacher across the country. The very best cooks sharing their secrets with you!

Favorite Recipes Press is proud to add the *Meats Cookbook Including Poultry and Seafood* to our ever-expanding line of Home Economics Teachers' Cookbooks. We hope this fine selection of recipes "makes the meal" for your family tonight!

*Mary June Blount*

FAVORITE RECIPES PRESS

# Board of Advisors

Favorite Recipes Press wants to recognize the following who graciously serve on our Home Economics Teachers' Advisory Board:

**Frances Rudd**
*Supervisor,* Home Economics
   Education
Arkansas Department of Education

**C. Janet Latham**
*Supervisor,* Home Economics
   Education
Idaho State Board of Vocational
   Education

**Catherine A. Carter**
*Head Consultant,* Consumer
   Homemaking Education
Illinois Division of Vocational
   and Technical Education

**Barbara Gaylor**
*Supervisor,* Home Economics
   Education Unit
Michigan Department of Education

**Louann Heinrichs**
*Home Economics Teacher*
Greenville High School
Greenville, Ohio

**Roberta Looper**
*1982 President,* National
   Association of Vocational
   Home Economics Teachers
Livingston, Tennessee

**Phyllis L. Barton**
*Past President,* National Association of
Vocational Home Economics Teachers
Alexandria, Virginia

# Contents

# MAKE THE MOST OF MEATS

For the novice approaching the meat counter, it's easy to panic. What a variety! So many types; so many cuts. It can be so confusing we can slip into a rut of preparing only familiar types of meats the same way day after day.

With the information and recipes found here, however, you'll soon feel more comfortable about buying a variety of meats and serving them in new and appetizing ways.

Starting with beef, the all-time favorite, this category also includes pork, lamb, veal—even game and variety meats. Dozens of delicious recipes certain to expand your meal-planning creativity!

## BEEF
From a juicy hamburger to elegant prime rib, beef is king of the dinner table. And with so many cuts available, it can fit every budget. However, knowing how to buy is the key to economical shopping.

### Beef Tips
- Look for beef cuts with a good covering of fat and generous marbling.
- Allow per serving: —¼ pound of boneless meat
                    —½ pound of bone-in meat
                    —¾ to 1 pound of boney meat
- Before taking advantage of that big meat sale, check your storage space.
- Do not keep fresh meat in market wrapper unless you plan to use it that day; to store meat, re-wrap loosely in aluminum foil or plastic wrap.
- Cook roasts fat side up.
- It's difficult to broil steaks accurately in a microwave.
- If you add salt to meat, do it at the end of the cooking time because it draws out the juices.

### Testing for Doneness
If you have no meat thermometer, try these time-honored tests:
- Press the surface of the meat with your finger: If it's soft, dents easily, but immediately resumes its shape, it is cooked *medium rare;* If meat remains firm under finger pressure, it's *well-done.*
- Prick meat to release juices! red juice means the meat is *rare;* pink juice means *medium rare;* colorless juice means the meat is *well-done.*

## PORK
As natural as a hot dog on the Fourth of July . . . as traditional as a Christmas ham studded with cloves . . . pork is versatile, tender, and truly a meat for all seasons. Second only to beef in popularity, it's a favorite American meat for breakfast, lunch, and dinner.

### Pork Tips
- When buying, make sure the fat is white and the lean portion pale pink. Both should be firm, not flabby.

- Don't salt pork before freezing.
- Cook bacon on broiler pan in oven. Grease goes to the bottom of the pan; bacon doesn't have to be turned.
- Cooked bacon can be frozen and reheated for later use.
- The greatest supply of fresh pork is available October-January.
- Score pork roasts yourself to make sure they're cut deep enough. Score through the outer skin and fat ¼ inch apart.

## VEAL

A delicate meat, veal is mild-flavored and exceptionally tender. However, it's probably one of the most misunderstood meats, because many cooks don't realize the variety of cuts available in addition to the traditional "cutlet."

The most tender veal comes from 6-12 week old milk-fed calves. Because of its expense, however, this veal is sold primarily to hotels and restaurants, while grocery stores stock older less tender cuts.

*Veal Tips*
- Look for veal that is grayish-pink, fine-grained and lean to buy. There should be no fat marbling.
- If meat becomes overcooked and dry, camouflage by grinding and serving in a rich sauce or in patties.
- Veal spoils easily, so it should be stored with great care.
- For an especially delicious roasted veal, insert long, thin strips of bacon at regular intervals throughout the veal.
- Use leftover veal for sandwiches, curried with rice, in casseroles.

# MEAT COOKING METHODS

*Broil*.................Generally a quick method. Slash fat edges of meat to prevent curling. Place on cold broiling pan rack. Cook 2 to 5 inches from source of heat.

*Braise*...............Brown meat slowly in small amount of hot shortening. (If desired, first coat meat with a small amount of all-purpose flour.) Pour off fat and season. Cover tightly and cook slowly in low temperature oven.

*Liquid Cooking*..For large, less tender meat cuts. Brown first in hot shortening, if desired. Cover meat with liquid. Season. Simmer in oven until tender.

*Panbroil*............Over medium heat, cook meat in uncovered skillet, without adding fat or water. Drain fat as it accumulates.

*Panfry*...............Brown slowly on both sides with a small amount of shortening in heavy, uncovered skillet.

*Roast*................Cook in uncovered roasting pan on oven rack. Place fat side up; season meat; add water or baste. Referred to as "baked" when cooking ham.

## COOKING MEAT

CUTS OF BEEF                    HOW TO COOK

| | Broil | Panbroil | Panfry | Roast | Braise | Cook in liquid |
|---|---|---|---|---|---|---|
| **BRISKET** | | | | | | |
| Corned | | | | | | x |
| Fresh | | | | | x | x |
| Stew | | | | | x | x |
| **ROASTS** | | | | | | |
| Chuck | | | | | x | |
| Pot | | | | | x | |
| Rib Eye | | | | x | | |
| Round | | | | | x | |
| Rump | | | | x | x | |
| Sirloin Tip | | | | x | x | |
| Standing Rib | | | | x | | |
| **SHORT RIBS** | | | | | x | x |
| Chuck | | | | | x | |
| **STEAKS** | | | | | | |
| Club | x | x | x | | | |
| Cube | x | | | | | |
| Flank | | | | | x | |
| Porterhouse | x | x | x | | | |
| Rib | x | x | x | | | |
| Round | | | | | x | |
| Sirloin | x | x | x | | | |
| Tenderloin (filet) | x | x | x | | | |
| T-Bone | x | x | x | | | |

| | Broil | Panbroil | Panfry | Roast | Braise | Cook in liquid |
|---|---|---|---|---|---|---|
| *FRESH* | | | | | | |
| CHOPS | x | | x | | x | |
| HAM | | | | x | | |
| ROAST | | | | | | |
|   Boston Butt | x | | x | x | | x |
|   Loin | | | | x | | |
|   Shoulder | | | | x | | |
| SAUSAGE | x | x | x | | | |
| SPARERIBS | x | | | x | x | |
| *SMOKED* | | | | | | |
| CHOPS | x | x | x | | x | |
| HAM | | | | | | |
|   Butt | x | | x | x | | x |
|   Half | | | | x | | |
|   Shank | | | | x | | |
|   Slice | x | x | x | x | | |
|   Whole | | | | x | | |
| PICNIC | | | | x | | x |
| ROASTS | | | | x | | |
| SAUSAGE | x | x | x | | | |
| SHOULDER BUTT | x | x | x | x | | x |
| BACON | | | | | | |
|   Canadian Style | x | x | x | x | | |
|   Salt Pork | | x | x | | | |
|   Slab Bacon | x | x | x | x | | |
|   Sliced Bacon | x | x | x | | | |
|   Spareribs | x | | | x | x | |

| | Broil | Panbroil | Panfry | Roast | Braise | Cook in liquid |
|---|---|---|---|---|---|---|
| CHOPS | | | x | | x | |
| CUBE STEAKS | x | x | x | | | |
| CUTLETS | | | x | | x | |
| GROUND | x | x | x | x | x | |
| ROASTS | | | | x | x | |
| STEAKS | | | x | | x | |

# Ground Beef

## Piquant Meat Loaf

1½ lb. ground beef
3 eggs, slightly beaten
¼ c. grated onion
½ c. finely chopped celery
½ c. evaporated milk
⅛ tsp. pepper
⅔ c. three-minute oats
1 tsp. salt
¾ c. catsup
6 tbsp. brown sugar
¼ tsp. nutmeg
1 tsp. dry mustard

Combine first 7 ingredients, salt and ½ cup catsup in bowl; mix well. Press into greased muffin pans. Combine brown sugar, remaining ¼ cup catsup, nutmeg and mustard; mix well. Spoon over meat loaves. Bake at 350 degrees for 45 to 55 minutes. Yield: 6-8 servings.

Lois Salter
Zwolle, Louisiana

## Economical Meat Loaf

2 slices bread
⅓ c. dry milk
1 lb. ground beef
Salt and pepper to taste
1 tbsp. minced onion
1 tbsp. Worcestershire sauce
1 egg, slightly beaten
1 slice bacon

Soften bread in ⅔ cup water in bowl. Add remaining ingredients, except bacon; mix well. Shape mixture into 1 or 2 loaves. Place in baking dish; cut bacon into thirds. Top loaves with bacon. Bake at 350 degrees for 1 hour. Yield: 6-8 servings.

Bernice J. Palmer
Preston, Mississippi

## Individual Beef Loaves

1  3-oz. can chopped mushrooms
1 egg, slightly beaten
¾ c. fine dry bread crumbs
1 lb. ground beef
1 tsp. onion salt
¼ tsp. pepper
⅛ tsp. oregano
¼ c. catsup
1 tsp. Kitchen Bouquet

Drain mushrooms, reserving liquid. Combine egg and reserved liquid in large bowl. Add crumbs; soak for 10 minutes. Add ground beef, mushrooms, seasonings and 2 tablespoons catsup; mix well. Shape into 4 loaves. Place in oiled shallow baking dish. Bake at 350 degrees for ½ hour or until lightly brown. Mix remaining catsup and Kitchen Bouquet in small bowl. Brush over loaves. Bake for 5 to 10 minutes longer. Yield: 4 servings.

Mrs. Hazel L. Seaton
Danville, Georgia

## Little Cheddar Loaves

1½ lb. ground beef
¾ c. oats
1 tsp. salt
½ c. grated sharp Cheddar cheese
¼ c. chopped onion
1 egg
¾ c. milk
1 tbsp. brown sugar
1 tbsp. prepared mustard
⅓ c. catsup

Combine first 7 ingredients in large bowl; mix well. Shape into 6 small loaves. Place in shallow baking pan. Combine remaining ingredients in bowl; mix well. Spread over tops of loaves. Bake at 350 degrees for about 35 minutes. Yield: 6 loaves.

Mrs. Mary Neighbors
Arthur, Illinois

## Italian Meat Loaf

2 slices each rye bread, white bread
1 lb. ground beef
1 med. onion, chopped
4 sprigs of parsley
3 tbsp. Parmesan cheese
1 egg
1 tsp. salt
½ tsp. pepper
2 tbsp. butter
1  8-oz. can tomato sauce
1 tsp. oregano

Soak bread in 1 cup water in large bowl for several minutes. Mash bread with fork. Add ground beef, onion, parsley, Parmesan cheese, egg, salt and pepper; mix well. Place in baking dish. Dot with butter. Bake at 350 degrees for ½ hour. Pour tomato sauce over meat loaf. Sprinkle with oregano. Bake 20 minutes longer. Yield: 4 servings.

*Mary J. Riehart*
*Pierce, Nebraska*

## Layered Meat Loaf

*1½ lb. ground beef*
*2½ tsp. salt*
*Pepper*
*2 eggs*
*2½ c. bread crumbs*
*½ c. milk*
*½ c. chopped celery*
*1 tbsp. each instant minced onion, parsley*
*1 tbsp. butter, melted*

Combine ground beef, 1½ teaspoons salt, ⅛ teaspoon pepper, 1 egg, ½ cup bread crumbs and milk in large mixing bowl. Blend well. Blend 2 cups bread crumbs, celery, onion, parsley, butter, 1 teaspoon salt and ⅛ teaspoon pepper in bowl. Layer meat mixture and dressing in 9 × 5 × 3-inch pan, using 2 layers meat mixture to layer dressing. Bake at 350 degrees for 50 minutes to 1 hour. Yield: 6 servings

*Anglee Smith*
*East Bernstadt, Kentucky*

## Lemon-Barbecued Loaves

*1 lb. ground beef*
*¼ c. lemon juice*
*1 egg, slightly beaten*
*½ c. stale bread crumbs*
*1 tsp. seasoning salt*
*1 tsp. dehydrated onion*
*½ c. catsup*
*⅓ c. (firmly packed) brown sugar*
*1 tsp. dry mustard*
*¼ tsp. each ground cloves, ground*
*    allspice*
*6 thin slices lemon*

Combine ¼ cup water and first 6 ingredients in bowl; mix well. Shape into 6 individual loaves. Place in greased baking pan. Bake at 350 degrees for 15 minutes. Combine next 5 ingredients. Cover loaves with mixture. Place lemon slice on each loaf. Bake for ½ hour

longer, basting occasionally with sauce. Yield: 6 servings.

*Mrs. Nancy R. Cumbow*
*Abingdon, Virginia*

## Olive Picnic Meat Loaf

*3 slices bread, crumbled*
*1 c. milk*
*1 egg*
*⅓ c. chopped onion*
*1½ tsp. salt*
*¼ tsp. each: pepper, ground sage,*
*    oregano leaves*
*¼ c. chopped parlsey*
*1½ lb. ground chuck*
*¼ c. chopped pimento-stuffed olives*
*4 hard-boiled eggs*
*10 lg. pimento-stuffed olives*

Combine bread, milk, egg, onion and seasonings in bowl. Let stand for 15 minutes. Add parsley, ground chuck and chopped olives; mix thoroughly. Turn meat mixture onto large piece of waxed paper. Spread to 11 × 9-inch rectangle. Place rows of hard-boiled eggs and whole olives at short end of meat mixture. Roll up meat jelly roll fashion. Seal ends of loaf. Place in shallow baking pan, seamside down. Bake in 350-degree oven for 50 minutes. Serve with Dijon mustard or catsup. Yield: 8 servings.

*Photograph for this recipe above.*

## Meat Loaf with Olive Stuffing

1 lb. ground beef
½ lb. each ground veal, ground pork
¼ tsp. pepper
2½ tsp. salt
1 tbsp. chopped onion
2 tbsp. butter
1½ c. dry bread crumbs
8 stuffed olives, sliced
1 egg, beaten
½ lb. sliced bacon

Combine beef, veal and pork in large bowl. Season with pepper and 2 teaspoons salt. Press meat into 8 × 11-inch rectangle on waxed paper. Saute onion in butter in skillet until onion is transparent. Add bread crumbs, remaining salt, olives and egg; mix well. Add ½ cup boiling water to mixture; mix well. Spoon dressing lengthwise down center of meat mixture. Roll meat to enclose dressing. Seal edges. Place meat roll in greased baking dish. Arrange bacon slices over top of roll. Bake at 325 degrees for 1 hour. Garnish with parsley and stuffed olives if desired. Yield: 12 servings.

*Catherine Dicks*
*University Park, New Mexico*

## Spicy Meat Loaf

1½ lb. ground beef
1 c. cracker crumbs
2 eggs, beaten
1 8-oz. can seasoned tomato sauce
½ c. finely chopped onion
2 tbsp. chopped green pepper
1½ tsp. salt
1 med. bay leaf, crushed
Dash of thyme, marjoram
2 green pepper rings, (opt.)
1 onion ring (opt.)

Combine first 10 ingredients in bowl; mix well. Shape mixture into loaf. Place in shallow baking dish. Press green pepper rings and onion ring into meat loaf. Bake at 350 degrees for 1 hour. Yield: 6-8 servings.

*Iona Ross*
*Freer, Texas*

## Meat Loaf Surprise

⅓ c. minced onion
1¼ lb. ground beef
Salt and Pepper to taste
1 c. bread crumbs
2 tbsp. chopped green pepper
1 tbsp. minced parsley
1 egg
½ c. milk
4 hard-boiled eggs
2 c. whipped potatoes
Paprika to taste

Saute onion in skillet. Combine with next 9 ingredients in large bowl; mix well. Spread half the mixture in well-greased 8¾ × 4¾ × 2½-inch loaf pan. Place hard-boiled eggs lengthwise down center of pan. Press remaining meat mixture firmly over top. Bake at 350 degrees for 1 hour. Unmold on ovenproof dish. Frost with whipped potatoes. Garnish with paprika. Bake unto browned. May substitute tomato sauce for milk. Yield: 8 servings.

*Leora Sayre*
*South Salem, Ohio*

## Apricot Meat Loaf

2 lb. ground beef
1 c. chopped dried apricots
½ c. dry bread crumbs
2 eggs
2 tbsp. chopped parsley
1½ tsp. salt
⅛ tsp. pepper
½ c. (firmly packed) brown sugar

Combine first 7 ingredients in bowl; mix well. Shape into loaf. Place in greased shallow baking pan. Bake at 350 degrees for 1 hour. Combine brown sugar and 1 teaspoon water in saucepan. Heat until sugar melts, stirring occasionally. Spread evenly over hot meat loaf. Bake for 5 to 10 minutes longer. Yield: 8 servings.

*Helen C. Sockman*
*Mechanicsburg, Pennsylvania*

## Meatballs in Buttermilk Sauce

1½ lb. ground beef
1 sm. onion, finely chopped
3 tbsp. chopped green pepper
⅓ c. sliced celery
1 c. cooked rice
1 tsp. salt
½ tsp. pepper

1 egg
1 2-oz. can mushroom stems & pieces
1 10½-oz. can mushroom soup
1 soup can buttermilk

Combine first 8 ingredients in large bowl; mix well. Shape into 12 balls. Place in greased 2-quart casserole. Drain mushrooms, reserving liquid. Combine reserved liquid with soup and buttermilk in bowl. Beat until smooth. Pour over meatballs. Add mushrooms. Bake at 350 degrees for 1 hour. Yield: 6 servings.

*Mrs. M. Judelle Jones*
*Turlock, California*

## Barbecued Meatballs

1 lb. ground beef
⅛ tsp. pepper
1 tsp. salt
⅔ c. milk
¾ c. oats
2 tbsp. shortening
½ c. catsup
2 tbsp. each Worcestershire sauce, vinegar

Combine first 5 ingredients in bowl; mix well. Shape into 12 meatballs. Brown on all sides in shortening in skillet. Combine remaining ingredients in bowl; mix well. Place meatballs in casserole. Pour sauce over top; cover. Bake at 350 degrees for ½ hour. Yield: 6-8 servings.

*Mrs. Julia Read Clark*
*Tracy City, Tennessee*

## Floppy Meatballs

2 lb. ground beef
2 eggs, beaten
1 c. fine bread crumbs
3 c. milk
1 onion, finely chopped
2 tsp. salt
¼ tsp. pepper
Flour
Shortening
1 can cream of mushroom soup

Combine first 7 ingredients in large bowl. Shape mixture into balls. Coat with flour; brown in hot shortening in Dutch oven. Combine soup with 1 cup water; pour over meatballs. Bake at 350 degrees for 1 hour.

*Mrs. Eleanore Dahl*
*Belgrade, Minnesota*

## Italian Spaghetti With Meatballs

1 med. onion, chopped
2 cloves of garlic, minced
2 tbsp. oil
2 c. tomatoes, mashed
1 6-oz. can tomato paste
4 tsp. oregano
2 tsp. salt
¼ tsp. pepper
1 lb. ground beef
4 slices bacon
2 hard-boiled eggs, chopped
1 slice bread, cubed
8 oz. spaghetti
Parmesan cheese

Saute onion and garlic in oil in large skillet. Add tomatoes, tomato paste, 3 teaspoons oregano, 1 teaspoon salt and pepper. Simmer for 1½ hours or until thick. Combine ground beef, remaining salt and oregano in bowl; set aside Cook bacon in skillet; drain, reserving drippings. Crumble bacon in bowl. Add eggs, bread cubes and 2 tablespoons reserved drippings. Shape into balls. Press meat mixture firmly around egg balls. Saute in bacon drippings for 10 minutes. Place meatballs in tomato sauce. Simmer for 10 minutes longer. Place cooked spaghetti on serving platter; pour meatballs and sauce over top. Sprinkle with Parmesan cheese. Yield: 6 servings.

*Mrs. Velma Cain*
*Burwell, Nebraska*

## Meatballs Wrapped In Bacon

1 lb. ground beef
½ tsp. salt
1 tsp. Worcestershire sauce
Dash of pepper
4 slices thin bacon

Combine ground beef, salt, Worcestershire sauce and pepper in bowl; mix well. Shape into 4 balls. Place 1 slice bacon around each meatball. Fasten with toothpick. Press meatball and bacon together until firm. Brown on all sides in skillet. Cover. Cook over low heat to desired degree of doneness. Yield: 4 servings.

*Mrs. Daisy Massey*
*Fredericksburg, Texas*

## Guisado

1½ lb. ground round
6 tbsp. dry bread crumbs
¼ c. grated cheese
Juice of 1 lemon
1 tbsp. parsley
1 egg, beaten
2 tbsp. shortening
Flour
1½ c. tomato juice
Salt to taste
½ tsp. chili powder
½ c. cooked elbow macaroni

Combine first 6 ingredients in bowl; mix well. Shape into walnut-sized meatballs. Brown in shortening in large skillet. Dip browned meatballs in flour; brown again in skillet. Add 1 cup boiling water, tomato juice and salt, stirring constantly. Cover. Simmer for 2 hours. Stir in chili powder and macaroni. Arrange on hot platter. Sprinkle with additional grated cheese. Yield: 6-8 servings.

Mrs. Jennie J. White
Rosemary, Alberta, Canada

## Meatball Pancakes

3 egg yolks, lightly beaten
½ lb. ground beef
¼ tsp. baking powder
½ tsp. salt
Dash of pepper
1 tsp. lemon juice
1 tbsp. each minced parsley, grated onion
3 egg whites, stiffly beaten

Combine first 8 ingredients in bowl; mix well. fold in stiffly beaten egg whites. Drop by spoonfuls onto greased hot griddle. Brown until puffed. Turn; brown remaining side. Serve immediately with mushroom sauce or creamed vegetables. Yield: 6 servings.

Mrs. Jo Belton
Marietta, Georgia

## Oriental Meatballs

1 lb. ground beef
¼ c. oatmeal
⅓ c. chopped onion
¾ tsp. salt
½ c. evaporated milk
1 No. 2 can bean sprouts
¼ c. cornstarch
½ c. soy sauce
1 4-oz. can mushrooms
1 pkg. frozen chopped spinach, thawed
4 c. hot cooked rice

Combine first 5 ingredients in bowl. Shape into balls. Saute in skillet. Drain bean sprouts, reserving liquid. Make a paste of cornstarch and ¼ cup water in small bowl. Stir in reserved liquid and soy sauce. Pour over meatballs. Bring to a boil over medium heat. Cover. Cook slowly for 20 minutes. Add mushrooms, bean sprouts and spinach. Cover. Simmer about 10 minutes or until tender. Serve over hot cooked rice. Yield: 8 servings.

Mrs. Edith Jones
Cusick, Washington

## Porcupine Meatballs

1 lb. ground beef
1 tbsp. onion salt
¼ tsp. pepper
½ tsp. chili powder
1 egg, beaten
⅓ c. rice
2 tbsp. oil
3 c. tomato juice

Combine ground beef and seasonings in bowl. Add egg; mix well. Stir in rice; blend well. Shape into 1½-inch balls. Brown meatballs in hot oil in skillet. Add tomato juice. Simmer for 35 to 40 minutes or until rice is cooked. Yield: 5 servings.

Mrs. L. L. Stewart
Otisville, Michigan

## Spicy Meatballs in Wine Sauce

½ c. chili sauce
1 can tomato paste
1 tbsp. paprika
¼ c. catsup
2 c. dry red wine
⅛ tsp. each thyme, curry powder, nutmeg
4 slices white bread, crusts removed
¾ c. milk
1 sm. onion, grated
1 tsp. salt
½ tsp. pepper
1½ lb. ground beef
1 c. flour
5 tbsp. bacon drippings

Combine first 5 ingredients with spices and 1 cup water in bowl; mix well. Soak bread in milk in bowl. Add next 4 ingredients; mix well. Shape ground beef mixture into bite-sized meatballs. Coat with flour. Warm half the wine sauce in a sauce-pan over low heat. Brown meatballs in bacon drippings in skillet over medium heat. Remove to warm wine sauce. Combine remaining sauce with pan drippings. Pour over meatballs; cover. Simmer for 1 hour, turning occasionally. Meatballs may be frozen after cooking and reheated later for 30 to 45 minutes.

*Mrs. Anna Marie Rittinger*
*St. Clair Shores, Michigan*

## Swedish Meatballs

1 lb. ground beef
½ lb. ground pork
½ c. minced onion
¾ c. dry bread crumbs
1 tbsp. minced parsley
1 tsp. Worcestershire sauce
1 egg
½ c. milk
2 tsp. salt
¼ tsp. pepper
¼ c. oil
¼ c. flour
1 tsp. paprika
¾ c. sour cream

Combine first 8 ingredients with 1½ teaspoon salt and ⅛ teaspoon pepper in large bowl; mix well. Shape into walnut-sized balls. Brown in oil in skillet. Remove meatballs; set aside. Combine flour, paprika, remaining salt and pepper; stir into pan drippings. Add 2 cups boiling water, stirring constantly. Return meatballs to gravy. Cook for 15 to 20 minutes or until tender. Remove from heat; blend in sour cream.

*Mrs. Carolyn Nordlund Arthur*
*Mayville, Wisconsin*

## Sweet and Sour Meatballs

2 eggs
3 tbsp. flour
½ tsp. each salt and pepper
1½ lb ground beef, shaped into balls
¾ c. oil
1½ c. chicken bouillon
3 lg. green peppers, diced
6 slices canned pineapple, diced
2 tbsp. cornstarch
2 tbsp. soy sauce
1 tbsp. Accent
¾ c. each vinegar, pineapple juice
¾ c. sugar

Combine eggs, flour, salt and pepper in bowl; mix well. Dip meatballs in batter; brown in oil in hot skillet. Remove meatballs; keep warm. Reserve 1 tablespoon pan drippings in skillet; add ½ cup bouillon, green peppers and pineapple. Cover. Cook over medium heat for 10 minutes. Stir in remaining ingredients. Bring to a boil, stirring constantly until thick. Add meatballs. Simmer for 15 minutes.

*Ann L. Walsh*
*Fairbanks, Alaska*

## Ground Beef-Bake Biscuit

½ lb. ground beef
½ c. quick oats
1 sm. clove of garlic, minced
Pepper to taste
⅔ c. tomato juice
¼ tsp. each salt, dill seed, monosodium
    glutamate
1 bouillon cube
3 tbsp. shortening
1 c. sliced onions
½ c. sliced mushrooms
¼ c. flour
½ tsp. Kitchen Bouquet
½ recipe biscuit dough

Combine first 5 ingredients in bowl with seasonings; mix well. Dissolve bouillon cube in ¼ cup boiling water; set aside. Shape ground beef mixture into 6 patties. Brown patties in shortening in Dutch oven. Remove; set aside. Brown onions and mushrooms in pan drippings. Stir in flour; cook until bubbly. Pour bouillon gradually into onion mixture, stirring constantly. Add Kitchen Bouquet. Cook over low heat until thick, stirring constantly. Return browned patties to Dutch oven. Spoon gravy over patties. Roll biscuit dough into circle ¼ inch thick and 1 inch smaller than Dutch oven. Cut dough into 6 wedges; arrange over gravy. Bake at 425 degrees for 20 to 25 minutes.

*Mary Sullivan Debevec*
*Chisholm, Minnesota*

## Broiled Salisbury Steaks

1 lb. ground beef
½ tsp. Worcestershire sauce
4 tbsp. barbecue sauce
1 c. crushed corn flakes
1 tbsp. Parmesan cheese
Salt and pepper to taste

Combine ground beef and remaining ingredients in bowl; mix well. Shape into patties. Place on broiler pan. Broil for 5 minutes on each side. Serve hot. Yield: 4-6 servings.

Mrs. Dixie Dunn Ruby
Charles Town, West Virginia

## Salisbury Steak with Mushroom Sauce

1 lb. ground beef
½ c. cream
1 tsp. salt
½ tsp. pepper
2 tbsp. bacon drippings
2 tbsp. flour
½ c. consomme
¼ to ½ dry red wine
1 tsp. Worcestershire sauce
2 tsp. chopped parsley
4-oz. can mushrooms

Mix ground beef wtih next 3 ingredients. Shape into patties. Brown patties in bacon drippings in skillet. Remove to heated platter. Add flour to pan drippings; stirring constantly, until smooth. Add consomme and wine. Bring to a boil. Cook, stirring constantly, until thick. Add remaining ingredients; mix well. Spoon over ground beef. Serve with rice or potatoes. Yield: 3-4 servings.

Mrs. Nancy K. Roop
Dodge City, Kansas

## Steakburger Deluxe

2 lb. lean ground chuck
Salt, pepper, garlic salt to taste
3 lg. onions, sliced
2 green peppers, sliced
1 stick butter, cut into 6 pieces
6 med. potatoes, sliced

Shape ground chuck into 6 patties. Place on heavy foil. Season to taste. Top each patty with 1 slice each onion, green pepper and butter. Arrange potatoes around patties. Seal foil.

Place in baking dish. Bake at 300 degrees for 1 hour or until tender. Yield: 6 servings.

Mrs. Lodena Waggoner
Hickory, Mississippi

## Tabasco Burgers

1½ lb. ground beef
1 tsp. dry mustard
2 tbsp. lemon juice
¼ tsp. Tabasco sauce
1 tsp. salt
1 tsp. paprika
2 tbsp. butter

Shape ground beef into 6 patties. Broil to desired degree of doneness. Place on hot platter. Combine remaining ingredients with 2 teaspoons water in skillet; stir until butter melts. Pour over patties. Yield: 6 servings.

Muriel Lehman Haig
Van Nuys, California

## Scalloped Pickle-Burger Bake

1 can cream of mushroom soup
¾ c. sweet pickle salad cubes
1 med. onion, chopped
4 med. potatoes, thinly sliced
1 lb. ground beef
1 egg, beaten
1 tbsp. dry bread crumbs
1 tsp. salt
Dash of pepper
1 12-oz. can whole kernel corn, drained
1 4-oz. package shredded Cheddar cheese

Combine soup, ½ cup pickle cubes, onion and ¼ cup water in medium bowl; blend well. Stir in potatoes. Spoon mixture into greased 12 × 8-inch baking dish. Cover with foil. Bake at 350 degrees for ½ hour. Combine ground beef with next 4 ingredients and remaining pickle cubes in bowl; mix well. Shape into 6 patties. Place in baking dish. Bake at 350 degrees for 15 minutes. Spread corn over potatoes. Top with ground beef patties. Sprinkle with cheese. Bake for 15 minutes longer or until potatoes are tender. Garnish with sweet gherkin slices. Yield: 6 servings.

Photograph for this recipe on page 17.

1½ tsp. salt
Dash of cayenne

Combine all ingredients in large bowl; mix well. Shape into 8 patties. Place on broiling rack. Broil about 5 inches from heat source for 10 minutes, turning once to brown both sides. Yield: 8 servings.

*Ouida M. Shows*
*Theodore, Alabama*

## Bunyan Burgers

1 egg
2 lb. hamburger
2 tbsp. Worcestershire sauce
1½ tsp. salt
½ tsp. garlic salt
Pepper
Grated cheese
Chopped dill pickle
Chopped onion (opt.)

Combine first 6 ingredients in bowl; mix well. Shape into 4 patties. Mix remaining ingredients. Spoon onto ½ of each patty. Fold hamburger to enclose filling. Seal edges. Place on broiler rack. Broil for 5 to 8 minutes. Yield: 4 servings.

*Colleen Lenz*
*New Prague, Minnesota*

## Campfire Kitchen

½ c. ground beef
2 slices onion
Salt and pepper to taste
1 slice green pepper
½ stalk celery, chopped
¼ chopped cabbage
½ med. carrot, grated
1 med. potato, sliced ¼ in. thick

Shape ground beef into large patty. Place onion on large piece of foil. Cover wth ground beef patty. Season with salt and pepper. Top with remaining ingredients and 1 tablespoon water. Wrap tightly. Grill for 1 hour or until vegetables are tender. May be baked at 350 degrees for 1 hour. Yield: 1 serving.

*Marilyn Q. Zakariasen*
*Drumheller, Alberta, Canada*

## Ground Beef Pepper Steak

1 lb. ground beef
1 tsp. salt
⅛ tsp. pepper
1 tsp. margarine
2 med. green peppers, cut in eighths
1 sm. clove of garlic, minced
1 tbsp. soy sauce

Mix ground beef, salt and pepper in bowl. Shape into 8 patties. Brown quickly on both sides in margarine in skillet. Remove patties to hot platter. Combine green peppers, garlic and soy sauce in skillet. Cook, stirring constantly for 2 to 3 minutes. Arrange on platter with patties. Serve with additional sauce. Yield: 4 servings.

*Mrs. E. L. Dennard*
*Hutchins, Texas*

## Brazilian Hamburgers

2 lb. ground beef
½ c. grated Parmesan cheese
1 c. finely chopped green onions
1 c. finely chopped parsley
2 eggs, beaten

## FarmHouse Hamburgers

1 tbsp. instant minced onion
2 lb. lean ground beef
2 eggs
2 tbsp. prepared horseradish, drained
1 tsp. salt
¼ tsp. sugar
1 tbsp. lemon juice
½ c. finely chopped pickled beets
½ c. light cream
1½ c. whole wheat bread crumbs
¼ c. oil
¼ c. butter

Combine onion and 1 tablespoon water in large bowl. Let stand until onion is soft. Add next 7 ingredients; mix well. Combine cream and bread crumbs; let stand 5 minutes. Add to ground beef mixture; mix thoroughly. Shape into 12 large patties. Brown beef patties in oil and butter in skillet, turning once. Yield: 12 servings.

Mrs. A. R. Sanders, Jr.
Fabens, Texas

## Nutburgers

6 slices bacon
1½ lb. ground beef
1 tsp. salt
6 tbsp. chopped nuts
3 tbsp. chopped parsley
2 tbsp. grated onion

Saute bacon in skillet; drain. Season ground beef with salt. Shape ground beef into 12 patties. Combine nuts, parsley and onions. Spread on 6 patties. Place 1 slice bacon on each patty. Top with remaining patties. Seal edges. Place patties on broiling rack. Broil about 8 minutes or until desired degrees of doneness. Yield: 6 servings.

Mary Elizabeth Kloos
La Mesa, California

## Oriental Hamburger Steaks

1½ lb. ground beef
¼ c. each oil, soy sauce
2 tbsp. catsup
1 tbsp. vinegar
¼ tsp. pepper

2 cloves of garlic
6 hamburger buns

Shape ground beef into 6 large patties. Place in 13 × 9½ × 2-inch baking dish. Combine remaining ingredients except buns in bowl; mix well. Pour over meat; marinate for 2 to 3 hours, turning occasionally. Place patties on grill 4 to 5 inches from hot coals. Grill for 8 minutes per side for medium or 1 to 12 minutes per side for well done. Serve on toasted hamburger buns. Yield: 6 servings.

Jessie D. Lombard
Windsor, Vermont

## Picnic Kabobs

1½ lb. ground beef
1 c. oats
1 egg, beaten
1 tsp. salt
1 tbsp. Worcestershire sauce
¼ c. tomato sauce
24 med. stuffed olives
4 med. tomatoes, each cut into 8 pieces
2 green peppers, each cut into 8 pieces
8 sm., whole cooked potatoes
8 button mushrooms
Barbecue sauce

Combine ground beef, oats, egg, salt, Worcestershire and tomato sauce in bowl; mix well. Shape small amount of meat mixture around each olive. Alternate 3 meatballs, 2 tomato wedges, 2 green pepper pieces, 1 potato and 1 mushroom on 8 skewers. Brush with barbecue sauce. Place kabobs over coals about 6 inches from source of heat. Cook for 5 to 7 minutes. Turn; brush with additional barbecue sauce. Cook for 3 to 4 minutes longer for medium doneness. Yield: 8 servings.

Mrs. Edith Blasi
Odessa, Texas

## Supper-on-a-Bread-Slice

1½ lb. ground beef
⅔ c. evaporated milk
½ c. cracker crumbs
1 egg
½ c. chopped onions
1 tbsp. mustard
1½ tsp. salt
¾ tsp. Accent
Dash of pepper

*1 loaf French bread, split lengthwise*
*2 c. grated pizza cheese*

Brown ground beef in skillet until crumbly. Combine next 8 ingredients; mix well. Spread evenly on cut surface of French bread. Wrap foil around crust, leaving filling uncovered. Place on cookie sheet. Bake at 350 degrees for 25 minutes. Sprinkle with cheese. Bake for 5 minutes longer. Yield: 16 servings.

*Clara M. Trout*
*Oakland, Iowa*

## Mozzarella Meat Whirl

*1½ lb. ground beef*
*½ c. soft bread crumbs*
*1 egg, slightly beaten*
*1 tbsp. mustard*
*⅛ tsp. pepper*
*3 tsp. salt*
*6 oz. mozzarella cheese, sliced*
*1 tsp. dried parsley*
*¾ c. catsup*
*1 tbsp. Worcestershire sauce*

Combine first 6 ingredients in bowl; mix well. Shape into 10 × 14-inch rectangle on waxed paper. Place mozzarella cheese slices over top. Sprinkle with parsley. Roll as for jelly roll, beginning with short end. Seal edges. Place in shallow baking dish, seam-side down. Combine ¾ cup water with catsup and Worcestershire sauce in small bowl; mix well. Pour over ground beef roll. Bake at 375 degrees for 1 hour and 10 minutes, basting frequently. Serve pan drippings in separate bowl for sauce. Yield: 8 servings.

*Mrs. Darlene Freadhoff*
*Valley City, North Dakota*

## Stuffed Picnic Rolls

*2 tbsp. shortening*
*1 sm. onion, chopped*
*1 lb. hamburger*
*Salt to taste*
*⅓ c. catsup*
*1 tbsp. Worcestershire sauce*
*1½ c. grated cheese*
*6 to 8 hamburger buns, split*
*1 tsp. prepared mustard*

Melt shortening in heavy frypan. Add onion. Saute until golden brown. Add hamburger.

Cook until lightly brown. Stir in next 4 ingredients: simmer for 10 minutes. Spread buns with mustard; fill with meat mixture. Wrap in foil; seal tightly. Bake in 275-degree oven until heated thoroughly. Yield 6-8 servings.

*Mrs. Mary Rice*
*Piedmont, South Carolina*

## Butterflake Pizzas

*½ lb. ground beef*
*2 tbsp. minced onion*
*1 tsp. thyme*
*¼ tsp. garlic salt*
*½ tsp. each leaf oregano, parsley flakes*
*Salt to taste*
*1 can butterflake-biscuits*
*1 can tomato sauce*
*¼ lb. sharp cheese, grated*

Saute ground beef and onion in large skillet. Add seasonings; mix well. Press 1 biscuit into each muffin cup. Add ½ to 1 teaspoon each ground beef mixture and tomato sauce. Sprinkle with cheese. Bake at 400 degrees for 7 to 12 minutes.

*Mrs. Margaret Leaphart*
*Bernice, Louisiana*

## Ground Beef Pizza Pie

*1 lb. ground beef*
*½ tsp. garlic salt*
*⅓ c. bread crumbs*
*⅔ c. milk*
*⅓ c. catsup*
*1 2-oz. jar mushrooms*
*¼ tsp. oregano*
*1 tbsp. Parmesan cheese*
*4 slices American cheese*

Mix first 4 ingredients together in bowl. Press against bottom and sides of 9-inch pie pan. Combine catsup, mushrooms, oregano and Parmesan cheese in small bowl. Spread over beef mixture. Garnish with American cheese. Bake at 400 degrees for ½ hour. Cut in wedges. Yield: 4 servings.

*Mrs. Jeanette Vetter*
*Kewaskum, Wisconsin*

## Spicy Pizza

½ tsp. yeast
2 c. flour
1 lb. sausage
2 8-oz. cans tomato paste
1 tsp. each whole oregano, anised
½ tsp. whole rosemary
1 tsp. each garlic salt, salt
1 med. onion sliced
¼ c. Parmesan cheese, grated
10 oz. Mozzarella cheese, grated

Dissolve yeast in ½ cup water in large bowl. Add flour; mix well. Let rest for 5 minutes. Shape into ball. Roll out into ¹/₁₆-inch thick rectangle. Place on large greased and floured cookie sheet. Brown sausage in skillet, stirring until crumbly. Drain. Add tomato paste, 1¼ cups water and spices; mix well. Spoon sauce evenly over dough. Top with onion. Sprinkle with Parmesan and mozzarella cheese. Bake at 425 degrees for 25 minutes. Yield: 4 servings.

Mrs. Joanne Beck
Cathlamet, Washington

## Chili Macaroni

2 lb. ground round
3 tbsp. oil
1 1-lb. 12-oz. can tomatoes
1 qt. tomato juice
2 c. chopped onions
1 clove of garlic, minced
Salt to taste
2 tbsp. chili powder
½ tsp. each ground cuminseed, oregano
    and pepper
1 bay leaf
1 15-oz. can red kidney beans
1 c. chopped mixed sweet pickles
2 c. elbow macaroni

Brown ground beef in oil in Dutch oven. Add next 10 ingredients. Simmer, covered, for 1 hour. Add kidney beans and pickles. Cook for ½ hour longer; remove bay leaf. Cook macaroni, using package directions; drain. Add to chili.

Myrtle Baker
Marbury, Alabama

## Italian Surprise

1 lb. ground beef
1 clove of garlic, minced

2 tbsp. chopped onion
1 tbsp. oil
1 can tomato soup
1 can tomato paste
½ tsp. each salt, pepper
¼ tsp. chili powder
1 sm. bottle whole mushrooms
1 bottle of stuffed green olives
½ lb. macaroni, cooked, drained

Brown ground beef, garlic and onion in hot oil in large skillet. Add soup, tomato paste, 1 tomato paste can water and seasonings. Simmer for 20 minutes. Add mushrooms and olives. Simmer for 10 minutes longer. Stir macaroni into ground beef mixture. Heat thoroughly. Yield: 5-6 servings.

Maudie White
Erie, Pennsylvania

## Manicotti Parmigiana

1 pkg. spaghetti sauce mix
1 1 lb. 12-oz. can whole tomatoes
1 8-oz. can tomato sauce
2 tbsp. garlic spread
1½ tsp. seasoned salt
8 manicotti shells
1 lb. ground beef
¼ c. chopped green pepper
8 oz. mozzarella cheese, diced
Parmesan cheese

Combine first 5 ingredients in large saucepan. Simmer for 20 minutes. Cook manicotti shells using package directions for about 7 minutes. Drain; set aside. Saute ground beef and green pepper in skillet. Drain. Stir in mozzarella cheese. Stuff manicotti shells with ground beef mixture. Pour ¾ of the sauce into 12 × 8 × 2-inch baking dish. Place manicotti shells over sauce. Top with remaining sauce. Sprinkle with Parmesan cheese. Bake at 375 degrees for 30 minutes. Yield: 4-8 servings.

Mrs. Sandra Faber
North Chicago, Illinois

## Pepper Steak-Cheddar Noodles

1½ lb. ground beef
¼ c. butter
⅓ c. chopped onion
1½ green peppers, cut in julienne strips
1 1-lb. can tomatoes
1 beef bouillon cube

1 tbsp. cornstarch
2 tbsp. soy sauce
1 tsp. sugar
½ tsp. salt
⅛ tsp. garlic powder
3 c. wide noodles
1 c. shredded Cheddar cheese

Saute ground beef in butter in skillet, stirring until crumbly. Remove from skillet. Saute onion and green pepper for 2 minutes. Add ground beef, tomatoes and bouillon cube. Blend 2 tablespoons water with cornstarch, soy sauce, sugar, salt and garlic powder. Add to skillet. Cook, stirring constantly, for 2 minutes. Cook noodles using package directions; drain. Toss with cheese. Serve Pepper Steak over Cheddar Noodles. Yield: 8 servings.

Mrs. Rena D. Marstiller
Valley Mills, Texas

### Spaghetti Platter

1 lg. onion, chopped
¼ c. oil
1 lb. ground beef
1 8-oz. can tomato sauce
2½ c. tomatoes
½ c. chopped celery
1 clove of garlic, minced
½ bay leaf
2 to 3 tsp. chili powder
1 tsp. salt
Dash of pepper
1 8-oz. package spaghetti
1 3-oz. package grated Parmesan cheese

Saute onion in hot oil in skillet. Add ground beef. Brown, stirring until crumbly. Add next 8 ingredients and 1 cup water. Simmer for 2 hours, stirring occasionally. Cook spaghetti according to package directions. Drain. Rinse with hot water; drain. Place spaghetti on large platter; Top with ground beef sauce. Toss to blend. Sprinkle with cheese. Yield: 6 servings.

Broxie C. Stuckey
Gordo, Alabama

### Savory Spaghetti Sauce

1 lb. ground beef
1 lg. green pepper, chopped
1 onion, chopped
1 qt. can Tomatoes, drained
3 tbsp. catsup
½ tsp. Worcestershire sauce

Few drops of Tabasco sauce
1 bay leaf
1 pkg. spaghetti, cooked

Brown ground beef, green pepper and onion in shortening in skillet. Combine remaining ingredients in saucepan. Bring to a boil. Add to ground beef mixture. Simmer for 3 to 4 hours. Serve over cooked spaghetti. Yield: 6 servings.

Lois O. Crabtree
Ceres, Virginia

### Western Spaghetti

1 lb. ground beef
3 c. tomato juice
1 tsp. salt
1½ pkg. spaghetti
1 c. grated American cheese
1 small bottle chopped salad olives
Worcestershire sauce to taste

Brown ground beef in skillet, stirring until crumbly. Add tomato juice and 1 cup water. Simmer for 15 minutes. Add salt and spaghetti. Cook for 1 hour or until tender. Add remaining ingredients. Cook until cheese is melted.

Mrs. Carol McBride
Waco, Texas

### Bayou Beef-Rice Dish

3 tbsp. shortening
3 tbsp. all-purpose flour
2 lg. onions, minced
3 lb. ground beef
½ c. minced celery
¾ c. minced green pepper
3 cloves of garlic, minced
2 bay leaves
Salt to taste
1 tsp. each cayenne pepper, pepper
2 c. rice, cooked
½ c. each chopped parsley, shallots

Melt shortening in large skillet. Add flour. Cook until lightly brown, stirring constantly. Add onions. Saute until transparent. Add next 8 ingredients. Cook, stirring constantly, until ground beef is lightly brown. Add 2 cups water. Simmer for 2 hours, adding additional water as needed to prevent sticking. Add rice, parsley and shallots. Heat thoroughly.

Sister Marian O. Carm
New Orleans, La.

## Curried Ground Beef and Rice

1 lb. ground beef
1 lg. onion, chopped
2 tbsp. oil
1 c. rice
1 can tomato soup
1 c. chopped potato
1 pkg. frozen peas
¼ tsp. garlic powder
½ tsp. each curry powder, salt

Saute ground beef and onion in oil in large fry-pan until onion is lightly browned. Add rice, soup and 2½ soup cans water; mix well. Add remaining ingredients. Cover. Bring to a boil. Simmer for 15 minutes. Garnish with sour cream or yogurt. Yield: 4 servings.

*Niva J. Reddick*
*Largo, Florida*

## Longhorn Tacos

1 lb. ground chuck
1 med. onion, chopped
1 clove of garlic, chopped
Salt and pepper to taste
20 tortillas
½ lb. longhorn cheese, grated
Shredded lettuce
1 sm. can taco sauce

Brown ground chuck with onion and garlic in skillet, stirring until crumbly. Season with salt and pepper. Drain; set aside. Keep warm. Melt enough shortening in small skillet to measure ½ inch deep. Cook tortillas in hot shortening until crisp on both sides. Fold over into half-moon shapes. Place 2 tablespoons ground chuck mixture in each tortilla. Add cheese and lettuce. Spoon sauce over lettuce. Yield: 5-6 servings.

*Mrs. Martha Brown Long*
*McCamey, Texas*

## Sloppy Joes

3 med. onions, diced
½ green pepper, diced
2 tbsp. bacon drippings
2 lb. ground beef
1 bottle of catsup
3 tbsp. Worcestershire sauce

Saute onions and green pepper in bacon drippings in skillet. Add ground beef. Cook over low heat for 20 minutes, stirring until crumbly. Add catsup and Worcestershire sauce; mix well. Cook for 5 minutes longer. Serve on hot cornbread slices.

*Mrs. Tillie Gandy*
*Weatherford, Texas*

## Best Barbecue

1 lb. ground beef
1 lg. onion, chopped
1 tbsp. each flour, sugar
1 tsp. salt
¼ tsp. pepper
1 bottle of catsup
1 tbsp. each mustard, Worcestershire sauce

Saute ground beef and onion over medium heat in skillet, stirring until crumbly. Add dry ingredients to beef; mix well. Stir in remaining ingredients until thoroughly combined. Heat through. Serve on hamburger buns. Yield: 10-12 servings.

*Mrs. Joan M. Hughes*
*Mumidia, Pennsylvania*

## Baked Tacos

1 lb. ground beef
¼ c. chopped onions
1 tsp. salt
½ c. taco sauce
1 c. tomato sauce
12 corn tortillas
1 c. grated longhorn cheese

Brown ground beef and onions in skillet; Drain. Stir in next 3 ingredients; mix well. Alternate layers of tortillas, cheese and ground beef mixture in 1½-quart casserole. Bake in 375-degree oven for ½ hour. Sprinkle with additional cheese if desired. Yield: 4 servings.

*Mrs. R. W. Shannon*
*Flagstaff, Arizona*

## Chow Mein-Cashew Casserole

1 lb. ground beef
1 med. onion, chopped
2 stalks celery, chopped
1 can chicken with rice soup
1 can cream of mushroom soup
1 8-oz. package chow mein noodles
1 c. salted cahews

Brown beef, onion and celery in skillet. Add soups and noodles. Place in buttered 2-quart casserole. Bake at 350 degrees for ½ hour. Sprinkle with cashews. Bake for 10 to 15 minutes longer. Yield: 6-8 servings.

*Mrs. Shirley Glenn*
*Circle Pines, Minnesota*

## Enchilada Bake

3 tbsp. flour
4 tsp. chili powder
3 tbsp. oil
1 lb. hamburger
½ c. chopped onion
1 tsp. salt
¼ tsp. pepper
½ tsp. garlic salt
12 tortillas
1 lb. Cheddar cheese, grated

Brown flour and chili powder in oil in skillet. Stir in 2 cups water gradually. Simmer for ½ hour. Brown hamburger with onion in separate skillet until crumbly. Add seasonings. Dip tortillas in chili powder mixture with tongs until softened. Fill center of tortilla with hamburger mixture. Sprinkle with cheese. Roll to enclose mixture. Place in baking dish. Sprinkle remaining cheese over top. Pour chili powder mixture over enchiladas. Bake at 350 degrees until cheese is melted. Serve hot.

*Marilyn Finger*
*Round Rock, Texas*

## Layered Enchilada Pie

1 lb. ground beef
1 c. chopped onion
1 clove garlic, minced
2 tbsp. butter
2 tsp. salt
¼ tsp. pepper
1 tbsp. chili powder
1¼ cans chopped olives
1 8-oz. can tomato sauce
6 tortillas, buttered
2 c. grated cheese

Brown ground beef, onion and garlic in butter in skillet. Add seasonings, olives and tomato sauce. Cover bottom of 2-quart casserole with meat mixture. Alternate layers of tortilla, meat mixture and cheese in casserole. Sprinkle with remaining cheese. Add ⅔ cup water; cover.

Bake at 400 degrees for ½ hour. Cut into quarters. Yield: 6 servings.

*Mrs. Betty Ferber*
*Covina, California*

## Easy Chili-Rice Casserole

1½ lb. ground beef
1 sm. onion, chopped
2 c. cooked rice
1 can cream of tomato soup
2 tsp. chili powder
1 c. English peas
½ c. crushed cheese crackers

Saute ground beef and onion in skillet. Add ½ cup water and remaining ingredients except crackers. Place in buttered 1½-quart casserole. Sprinkle cracker crumbs over top. Bake at 375 degrees for 20 to 25 minutes. Yield: 4-6 servings.

*Mrs. Grace Callaway*
*Greensboro, Georgia*

## Hamburger Hot Dish

1 lb. hamburger
1 8-oz. can tomato soup
1 No. 303 can corn
1 c. shredded cheese
2 c. chopped potatoes
Salt and pepper to taste

Brown hamburger in skillet, stirring until crumbly. Combine soup, corn and cheese in bowl; mix well. Alternate layers of potatoes, hamburger, tomato mixture and seasonings in casserole until all ingredients are used. Bake at 350 degrees for 1 hour. Yield: 8 servings.

*Ilene Bastian*
*Tyler, Minnesota*

## Meal-In-A-Casserole

1 No. 2½ can tomatoes
1 to 1½ lb. ground beef
2 c. thinly sliced potatoes
1 lg. onion, sliced
1 No. 2 can peas
Salt and pepper to taste

Drain tomatoes, reserving juice. Layer ground beef, potatoes, onions, peas, tomatoes and seasoning in 8 × 11-inch casserole. Add tomato juice as needed to prevent dryness during baking. Bake at 350 degrees for 2 hours.

*Mrs. Helen E. Zeh*
*Prattsburg, New York*

## Oriental Beef Casserole

1 lb. ground beef
1 med. onion, chopped
2 tbsp. butter
1 7-oz. package frozen Chinese pea pods,
    thawed
1 10-oz. can cream of mushroom soup
3 tbsp. milk
1 tbsp. soy sauce
⅛ tsp. pepper
1 sm. can chow mein noodles

Saute ground beef and onion in butter in skillet until brown and crumbly. Spoon into greased 1½-quart casserole. Spread pea pods over ground beef. Combine soup, milk, soy sauce and pepper in bowl. Pour over ground beef mixture. Sprinkle with noodles. Bake at 375 degrees for 25 minutes. Yield: 3 servings.

Mrs. Diana S. Moniz
Sepulveda, California

## Baked Vermicelli Casserole

¾ lb. each ground beef, pork
2 onions, chopped
⅓ c. diced green pepper
3 stalks, celery, diced
Salt and pepper to taste
1 4-oz. package vermicelli, cooked,
    drained
1 or 2 cans stewed tomatoes
1 can cream of celery soup
1 tbsp. Worcestershire sauce
2 c. grated Cheddar cheese
1 2½-oz. jar mushroom stems and pieces,
    drained

Brown beef and pork in large skillet, stirring frequently. Add onions, green pepper, celery, salt and pepper. Cook until vegetables are tender, stirring frequently. Add vermicelli, tomatoes, soup and Worcestershire sauce; mix well. Spoon into 9 × 13-inch baking dish. Bake in preheated 350-degree oven for ½ hour. Sprinkle cheese and mushrooms over top. Bake until cheese is melted. Almonds may be added with cheese and mushrooms.

Mrs. Mildred Anderson
Moorhead, Minnesota

## German Casserole

1½ lb. hamburger
1 green pepper, chopped
1 8-oz. package noodles, cooked
1 can whole kernel corn
2 cans cream of chicken soup
Salt and pepper to taste
1 8-oz. package process cheese, diced

Brown hamburger and green pepper in large skillet over low heat, stirring until crumbly. Add noodles corn, soup, salt and pepper. Reserve ½ cup cheese. Add remaining cheese to hamburger mixture; mix well. Pour into greased baking dish. Top with reserved cheese. Bake at 350 degrees for ½ hour.

Mrs. Vivian Hallett
Tower Hill, Illinois

## Sour Cream Lasagna

1 8-oz. package lasagna noodles
1½ lb. hamburger
1 tsp. salt
Dash of pepper
¼ tsp. garlic salt
¼ tsp. liquid smoke
1 8-oz. can tomato sauce
1 tbsp. brown sugar
1 c. cottage cheese
1 12-oz. carton sour cream
6 green onions, chopped
¾ c. grated sharp Cheddar cheese

Cook noodles according to package directions. Rinse, drain. Brown hamburger in skillet. Add next 6 ingredients; mix well. Cook for 5 minutes; remove from heat. Combine noodles with next 3 ingredients. Alternate layers of noodle mixture and meat mixture in 2-quart baking dish, ending with meat mixture. Top with Cheddar cheese. Bake at 350 degrees for ½ hour or until heated through.

Elizabeth Alderson
Meriden, Kansas

## Mock Ravioli

1½ lb. ground beef
3 lg. onions, finely chopped
1 lg. clove of garlic, finely chopped
Salt and pepper to taste
1 No. 2 can spinach
1 tsp. each rosemary, oregano and sage

½ c. parsley
1 can mushroom slices
2 cans tomato sauce
1 lb. shell macaroni, cooked
1 c. diced cheese

Saute ground beef, onions, garlic, salt and pepper in skillet. Combine spinach, herbs, parsley, mushrooms and tomato sauce in heavy saucepan; mix well. Cook 1½ hours over low heat. Layer meat mixture, macaroni and spinach mixture in greased casserole. Top with cheese. Bake at 350 degrees for 20 minutes.

*Mrs. Marlene Figone*
*Manteca, California*

## More

1 lb. ground beef
½ c. each chopped onions, green pepper
1 c. chopped celery
1 5-oz. package egg noodles, cooked
1 8-oz. can tomato sauce
1 12-oz. can niblet corn
2 tbsp. chili powder
Salt and pepper to taste
1 c. grated cheese

Brown ground beef in shortening in skillet, stirring until crumbly. Add onions, green pepper and celery. Cook over low heat for several minutes. Add noodles, tomato sauce, corn, chili powder, salt and pepper; mix well. Spoon into baking dish. Top with grated cheese. Bake at 350 degrees for 20 minutes.

*Mrs. Clifford E. Wheeler*
*Woodville, Mississippi*

## Party Casserole

1 lb. ground beef
½ c. chopped onion
¾ c. milk
1 8-oz. package cream cheese, cubed
8 oz. cooked noodles
1½ c. whole kernel corn, drained
1 can condensed cream of mushroom
    soup
¼ c. chopped pimento
1½ tsp. salt
Dash of pepper

Saute ground beef in large skillet. Add onion. Cook until tender. Stir in milk and cheese until blended. Add remaining ingredients; mix well.

Pour into 2-quart casserole. Bake at 350 degrees for 30 minutes. May freeze and bake later at 350 degrees for 1 hour and 45 minutes.

*Alma L. Wells*
*Hammond, Louisiana*
*Marjorie Bough*
*Edwardsville, Illinois*

## Savory Spaghetti Casserole

½ c. chopped onion
¼ c. chopped green pepper
2 tbsp. butter
1 lb. ground beef
1 can cream of mushroom soup
1 can cream of tomato soup
1 clove of garlic, minced
1 c. shredded sharp cheese
½ lb. spaghetti, cooked, drained

Saute onion and green pepper in butter in skillet until tender. Add ground beef. Brown, stirring until crumbly. Add soups, 1 soup can water and garlic; mix well. Heat thoroughly. Blend ½ cup cheese and spaghetti in 3-quart casserole. Add beef mixture. Top with remaining cheese. Bake at 350 degrees for ½ hour or until bubbly. Yield: 4-6 servings.

*Mrs. Phyllis Buchanan*
*Valier, Illinois*

## Spanish Delight

1 lg. onion, chopped
1 lg. green pepper, chopped
3 tbsp. oil
1 lb. ground beef
1 No. 303 can cream-style corn
1 10½ oz. can tomato soup
1 3-oz. can mushroom pieces
1 tsp. each seasoning salt, chili powder
⅛ tsp. pepper
1 tsp. Worcestershire sauce
1 c. grated Cheddar cheese

Saute onion and green pepper in oil in skillet for 3 minutes. Add ground beef. Stir fry until beef is brown. Stir in corn, soup, mushrooms, seasonings, Worcestershire sauce and ½ cup cheese. Pour into 9 × 13 × 10-inch baking dish. Sprinkle with remaining cheese; cover. Bake at 350 degrees for 30 to 40 minutes. Remove cover. Bake for 10 to 15 minutes longer.

*Mrs. Marguerite Woods*
*Modesto, California*

## Twenty-Minute Hamburger Casserole

1 lb. hamburger
1 sm. onion, chopped
1 16-oz. can mixed vegetables
1 10½-oz. can tomato soup
1 can whole mushrooms

Brown hamburger and onion in skillet, stirring until crumbly. Pour into 1-quart casserole. Add remaining ingredients; mix well. Bake at 375 degrees for 20 minutes. Yield: 2-4 servings.

*Mrs. Lynne Hatle*
*Ashley, Michigan*

## Water Chestnut Casserole

1 lb. ground beef
Salt and pepper to taste
1 med. onion, chopped
½ green pepper, finely chopped
Butter
1 can cream of celery soup
½ can evaporated milk
1 8-oz. box fine noodles, cooked
1 can water chestnuts, drained, thinly
    sliced
1 sm. jar pimentos
Italian-style bread crumbs

Saute ground beef with seasoning, onion and green pepper in butter in skillet. Mix soup and milk in large bowl. Add ground beef mixture and next 3 ingredients; mix well. Pour into casserole. Sprinkle bread crumbs over top. Dot with butter. Bake at 350 degrees for ½ hour.

*Mrs. Helen Lee*
*Falls Church, Virginia*

## Western Chili Casserole

1 lb. ground beef
1 lg. onion, chopped
½ c. chopped celery
1 15-oz. can Mexican-style chili beans
½ tsp. each seasoned salt, chili powder
2 c. crushed corn chips
1¼ c. grated Cheddar cheese
Pitted ripe olives

Saute ground beef in skillet; add onion and celery. Cook until tender; drain. Add beans and seasonings. Reserve ½ cup corn chips and ¼ cup Cheddar cheese. Line bottom of 2-quart casserole with a small amount of remaining chips. Layer cheese and chili with chips until all ingredients are used. Sprinkle center with reserved cheese. Place reserved chips around edge. Top with olives. Bake at 350 degrees for 20 minutes or until heated through.

*Charlyene Deck*
*Exeter, California*

## Upside Down Bake

1 lb. hamburger
¼ c. chopped onion
1 tsp. salt
½ tsp. chili powder
¼ c. catsup
1 12-oz. can golden whole corn
1 recipe corn bread batter

Combine first 5 ingredients in skillet. Cook until hamburger is crumbly and brown. Push hamburger to edge of skillet, forming ring. Pour corn into center. Pour corn bread batter evenly over hamburger mixture and corn. Bake at 425 degrees for 20 to 25 minutes or until corn bread tests done. Remove from oven. Let stand for 5 minutes. Turn onto hot serving plate.

*Mary Emma Briston*
*Yale, Oklahoma*

## Tamale Casserole

¾ c. cornmeal
1½ tsp. salt
1¾ c. evaporated milk
¾ lb. ground beef
6 tbsp. finely chopped onions
2½ tbsp. shortening
¾ c. canned tomatoes
⅛ tsp. pepper
2 tbsp. chili powder

Combine cornmeal and ¾ teaspoon salt in saucepan. Add evaporated milk and 1½ cups water gradually; mix well. Bring to a boil. Cook until mixture is thick, stirring constantly. Cover; cool. Brown ground beef and onions in shortening in skillet for about 5 minutes. Add tomatoes, pepper, chili powder and remaining salt. Cook until mixture is well blended, stirring constantly. Spread half the cornmeal mixture in baking dish. Cover with ground beef mixture. Top with remaining cornmeal mixture. Bake at 350 degrees for 45 minutes or until brown.

*Mrs. Jimmie Cain*
*Thrall, Texas*

## Ranch-Style Bean Bake

*1 lb. hamburger*
*2 onions, chopped*
*½ stick margarine*
*2 cans pork and beans*
*3 cans ranch-style beans*
*¼ c. prepared mustard*
*1 c. (firmly packed) brown sugar*
*¼ c. maple syrup*
*1 c. catsup*

Brown hamburger with onion in margarine in Dutch oven. Add remaining ingredients; mix well. Bake at 300 degrees for 2 hours. May be simmered slowly on top of stove. Yield: 20 servings.

*Nellie S. Moore*
*Perrin, Texas*

## Beef and Bean Barbecue

*1 lb. ground beef*
*¼ c. diced green pepper*
*½ c. each minced onion, diced celery*
*1 8-oz. can tomato sauce*
*1 clove of garlic, minced*
*2 tbsp. wine vinegar*
*1 tsp. dry mustard*
*½ tsp. thyme*
*1 tbsp. brown sugar*
*2 tbsp. Worcestershire sauce*
*Salt and pepper to taste*
*1 No. 2 can pork and beans*

Brown ground beef with vegetables in hot shortening in skillet. Add remaining ingredients except pork and beans. Blend well. Simmer for 5 minutes. Pour pork and beans into 1½-quart casserole. Spoon beef mixture on top. Bake at 375 degrees for 45 minutes. Yield: 6-8 servings.

*Mrs. Marian S. Hanchett*
*Ely, Nevada*

## Calico Beans

*1 lb. hamburger*
*¼ lb. bacon, cut into squares*
*½ c. chopped onion*
*1 No. 2 can kidney beans*
*1 No. 2 can lima beans*
*1 No. 2 can pork and beans*
*¼ c. sugar*
*¼ c. (firmly packed) brown sugar*

*1 tsp. each salt, dry mustard*
*½ c. catsup*
*1 tbsp. vinegar*

Brown hamburger, bacon and onion in Dutch oven. Drain. Drain beans, reserving liquid. Add beans to hamburger mixture; mix well. Add remaining ingredients with enough reserved liquid for desire consistency; mix well. Bake at 350 degrees for 40 minutes. Yield: 6-8 servings.

*Luella Sunderman*
*Estherville, Iowa*

## Hamburger-Bean Dish

*1 lb. hamburger*
*1 onion, chopped*
*1 tbsp. Worcestershire sauce*
*2 tbsp. chili powder*
*2 tsp. salt*
*1 can tomatoes*
*1 can kidney beans*
*1 c. crushed potato chips*

Brown hamburger and onion in skillet, stirring until crumbly. Add remaining ingredients except potato chips. Pour into casserole. Top with potato chips. Bake at 375 degrees for 25 minutes. Yield: 6 servings.

*Mrs. Petrena Forsythe*
*Fredonia, Kansas*

## Tara's Casserole

*1 lb. hamburger*
*1 med. onion, chopped*
*1½ tsp. salt*
*¼ tsp. pepper*
*1 tsp. sugar*
*10 stuffed olives, sliced*
*1 can French-style green beans, drained*
*1 No. 2½ can tomatoes*
*1 pkg. instant mashed potatoes*
*⅛ c. grated cheese*

Brown hamburger and onion in skillet, stirring until crumbly. Add next 6 ingredients, mix lightly. Pour into casserole. Prepare mashed potatoes, using package directions. Spoon around edges of casserole. Sprinkle potatoes with grated cheese. Bake at 350 degrees until golden brown. Yield: 6 servings.

*Eleanor Sturman*
*New Milford, Pennsylvania*

## Cabbage Rolls and Kraut

1 lg. head cabbage
1 med. onion, chopped
3 tbsp. butter
1 c. solid-pack tomatoes
1 c. tomato puree
1 clove of garlic, minced
Salt
¼ c. rice
1 lb. ground chuck
½ tsp. each onion powder, garlic powder,
    allspice
1 No. 303 can sauerkraut, drained
¼ c. (firmly packed) brown sugar

Trim outer leaves from cabbage; reserve. Remove core. Steam cabbage in boiling water in saucepan, core-side down, until tender. Drain; cool. Saute onion in butter in saucepan. Add tomatoes, puree, garlic, and ½ teaspoon salt. Cover. Simmer for 10 minutes. Cook rice in ½ cup boiling water and ⅛ teaspoon salt, until tender. Combine rice with ground chuck and seasonings in bowl; mix well. Stir in 1 cup tomato sauce. Layer sauerkraut in baking pan; sprinkle with brown sugar. Remove leaves from cabbage. Place ½ cup rice mixture at base of each leaf. Fold sides in; roll up to enclose fillings. Arrange seam side down on sauerkraut. Pour remaining sauce over rolls. Place coarse leaves on top. Bake at 350 degrees for 1 hour.

*Mrs. Lucilare Ansel*
*San Francisco, California*

## Baked Stuffed Tomatoes

6 to 8 tomatoes
1 lb. ground chuck
Margarine
½ c. chopped onion
1 No. 2 can tomatoes
1 tsp. each parsley flakes, dried mint, salt
½ c. rice
1 tbsp. brown sugar

Cut tops from tomatoes; reserve tops. Scoop out pulp. Wash tomatoes. Invert to drain. Brown ground chuck in margarine in skillet, stirring until crumbly. Add onion. Cook until transparent. Add remaining ingredients. Bring to a boil. Spoon ground chuck mixture into tomato shells. Replace reserved tops. Place in baking dish. Bake at 350 degrees for 1½ hours.

*Cleo Codas*
*Durham, North Carolina*

## Corn Chowder Casserole

1 lb. hamburger
⅓ c. finely diced onion
3 c. cooked macaroni
½ c. shredded American cheese
2 c. cream-style corn
1 tsp. salt
½ tsp. pepper

Brown hamburger and onion in skillet; drain. Add to remaining ingredients in large bowl; mix well. Place in well-greased casserole. Bake at 350 degrees for 20 to 30 minutes or until bubbly. Yield: 6-8 servings.

*Mrs. Jim Eckhout*
*Ansley, Nebraska*

## Kraut Squares

1 lb. ground beef
1 c. chopped cabbage
1 onion, chopped
1 pkg. hot roll mix

Combine ground beef, cabbage and onion in heavy saucepan; mix well. Cover. Steam until ground beef loses red color and cabbage is tender. Prepare hot roll mix according to package directions. Roll out on lightly floured surface to ¼-inch thickness. Cut into squares. Spoon cabbage mixture onto dough. Fold dough over filling. Seal edges. Let rise for 1 hour. Bake at 375 degrees for 25 minutes. Yield: 12 servings.

*Mrs. Lanell Long*
*Grand Prairie, Texas*

## Squash Delight

1 med. squash, cut in half, seeded
½ lb. ground beef
1 egg, beaten
1 med. onion, chopped
1 tbsp. salt
1 tsp. pepper

Arrange squash, cut-side down, in baking pan. Add a small amount of water. Bake at 350 degrees for 20 minutes. Turn cut-side up. Combine remaining ingredients in bowl; mix well. Fill center of squash with beef mixture. Bake for 40 minutes longer. Yield: 2 servings.

*Mrs. Bill Young*
*North Bend, Nebraska*

# Beef and Veal

## Beef-Biscuit Pie

½ recipe baking powder biscuits
1 c. cooked diced beef
½ c. diced celery
½ c. meat stock
¼ tsp. onion salt
1 c. grated cheese

Roll biscuit dough to ⅜-inch thickness on lightly floured board. Press into bottom and sides of 9-inch baking dish. Combine beef, celery, stock and onion salt in bowl; mix well. Spoon into pastry. Bake at 425 degrees for 15 minutes. Reduce temperature to 350 degrees. Add cheese. Bake for 5 minutes longer.

Era H. Sanders
College Park, Georgia

## Bubble and Squeak

4 tsp. salt
2 tsp. pepper
12 slices cold roast beef
4 tbsp. butter
1 head cabbage, finely chopped
½ tsp. nutmeg
2 tbsp. vinegar

Mix 2 teaspoons salt and 1 teaspoon pepper. Sprinkle over beef. Brown beef on both sides in 2 tablespoons butter in skillet. Remove beef. Set aside in warm place. Melt remaining butter in skillet. Add cabbage, remaining salt, pepper and nutmeg. Cook over medium heat until cabbage is lightly brown, stirring constantly. Sprinkle with vinegar. Cook for 1 minute longer. Serve with warm beef.

Mrs. Jean Mizak
Bridgeport, Connecticut

## Panbroiled Steak

1 or 2 sirloin steaks
4 tbsp. margarine
Juice of 1 lemon
1 tbsp. garlic salt

Brown steaks on both sides in margarine in heavy skillet over high heat. Reduce heat to medium. Add lemon juice and garlic salt. Cook for 10 to 15 minutes for well done steak. Yield: 2 servings.

Mrs. Jean Fite Moore
Clarksdale, Mississippi

## Marinated Chuck

½ c. oil
4 tbsp. lemon juice
½ tsp. each garlic powder, dry mustard, pepper
4 tbsp. Worcestershire sauce
2 tbsp. catsup
Dash of Tabasco sauce
1 boneless chuck steak, 2 in. thick

Combine all ingredients except chuck in jar. Cover tightly. Shake for 5 minutes. Place chuck in shallow dish. Cover with sauce. Marinate for 24 hours in refrigerator. Broil on rack until chuck reaches desired degree of doneness.

Barbara McDonald
Canaan, Vermont

## Beef Mortoun

2½ lb. cooked round roast, thinly sliced
2 onions, chopped
2 tbsp. butter
2 tbsp. flour
1 c. beef stock
Salt and pepper to taste
Bread crumbs

Place roast slices in greased casserole. Brown onions in butter in small skillet. Add flour; blend well. Add beef stock. Cook until slightly thick, stirring constantly. Add salt and pepper; pour over beef. Sprinkle with bread crumbs. Bake in 350-degree oven for ½ hour. Yield: 6 servings.

Mrs. Flora Schneider
Lititz, Pennsylvania

## Steak Blue Cheese

1  4-lb. sirloin steak, 1 in. thick
½ c. corn oil
¼ c. blue cheese, crumbled
½ c. lemon juice
1 tbsp. Worcestershire sauce

Score fat on edge of steak; place steak in shallow dish. Mix remaining ingredients in bowl; pour over steak. Marinate in refrigerator overnight. Drain steak; reserve marinade. Place steak on broiling rack. Broil steak 6 inches from heat source for 15 minutes on each side for medium rare, 20 minutes on each side for well done. Baste with marinade every 5 minutes. Yield: 6 servings.

*Mrs. Marilyn Musgrave*
*Robinson, Illinois*

## Steak Roll-Ups

*2-lbs. thinly sliced round steak*
*2 c. bread stuffing*
*2 tbsp. shortening*
*1 10½-oz. can cream of mushroom soup*
*½ c. sour cream*

Pound steak to flatten. Cut steaks into 8 pieces long enough to roll. Place ¼ cup stuffing near center of each piece. Roll jelly roll fashion; fasten with toothpick. Brown in shortening in Dutch oven. Add soup and ½ cup water; cover. Cook over low heat for 1½ hours or until tender, basting occasionally. Remove steak roll-ups from Dutch oven. Stir sour cream into sauce. Serve over roll-ups. Yield: 4 servings.

*Zedith Ogilbee*
*Lawton, Oklahoma*

## Teriyaki Steak

*3-lb. round steak*
*½ c. soy sauce*
*2 tbsp. brown sugar*
*1 clove of garlic*
*1 sm. piece of gingerroot*

Freeze steak for 1 hour. Slice thinly cross grain. Combine remaining ingredients in shallow dish; add steak slices. Marinate for ½ hour. Place on broiler rack. Broil 4 inches from heat source for 7 to 9 minutes. or until brown, turning to brown other side. Serve immediately. Yield: 6 servings.

*Mrs. Kathryn Whitten*
*Hanford, California*

## Beef Kabobs

*1 lb. lean beef, cut into 1½-in. cubes*
*¾ tsp. salt*
*½ tsp. each pepper, oregano*
*½ c. olive oil*
*8 ripe olives, pitted*
*2 onions, quartered*
*2 tomatoes, quartered*

Place beef cubes in bowl. Add salt, pepper and oregano to olive oil; sprinkle over beef. Refrigerate for 1 hour. Skewer beef cubes, olives and vegetables alternately using ¼ of each on each skewer. Place skewers on broiler rack. Broil until beef is brown, turning to brown evenly. Remove from skewers onto serving plate. Yield: 4 servings.

*Georgamy K. Campbell*
*Las Vegas, Nevada*

## Beef Curry with Sour Cream

*2 lb. beef steak, cut into 1½ in. cubes*
*2 onions, sliced*
*1 tbsp. curry powder*
*Salt and pepper to taste*
*1 c. red wine*
*1 c. consomme*
*½ pt. sour cream*
*1 tbsp. horseradish*

Combine first 6 ingredients in Dutch oven. Bring to a boil. Cover. Bake at 350 degrees for 2 hours or until tender. Stir in sour cream and horseradish. Serve over buttered noodles or rice. Yield: 8 servings.

*Mrs. Dorothy Deare O'Rear*
*Bellevue, Washington*

## Beef Bourguignon

*12 sm. onions*
*3 tbsp. shortening*
*2 lb. beef, cubed*
*1 tbsp. flour*
*2 c. red wine, heated*
*1 clove of garlic*
*Orange peel, bay leaf, thyme, nutmeg, to taste*
*Salt to taste*

Brown onions in shortening in skillet. Remove onions; set aside. Brown beef in pan drippings. Sprinkle flour over beef; stir well. Stir in remaining ingredients. Cover. Cook over low heat for 3½ hours. Add onions. Cook for 12 minutes longer. Garnish with parsley.

*R. Lehulze*
*San Francisco, California*

## Beef Stroganoff

3-lb. lean sirlon tip beef
3 tbsp. butter
1 lg. onion, thinly sliced
4 tbsp. flour
1 can consomme
1 can tomato soup
1 8-oz. can mushroom stems and pieces,
    drained
1 tsp. Worcestershire sauce
Salt and pepper to taste
1 carton sour cream
½ tsp. paprika

Cut beef across grain into narrow 2-inch long strips. Brown beef in butter in large skillet. Add onion; cook 2 to 3 minutes. Sprinkle flour over beef; stir well. Add consomme and soup. Cook until sauce thickens, stirring constantly. Add mushrooms, Worcestershire sauce, salt and pepper; cover. Simmer for 1 hour or until tender, stirring occasionally. Stir in sour cream and paprika. Serve over noodles or rice.

*Mrs. Margaret Hollingsworth*
*Mentevallo, Alabama*

## Family-Style Cornish Pasty

4 c. flour
2 tsp. salt
1½ c. shortening
2 eggs
2-lb. sirloin steak, cut in ½ in. cubes
6 med. potatoes, quartered and sliced
6 med. onions, chopped
½ c. suet, chopped
Salt and pepper to taste
¼ c. butter, cut-up

Sift flour and salt together in bowl. Cut in shortening until crumbly. Beat ⅞ cup cold water and eggs together in bowl. Stir into flour mixture. Roll out half the pastry into rectangle to fit 9 × 15 × 2½-inch baking pan; place in pan. Mix steak cubes, vegetables and suet together in large bowl. Add salt and pepper; mix well. Spoon into pastry; dot with butter. Roll remaining pastry to fit; cover pie. Seal edges. Cut slits in top. Bake in preheated 400-degree oven for 30 minutes. Reduce temperature to 350 degrees. Bake for 1½ hours longer. Cut into squares.

*Mrs. Marian Ahlgrimm*
*Mineral Point, Wisconsin*

## Barbecued Pot Roast

1 8-oz. can tomato sauce
½ c. beef broth
1 onion, chopped
Paprika, garlic powder, salt to taste
1 5-lb. pot roast
¼ c. each vinegar, catsup
2 tsp. Worcestershire sauce
1 tsp. mustard

Combine first 3 ingredients with paprika, garlic powder and salt in bowl; mix well. Place roast in large bowl. Pour marinade over roast. Cover; refrigerate for 12 hours. Remove roast from marinade. Brown roast slowly in hot shortening in Dutch oven. Add remaining ingredients to marinade; mix well. Pour over roast; cover. Simmer for 2½ hours or until tender. Yield: 8 servings.

*Mrs. Linda Knutson*
*Casselton, North Dakota*

## Beef Pot Roast With Vegetables

1 3-lb. chuck roast
½ tsp. pepper
4 tsp. salt
¼ c. oil
6 med. onions, peeled
6 med. carrots, scraped
6 med. potatoes, peeled, cut in half
¼ c. flour

Sprinkle roast with pepper and 2 teaspoons salt. Brown roast slowly in hot oil in Dutch oven for about 15 minutes on each side. Reduce heat; add ½ cup water. Cover. Simmer for 1½ hours, adding water as needed to prevent sticking. Add onions; cook for ½ hour longer. Add carrots and potatoes; sprinkle with remaining salt. Simmer for ½ hour longer or until tender. Remove to serving platter. Combine flour and 3 cups water in bowl. Add to pan drippings gradually. Cook until thick, stirring constantly. Serve with roast.

*Mrs. Joyce Morehead*
*Arkadelphia, Arkansas*

## Boeff Chandlier

1 3-lb. arm roast
Salt and pepper to taste
Sugar

1 tsp. each butter, oil
½ to 1 c. tomato sauce
1 tsp. Tabasco sauce
½ tsp. garlic salt
1 tsp. Worcestershire sauce
1 tbsp. brown sugar
½ tsp. each curry powder, pepper
½ c. dry Sherry
¼ tsp. smoked salt

Season roast with salt and pepper; sprinkle with sugar. Brown roast on both sides in butter and oil in skillet. Place roast in large foil-lined baking pan. Add remaining ingredients to oil in skillet. Bring to a boil. Pour over roast; seal foil. Bake at 250 degrees for 3½ hours. Venison may be substituted for roast. Yield: 6-8 servings.

*Fern S. Zimmerman*
*Clayton, New Mexico*

## Country-Style Beef Roast

*Flour*
*Salt and pepper to taste*
*1  4 to 5-lb. beef roast*
*1 onion (opt.)*

Combine flour and seasonings. Rub roast with seasoned flour. Place on rack in baking pan. Add water to depth of 2 inches. Bake in 350-degree oven until tender. Add additional water as needed to prevent sticking. Add onion during last hour of cooking. Remove roast to serving platter. Make gravy using pan drippings. Yield: 6-8 servings.

*Bernice M. Baker*
*Ruffin, North Carolina*

## Highland Pot Roast

*1  2-lb. beef rump roast*
*2 tbsp. shortening*
*8 potatoes, peeled*
*2 stalks celery, cut in 2-in. pieces*
*4 med. carrots, quartered lengthwise*
*1 tbsp. salt*
*¼ tsp. pepper*
*16 dried apricots, washed*
*1 c. sliced mushrooms*
*1 c. catsup*

Brown roast in shortening in Dutch oven over medium heat. Arrange vegetables, except mushrooms, around roast. Add seasonings.

Arrange apricots and mushrooms over roast. Top with catsup; cover. Bake in 325-degree oven for 2 hours or until tender, basting occasionally. Yield: 8 servings.

*Mrs. Wendell Bachmann*
*Colo, Iowa*

## Pot Roast Jardiniere

*1  3 to 4-lb. pot roast*
*1  10½-oz. can beef broth*
*1 tsp. salt*
*¼ tsp. each pepper, crushed rosemary*
*4 sm. carrots, halved lengthwise*
*2 med. turnips, quartered*
*8 sm. white onions*
*¼ c. flour*

Brown roast on all sides in large heavy skillet. Add broth; cover. Cook over low heat for 2½ hours. Add seasonings and vegetables. Cook, covered for 1 hour longer or until meat and vegetables are tender. Remove roast and vegetables to heated platter. Garnish with parsley. Blend ¼ cup water gradually into flour in small bowl. Stir slowly into pan drippings. Cook until thickened, stirring constantly. Yield: 6 servings.

*Mrs. Ned R. Mitchell*
*Charleston, South Carolina*

## Sauerbraten

*1  4 to 5-lb. chuck roast*
*¼ c. chopped onion*
*2 tsp. salt*
*2 tbsp. mixed pickling spices*
*1 c. red wine vinegar*
*½ c. (firmly packed) brown sugar*
*3 tbsp. flour*
*12 gingersnaps, crumbled*

Brown roast slowly on all sides in oil in heavy skillet. Add 3 cups water and remaining ingredients except gingersnaps. Simmer for 3 to 4 hours. Remove roast; keep warm. Strain pan drippings to measure 4 cups; return to skillet. Add gingersnaps. Cook, stirring until smooth and slightly thick. Yield: 8 servings.

*Barbara S. Fifer*
*Dover, Delaware*

## Tasty Beef Chuck Roast

1 3 to 4-lb. chuck roast
½ tsp. each salt, pepper
2 tsp. mustard
2 to 3 tbsp. flour
2 tbsp. oil

Rub roast with salt and pepper. Spread with mustard. Coat with flour. Brown roast in oil in Dutch oven. Cover. Bake in 325-degree oven for 2 hours or until tender. Yield: 6 servings.

Mrs. Virginia S. Sharbutt
Vincent, Alabama

## Barbecued Short Ribs

1½ to 2 lb. short ribs
2 stalks celery, chopped
1 med. onion, minced
1 tbsp. sugar
½ c. catsup
1 tbsp. vinegar
¼ tsp. Tabasco sauce
¼ tsp. chili powder
Pepper to taste
½ tsp. salt

Place short ribs in Dutch oven. Combine remaining ingredients with 1 cup water in bowl; mix well. Pour over short ribs. Add additional water to cover. Bake, covered, at 350 degrees for 2 to 3 hours or until tender. Yield: 4 servings.

Mrs. Phyllis I. Pope
Rib Lake, Wisconsin

## Cantonese Short Ribs

1 lb. 4 oz. can sliced pineapple
3 lbs. short ribs, cut into serving pieces
2 tbsp. oil
⅓ c. soy sauce
Brown sugar
1 tsp. ginger
Melted butter

Drain pineapple, reserving juice. Brown ribs in hot oil in heavy skillet. Add enough water to reserved juice to measure 2 cups. Combine juice mixture, soy sauce, 1 tablespoon brown sugar, and ginger in bowl. Mix well. Pour over ribs. Cover. Simmer for 3 hours or until tender. Brush pineapple slices with melted butter. Brown lightly under broiler. Arrange ribs on

hot platter. Garnish with broiled pineapple slices. Yield: 6 servings.

Lucile K. Lawson
Hayfork, California

## Baked Stuffed Flank Steak

1½ c. soft bread crumbs
1 tsp. salt
⅛ tsp. pepper
¼ c. each diced turnip, carrot, celery, onion
1 2-lb. flank steak, scored
¼ c. flour
¼ c. pan drippings

Combine bread crumbs, seasonings and vegetables in bowl; mix well. Place mixture on steak: roll so slices may be cut across grain. Fasten roll with toothpicks. Roll in flour. Brown in pan drippings in Dutch oven. Add a small amount of water; cover. Bake at 325 degrees for 1½ hours. Yield: 6-8 servings.

Gloria Ann Page
Dodge City, Kansas

## Barbecued Steak

¾ c. flour
1 tsp. salt
¼ tsp. pepper
1½-lb. round steak, cut into serving pieces
2 tbsp. shortening
2 tbsp. each vinegar, brown sugar, Worcestershire sauce
¾ c. chili sauce
¼ tsp. chili powder

Combine flour, salt and pepper. Pound seasoned flour into steak. Brown steak over low heat in shortening in Dutch oven. Combine remaining ingredients with ¼ cup water in bowl; mix well. Pour over steak; cover. Bake at 325 degrees for 45 minutes. Remove cover. Bake for 15 minutes longer or until tender.

Mrs. Norma Dubbe
Sturgis, South Dakota

## Beef With Cucumbers

2-lb. flank steak
¼ c. cornstarch
4 tsp. salt
Dash of pepper

¾ c. oil
8 cucumbers, peeled
1 c. chicken bouillon
2 tbsp. scallions

Cut steak into ⅓-inch strips. Place in large bowl. Sprinkle cornstarch, 2 teaspoons salt, pepper and ½ cup oil over steak strips. Mix thoroughly. Stir-fry steak in remaining oil and salt in heavy skillet. Quarter cucumbers lengthwise; slice thinly diagonally. Add to steak mixture with bouillon; cover. Cook over medium heat for 5 minutes or until cucumbers are tender-crisp. Add scallions. Serve immediately over hot rice. Yield: 8-10 servings.

*Naomi Mayes*
*Richville, Kentucky*

## Beef Grenadine

*2  4-oz. beef filets, ½ in. thick*
*Flour*
*1 tsp. butter*
*2 lg. mushrooms*
*Pinch of salt*
*1 tsp. red wine*
*3 tbsp. beef broth*

Coat filets with flour. Saute in butter in skillet for 3 minutes on each side. Add mushrooms and salt; saute for 2 minutes longer. Add wine and beef broth; simmer until sauce is slightly thick.

*Mrs. June Letcher*
*Mount Shasta, California*

## Country-Fried Steak

*1 tsp. salt*
*¼ tsp. each pepper, paprika*
*1 c. flour*
*1 egg*
*1-lb. round steak, cut in 4 pieces*
*2 c. milk*

Combine dry ingredients in bowl. Mix egg with 2 tablespoons water in separate bowl. Dip steak in seasoned flour, egg mixture and again in flour. Brown steak in shortening in skillet. Cover. Cook over low heat for 20 to 30 minutes or until tender. Remove steak. Blend remaining seasoned flour into pan drippings. Add milk. Cook, stirring constantly, for 1 minute or until thickened. Serve with steak.

*Mrs. Lynn F. Fite*
*Mount Holly, Arkansas*

## Chafing Dish Steak Bites

*1  4-lb. sirloin steak*
*Seasoned meat tenderizer*
*1 clove of garlic, cut in half*
*1 c. cooking Sherry*
*½ c. margarine, melted*
*1 tbsp. dry mustard*
*½ tsp. garlic salt*
*1 tbsp. Worcestershire sauce*
*⅛ tsp. each pepper, hot sauce*
*1 tbsp. liquid smoke*
*1 sm. can mushroom stems*

Sprinkle steak with meat tenderizer; rub with garlic on both sides. Marinate in Sherry in shallow dish for ½ hour on each side. Drain, reserving ⅓ cup marinade. Place steak in broiler pan. Broil steak until medium-well done. Cut into bite-sized pieces. Place in chafing dish. Combine reserved marinade with remaining ingredients. Pour over steak; heat. May prepare day before serving. Heat through just before serving. Yield: 5 servings.

*Mrs. Pattye Warren*
*Oxford, Mississippi*

## Creole Steak

*1  2-lb. round steak, 1 in. thick*
*3 tbsp. shortening*
*4 tbsp. flour*
*1 lg. onion, chopped*
*1 can tomato sauce*
*1 tbsp. Kitchen Bouquet*
*1½ tbsp. Worcestershire sauce*
*Salt and pepper to taste*
*1 green pepper, chopped*
*½ c. chopped celery*
*3 tbsp. chopped green onion tops*
*3 tbsp. chopped parsley*

Brown steak on both sides in 1 tbsp. shortening in large skillet. Remove from skillet; set aside. Add remaining shortening to skillet. Add flour, stirring constantly until golden brown. Add onion; cook until wilted. Add 2 cups water gradually to flour mixture, stirring constantly. Stir in tomato sauce, Kitchen Bouquet, seasoning, green pepper and celery; mix well. Return steak to skillet, spooning sauce over steak. Cover. Simmer until meat is tender. Add green onion tops and parsley. Simmer for 15 minutes longer. Serve with rice or mashed potatoes.

*Mrs. Odessa N. Smith*
*Baton Rouge, Louisiana*

## Corned Beef and Cabbage

½ c. chopped parsley
1 c. chopped celery
1 lg. green pepper, chopped
1 lg. onion, chopped
1 tsp. garlic powder
2 tbsp. oil
1 can corned beef, crumbled
1  2-lb. cabbage, cut into eighths
1 lg. can tomatoes
¼ c. Worcestershire sauce
Salt and peppr to taste

Saute first 5 ingredients in oil in Dutch oven for 5 minutes. Reduce heat to low. Add corned beef. Separate cabbage leaves. Add to corned beef. Stir in remaining ingredients. Add water to cover cabbage. Bring to a boil. Reduce heat to medium; cover. Cook until cabbage is tender.

Lynda Dean
Vidor, Texas

## Corned Beef

3 lb. beef brisket
4 tbsp. brown sugar
3 tbsp. salt
½ tsp. salt peter

Place brisket in large bowl. Dissolve brown sugar, salt and salt peter in 1 cup water. Pour over brisket; add additional water to cover. Refrigerate for 4 days, turning brisket once each day. Transfer brisket and marinade to Dutch oven. Simmer for 5 minutes; skim. Cook slowly until tender allowing 1 hour per pound. Yield: 6 servings.

Mrs. Edna A. Bouland
Lee, Florida

## Stuffed Veal Rolls

½ lb. ground chuck
1 hard-boiled egg, chopped
⅓ c. chopped stuffed olives
2 sm. cloves of garlic, minced
¼ c. chopped parsley
⅛ tsp. nutmeg
1 egg, beaten
1½ lb. veal, cut for scallopine
¼ c. olive oil
1 med. onion, chopped
⅓ c. almonds, chopped
1 16-oz. can tomatoes
½ tsp. salt
Dash of pepper
2 tbsp. dry Sherry
Whole pimento-stuffed olives
3 slices white bread, toasted, cut in half

Combine first 7 ingredients in bowl; mix well. Spread each piece of veal with meat mixture. Roll as for jelly roll. Secure with toothpicks. Brown veal rolls on all sides in olive oil in large skillet. Remove to shallow baking dish. Saute onion and almonds in pan drippings until onion is tender. Stir in next 4 ingredients; mix well. Pour over veal; cover. Bake in 350-degree oven for 45 minutes. Remove cover. Bake for 15 minutes longer. Garnish with olives and toast. Use pan drippings to make gravy. Serve with veal. Yield: 6 servings.

*Photograph for this recipe below.*

## Breaded Veal Cutlet

3 tbsp. grated Parmesan cheese
1 egg, beaten
1 tsp. minced parsley
Salt to taste
½ tsp. pepper
¼ tsp. grated nutmeg
½ c. milk
Flour
4 6-oz. veal cutlets, pounded thin
6 tbsp. butter
Juice of 1 small lemon

Combine first 7 ingredients with 2 tablespoons flour in bowl. Blend until smooth. Coat veal with flour; dip into egg mixture. Brown in 4 tablespoons butter in skillet. Remove cutlets to heated serving platter. Add remaining butter to skillet. Stir in lemon juice. Pour over cutlets. Garnish with parsley. Yield: 4 servings.

*Claudia Thomsen*
*Ashton, Idaho*

## Cheese-Veal Pie

2 c. sifted flour
1½ tsp. each garlic salt, oregano
7 tbsp. grated Parmesan cheese
¾ c. butter
1 1-lb. veal steak, cut in bite-sized pieces
2 c. tomatoes
1 c. tomato sauce
¼ c. chopped onion
1 tbsp. sugar
½ tsp. salt
Dash of pepper
4 slices Cheddar cheese

Sift 1½ cups flour with 1 teaspoon garlic salt in bowl. Add 1 teaspoon oregano and 4 table-spoons Parmesan cheese. Cut in ½ cup butter until crumbly. Sprinkle 4 to 5 tablespoons cold water over top; stir with fork until ingredients are moistened. Roll ⅔ of the dough on floured surface to 11-inch circle. Fit into pie pan. Coat veal with remaining flour. Brown in remaining butter in skillet. Stir in remaining ingredients except Cheddar cheese. Cover. Simmer for ½ hour or until tender. Turn into pastry shell. Top with Cheddar cheese. Roll out remaining dough into circle ⅛ inch thick. Place over pie; flute edges. Bake at 400 degrees for ½ hour.

*Mrs. Linda Adams*
*Duncannon, Pennsylvania*

## Easy Veal Cordon Bleu

8 3-oz. veal steaks, tenderized
4 thin slices ham
4 slices Swiss cheese
1 egg
Salt, pepper, garlic salt, onion salt to
   taste
1 c. cracker crumbs
½ c. oil
1 c. medium white sauce
1 c. sliced mushrooms
1 tbsp. grated onion

Layer 1 veal steak, 1 slice ham, 1 slice cheese and 1 veal steak. Press edges together securely. Beat egg with 1 tablespoon water in bowl. Dip steak stacks into egg mixture. Sprinkle with seasonings. Roll in cracker crumbs. Saute on each side in hot oil in skillet until golden brown. Transfer to casserole. Bake in preheat-ed 325-degree oven for ½ hour. Combine remaining ingredients in saucepan. Cook for about 3 minutes, stirring occasionally. Serve over steaks. Yield: 4 servings.

*Mrs. Dorothy Wuertz*
*Los Angeles, California*

## Mock Veal Scallopini

3 med. onions, chopped
Shortening
⅔ c. pancake mix
1 tsp. salt
½ tsp. pepper
2-lb. veal cutlets, thinly sliced
1 10½-oz. can beef consomme
1 clove of garlic, crushed
¼ tsp. rosemary

Brown onions lightly in 3 tablespoons shorten-ing in skillet; place in shallow casserole. Combine pancake mix, salt and pepper in bowl; dredge veal in pancake mixture. Reserve remaining pancake mixture. Brown veal on both sides in small amount of shortening in skillet; place on onions. Combine consomme, garlic, rosemary and remaining pancake mix-ture in skillet. Bring to a boil, stirring con-stantly. Pour over veal. Bake at 350 degrees for 45 minutes or until veal is tender. Yield: 6 servings.

*Grace W. Beaulieu*
*Dracut, Massachusetts*

## Veal-Cheese Roll-Ups

½ c. cracker crumbs
1 c. shredded mozzarella cheese
1 tbsp. minced onion
1 tsp. basil leaves
Salt and pepper to taste
1-lb. veal cutlets, tenderized
1 ½ c. tomato sauce
2 slices bacon
½ c. mushrooms, sauteed

Combine cracker crumbs, ½ cup cheese, onion, basil, salt and pepper in bowl; mix well. Spread over veal. Roll up as for jelly roll; fasten with toothpicks. Place roll-ups in baking dish. Cover with tomato sauce, bacon and mushrooms. Bake at 350 degrees for 1 hour. Sprinkle roll-ups with remaining cheese. Bake for 15 minutes longer.

*Phyllis Richards*
*Mill Hall, Pennsylvania*

## Veal Fricassee

1-lb. veal
Salt
1 clove
1 bay leaf
3 tbsp. butter
5 tbsp. flour
¼ c. white wine
1 egg yolk
1 tsp. capers
⅛ tsp. pepper

Simmer veal, ½ teaspoon salt, clove and bay leaf in 4 cups water in large saucepan until tender. Drain; reserve 2½ cups broth. Melt butter in saucepan. Stir in flour; cook until bubbly. Add broth gradually, stirring until thickened. Blend in wine. Add remaining ingredients and ⅛ teaspoon salt. Stir in veal. Heat for 15 to 20 minutes. Yield: 4 servings.

*Mrs. June Barnett*
*Onekama, Michigan*

## Veal Parmesan

¼ c. enriched flour
½ tsp. each garlic salt, paprika
1 tsp. salt
Dash of pepper
4 veal loin chops, ¾ inch thick
½ c. fine dry bread crumbs
¼ c. grated Parmesan cheese
1 egg, beaten
2 tbsp. olive oil
4 thin slices mozzarella cheese
1 lb. tiny new potatoes, scraped
1 8-oz. can seasoned tomato sauce
1½ tbsp. crushed oregano

Combine flour and seasonings; coat chops with mixture. Mix bread crumbs and Parmesan cheese in small bowl. Dip chops in egg then crumb mixture. Brown chops slowly in hot oil in skillet. Place slice of mozzarella cheese over each chop; arrange potatoes around veal. Pour tomato sauce over cheese; sprinkle with oregano. Cover. Simmer for 50 minutes or until meat and potatoes are tender. Yield: 4 servings.

*Mrs. Mary Kay S. Bisignani*
*Greensburg, Pennsylvania*

## Veal Rolls Continental

1 1¼-lb veal steak, ¼ in. thick
1 tbsp. prepared mustard
¼ c. grated Parmesan cheese
2 tbsp. snipped parsley
1 tsp. salt
1 sm. onion, finely diced
6 tbsp. butter
4 slices bread, cubed
1 tbsp. flour
1 tsp. paprika

Cut veal into 4 pieces. Spread each with mustard. Sprinkle with cheese, parsley and salt. Saute onion in 2 tablespoons butter in skillet until tender. Add bread; mix well. Sprinkle over veal. Roll as for jelly roll. Tie securely with string. Coat veal rolls with flour seasoned with paprika. Reserve leftover flour. Brown veal rolls in remaining butter in skillet. Add ½ cup water; cover. Simmer for ½ hour or until veal is tender. Transfer to heated serving platter. Remove string. Sift remaining flour mixture into liquid in skillet. Coat until thick, stirring constantly. Garnish with snipped parsley. Yield: 4 servings

*Mrs. E. Wasson*
*Bridgeton, New Jersey*

# Pork

## Bacon Pie

1½ c. sifted flour
1½ tsp. salt
⅓ c. shortening
¼ lb. bacon, cut into 1-in. pieces
2 tsp. chopped parsley
2 hard-boiled eggs, chopped
Rind of ½ lemon, grated
⅔ c. bouillon
Milk

Sift flour and ½ teaspoon salt into bowl. Cut in shortening until crumbly. Add 3 tablespoons water; mix well. Let stand for several minutes. Roll out on floured surface. Cover bottom of greased casserole with half of pastry. Arrange next 4 ingredients over pastry. Add 1 teaspoon salt and bouillon. Top with remaining pastry. Seal tightly. Brush with milk. Bake at 400 degrees for 30 minutes. Reduce temperature to 350 degrees. Bake for 1 hour longer. Yield: 6 servings.

Betty Mac Spadden
Salinas, California

## Easy Quiche Lorraine

8 slices crisp-fried bacon, crumbled
1 9-in. pastry shell, partially baked
½ lb. Swiss cheese, shredded
1 tbsp. flour
½ tsp. salt
Dash of nutmeg
3 eggs, beaten
1¾ c. milk

Reserve 2 tablespoon bacon. Place remaining bacon in pie shell. Add cheese. Combine next 5 ingredients; mix well. Pour over cheese. Sprinkle reserved bacon on top in circle. Bake at 325 degrees for 35 to 40 minutes. Cool for 25 minutes before serving. Yield: 6 servings.

Deborah Mabon
Hughesville, Pennsylvania

## Hunter's Stew

1 lb. sliced bacon, quartered
1 lb. sliced ham, cubed
1 No. 2 can lima beans
1 No. 2½ can tomatoes
1 No. 2 can whole kernel corn
1 can sliced mushrooms
2 med. cans spaghetti

Saute bacon and ham in skillet. Add vegetables, mushrooms and spaghetti. Cook for 20 minutes. Serve over toast. Yield: 8-12 servings.

Sue Belle Nance
Manila, Arkansas

## Bacon Rolls

1 c. bread crumbs
2 tbsp. butter, softened
¼ c. each nuts, raisins
Dash of pepper
½ tsp. each sage, salt
12 slices Canadian bacon
¾ c. tomato juice

Combine all ingredients except bacon and tomato juice in bowl; mix well. Spread on bacon slices. Roll as for jelly roll. Secure with toothpick. Place rolls in muffin tins. Pour 1 tablespoon tomato juice over each roll. Bake at 350 degrees for 45 minutes. Yield: 6 servings.

Mrs. Ruth Marie Scaggs
Greensboro, Pennsylvania

## Cranberry-Glazed Canadian Bacon

10 slices Canadian bacon, ¼ inch thick
1 tbsp. grated orange rind
½ tsp. sugar
⅛ tsp. cloves
Dash of nutmeg
1 c. whole cranberry sauce

Arrange Canadian bacon in 11¾ × 7½ × 1¾-inch baking dish. Combine orange rind and spices in small bowl; mix well. Sprinkle over bacon. Spread cranberry sauce over bacon. Bake at 350 degrees for 25 minutes.

Sandra M. Cuchna
Reedsburg, Wisconsin

## Canadian Bacon With Orange Sauce

12 slices Canadian bacon, ¼ in. thick
6 thin slices onion
6 orange slices, peeled
2 tsp. sugar
1 tbsp. cornstarch
1 c. orange juice
1 orange, peeled, sectioned
2 tsp. grated lemon rind

Arrange 6 slices bacon in greased, shallow 1½-quart baking dish. Top each with onion slice, orange slice and additional slice of bacon. Bake in 300 degree oven for ½ hour. Mix sugar and cornstarch in saucepan. Blend in orange juice, mixing well. Cook until thick and clear, stirring constantly. Stir in orange sections and lemon rind. Serve over bacon. Yield: 6 servings.

*Mrs. Twila Shankland*
*Westminster, Colorado*

## Asparagus-Ham Casserole

*3 tbsp. butter, melted*
*3 tbsp. flour*
*½ tsp. salt*
*¼ tsp. pepper*
*1 c. milk*
*1 No. 1 can asparagus, drained*
*½ c. diced ham*
*½ c. grated cheese*
*3 hard-boiled eggs, sliced*
*½ c. bread crumbs*

Blend butter, flour, salt and pepper in saucepan. Stir in milk gradually. Cook over low heat until thickened, stirring constantly. Alternate layers of asparagus, ham, cheese and egg slices in casserole, pouring white sauce over each layer. Top with crumbs. Bake at 400 degrees for 10 minutes or until browned. Yield: 6-8 servings.

*Mrs. Christine Moore*
*Lena, Mississippi*

## Baked Ham Roll-Ups

*1½ c. ground ham*
*⅓ c. finely chopped celery*
*5 tbsp. mayonnaise*
*8 slices bread, crusts removed*
*¼ c. butter, melted*
*1 can Cheddar cheese soup*
*½ soup can milk*

Combine ham, celery and mayonnaise in bowl; mix well. Brush 1 side of bread slices with butter. Spread with ham mixture. Roll as for jelly roll. Secure with toothpicks. Arrange rolls on cookie sheet. Brush with remaining butter. Bake in 425-degree oven for about 12 minutes. Mix soup and milk in saucepan; heat thoroughly. Serve with roll-ups.

*Rosalie Wentzell*
*Stettler, Alberta, Canada*

## Cheese-Topped Ham Sandwich

*6 slices ham*
*6 slices pineapple, drained*
*1  10-oz. can Cheddar cheese soup*
*3 English muffins, split*

Brown ham and pineapple in butter in skillet. Heat soup in saucepan. Toast muffin halves. Top each muffin half with ham, pineapple and hot cheese sauce. Yield: 6 servings.

*Marilyn Oelschlager*
*Flanagan, Illinois*

## Cuban Casserole

*1 med. onion, chopped*
*½ green pepper, chopped*
*1 lg. ham slice, diced*
*1 bay leaf*
*⅛ tsp. salt*
*2 tbsp. oil*
*½ c. black beans, cooked, drained*
*1 c. rice, cooked*

Saute first 5 ingredients in oil in skillet. Combine mixture with beans and rice in large casserole; toss lightly. Cover. Bake at 350 degrees for ½ hour or until bubbly.

*Josephine M. Jones*
*Anton, Colorado*

## Glazed Ham Balls

*½ lb. ground ham*
*¾ lb. ground pork*
*⅔ c. oats*
*1 egg, beaten*
*½ c. milk*
*⅓ c. (firmly packed) brown sugar*
*2 tbsp. flour*
*1 tsp. dry mustard*
*⅔ c. fruit juice*
*2 tbsp. vinegar*
*6 whole cloves*
*⅓ c. dark syrup*

Combine first 5 ingredients in bowl; mix well. Chill thoroughly. Shape into small balls. Place in shallow baking pan. Bake at 300 degrees for 1 hour. Drain. Combine remaining ingredients in saucepan. Cook over medium heat, stirring occasionally until slightly thick. Pour over ham balls. Bake for 15 minutes longer.

*Josephine Tupy*
*New Prague, Minnesota*

## Ham Casserole Maison

1 c. cooked ham, diced
1 c. cooked rice
1 med. onion, chopped
1 c. tomatoes, undrained
1 sm. can mushrooms (opt.)
1 sm. green pepper, diced (opt.)
Salt and pepper to taste
1 c. bread crumbs
½ stick butter

Layer ham, rice and onion in greased casserole. Add tomatoes, mushrooms and green peppers. Season with salt and pepper. Sprinkle bread crumbs over top. Dot with butter. Bake at 350 degrees until brown. Yield: 6 servings.

*Cathie Miller*
*Jackson, Mississippi*

## Ham and Egg-Filled Crepes

1½ c. milk
4 eggs
½ tsp. salt
2 c. flour
¼ c. margarine, melted
1 can cream of chicken soup
1 c. sour cream
1 c. cubed cooked ham
4 hard-boiled eggs, chopped
1 tbsp. chopped chives
¼ tsp. dry mustard
¼ c. grated Parmesan cheese

Place 1 cup water, 1 cup milk, eggs, salt, flour and margarine in blender container. Process at high speed for 1 minute. Scrape sides of container. Process for 3 seconds longer. Cover. Refrigerate for 2 hours. Bake on greased griddle over medium-high heat until brown on both sides, using 3 tablespoons batter for each crepe. Keep warm. Combine ½ can soup with remaining ingredients except cheese and milk in bowl; mix well. Place 3 tablespoons ham mixture on each crepe. Roll as for jelly roll. Place in shallow, oblong baking dish, seam-side down. Mix remaining soup and milk in bowl. Pour over crepes. Sprinkle with cheese. Bake in preheated 350-degree oven for about 20 minutes. Yield: 16 crepes.

*Ethel E. Teves*
*Bakersfield, California*

## Chili-Ham Loaf

1-lb. lean smoked ham, ground
2-lb. lean fresh pork, ground
2 eggs, slightly beaten
1½ c. cracker crumbs
½ c. chili sauce

Combine all ingredients in large bowl; mix well. Pack firmly into 9 × 5 × 3-inch loaf pan. Place in pan of hot water. Bake at 350 degrees for 1½ hours. Remove from pan. Slice to serve.

*Mrs. Hazel Speake*
*Albuquerque, New Mexico*

## Glazed Ham Loaf

1 c. bread crumbs
1 c. milk
2 eggs
1 lb. each ground ham, pork, veal
1¼ c. (firmly packed) brown sugar
¼ c. vinegar
6 cloves
½ tsp. dry mustard

Combine first 3 ingredients with ham, pork and veal in large bowl; mix well. Place in large loaf pan. Combine remaining ingredients with ¼ cup water in saucepan. Bring to a boil, stirring occasionally. Boil for 1 minute. Pour over loaf. Bake at 350 degrees for 1 hour.

*Judith Woodland*
*Lansing, Michigan*

## Ham Loaf and Raisin Sauce

1½ lb. ground smoked ham
2 lb. ground pork
1 c. each milk, tomato juice
1 c. cracker crumbs
2 tbsp. each flour, brown sugar
2 tbsp. butter
1 c. apple cider
¼ c. raisins
⅛ tsp. salt

Combine first 5 ingredients in bowl; mix well. Shape into loaf. Place in 7 × 10-inch baking pan. Bake at 325 degrees for 1 hour and 40 minutes. Combine flour and butter in bowl. Stir in cider gradually, blending well. Add remaining ingredients; mix well. Spread over ham loaf. Bake for 15 minutes longer.

*Mrs. Theresa H. Smith*
*Warner Robins, Georgia*

## Ham Tetrazzini

6 tbsp. butter
6 tbsp. flour
2 c. milk
⅛ tsp. pepper
¼ tsp. marjoram
½ c. grated sharp cheese
1 4-oz. can sliced mushrooms, drained
2 tbsp. chopped pimento
2 c. diced cooked ham
1 8-oz. package spaghetti, cooked
1 c. buttered bread crumbs

Melt butter in saucepan. Blend in flour. Stir in milk gradually. Add pepper and marjoram. Cook until thick, stirring constantly. Stir in cheese, mushrooms, pimento and ham. Place spaghetti in greased 2-quart casserole. Pour ham mixture over spaghetti. Sprinkle with bread crumbs. Bake at 350 degrees for 20 to 30 minutes. Yield: 6-8 servings.

Mrs. Miriam Bobo Templeton
Gray Court, South Carolina

## Ham in Tropical Barbecue Sauce

1 c. (firmly packed) brown sugar
3 tbsp. catsup
2 tbsp. bell pepper flakes
1 tbsp. soy sauce
1 tsp. dry mustard
1 c. crushed pineapple
1½ tbsp. cornstarch
3 center ham slices

Combine 1 cup water with first 6 ingredients in saucepan. Simmer for 10 minutes. Mix cornstarch and ¼ cup cold water. Add to sauce. Cook until clear, stirring constantly. Grill ham over charcoal, basting frequently with sauce. Yield: 8-10 servings.

Mrs. Jean H. Keithley
Peoria, Illinois

## Plantation-Style Ham Slice

1 c. (firmly packed) brown sugar
1 tsp. dry mustard
1 center slice ham, 2 in. thick
1¼ c. pineapple juice

Mix ¾ cup brown sugar with mustard in small bowl. Rub both sides of ham with mixture. Place ham in baking dish. Sprinkle with remaining brown sugar. Add pineapple juice.

Bake at 350 degrees for 2 hours or until tender, basting occasionally. Yield: 6-8 servings.

Mrs. Sanders McWhorter
Roxboro, North Carolina

## Sauerkraut-Ham Balls

1 med. onion, chopped
½ clove of garlic, chopped
¼ c. margarine
¼ c. flour
½ c. beef broth
1½ c. ground cooked ham
3 c. chopped sauerkraut, drained
1 tbsp. chopped parsley
2 eggs, beaten
¼ c. milk
Dry bread crumbs
Oil for frying

Saute onion and garlic in margarine in skillet until transparent. Blend flour and broth until smooth. Add to onions. Cook, stirring constantly, for 1 minute. Stir in ham, sauerkraut and parsley. Cook until thick, stirring constantly. Place in bowl. Chill until firm enough to handle. Shape into 1-inch balls. Mix eggs and milk in bowl. Dip ham balls into egg mixture; roll in bread crumbs. Fry in deep hot fat, 340 degrees on thermometer, until brown. Drain. Yield: 6 dozen.

Jenny L. Curtis
Orrville, Ohio

## Southwestern Ham Steak

1 2-lb. ham steak
2 tbsp. corn oil
2 tsp. each pickle liquid, molasses
⅛ tsp. each cloves, ginger
1 c. sour cream
2 sm. dill pickles, diced

Brown ham steak over high heat in oil in skillet. Place in baking dish. Mix 4 tablespoons water with remaining ingredients except sour cream and pickles. Add to pan drippings; mix well. Pour over ham. Bake at 350 degrees for 50 minutes. Remove ham to heated serving platter. Add sour cream and pickles to pan drippings; blend well. Pour over ham. Serve immediately. Yield: 4 servings.

Mrs. Anona Moore
Alvin, Texas

### Tangy Ground Ham Casserole

1 stick butter, melted
½ c. flour
1 c. evaporated milk
1½ c. ham broth
3 c. cooked ground ham
1 tsp. salt
½ tsp. each paprika, pepper, cayenne
    pepper
1 med. onion, finely chopped
1½ c. finely chopped celery
1 tsp. Worcestershire sauce
1 tbsp. mustard
Juice of 1 lemon
1 can biscuits (opt.)

Combine first 4 ingredients and 1 cup water in saucepan; mix well. Cook over medium heat until thick, stirring constantly. Add ham and seasoning. Simmer over low heat; stir occasionally. Combine 2 cups boiling water and remaining ingredients except biscuits in saucepan. Simmer until just tender. Combine mixtures; pour into large greased casserole. Top with biscuits. Bake at 400 degrees until biscuits are brown. Yield: 8-10 servings.

Juliet W. Jenkins
Sumter, South Carolina

### Glazed Ham

1 cooked ham
Pineapple rings
Candied cherries
½ c. wine vinegar
¼ c. dry red wine
¼ c. (firmly packed) brown sugar
½ tsp. pepper
¼ tsp. cloves
1 tbsp. Worcestershire sauce
1 tsp. each dry mustard, ginger

Decorate ham with pineapple rings and cherries. Mix remaining ingredients together in bowl. Brush on ham. Bake in 350-degree oven for 1 hour, basting frequently.

Mrs. D. W. Sullivan
Granum, Alberta, Canada

### Honey-Glazed Ham

1 6-lb. smoked ham
⅓ c. honey
⅓ c. (firmly packed) brown sugar
¼ c. orange juice concentrate

Score ham. Place ham, fat-side up, on rack in shallow baking pan. Bake at 325 degrees for 3 hours. Combine remaining ingredients in bowl; mix well. Baste ham with mixture during last ½ hour. Yield: 12 servings.

Mrs. Jeanette H. Stabler
St. Matthews, South Carolina

### Jezebel Ham

1 ham, baked
1 c. each apple jelly, pineapple preserves
1 tsp. pepper (opt.)
½ to ¾ c. horseradish mustard

Score ham. Combine remaining ingredients in saucepan. Heat, stirring until smooth. Coat ham generously with sauce. Bake at 350 degrees until glazed. Serve remaining sauce with sliced ham.

Carolyn Hancock
Monroe, Louisiana

### Missouri Baked Ham

1 10 to 12-lb. ham
Cinnamon
Whole cloves
½ lb. brown sugar
1 tbsp. prepared mustard
1½ c. vinegar

Simmer ham for 1 hour. Trim fat. Place ham in baking pan, trimmed-side up. Score. Sprinkle with cinnamon; stud with cloves. Spread brown sugar over ham. Add mustard and 1½ cups boiling water to vinegar. Pour into baking pan; cover. Bake at 325 degrees for 3 hours.

Jane Parnell
Fort Sumner, New Mexico

### Savory Fresh Ham Roast

2 tsp. salt
1 tsp. pepper
1 tsp. paprika
¼ tsp. garlic salt
1 tsp. rosemary leaves
1 tbsp. steak sauce
1 12-lb. leg of pork, boned
⅓ c. chopped parsley
⅓ c. chopped black olives
⅓ c. chopped green onions
3 canned pimentos, chopped

Combine first 6 ingredients in bowl; mix well. Rub half the mixture over inside of pork.

Combine remaining ingredients; stuff pork with pimento mixture. Tie securely. Score fat and skin. Rub remaining salt mixture over pork. Place pork, fat-side up, on rack in shallow baking pan. Bake in 325-degree oven for 4½ hours or to 185 degrees on meat thermometer.

*Karen L. LeClair*
*Olivet, Michigan*

## Southern Baked Ham

1  3 to 4-lb. picnic ham
5 c. milk
2 tbsp. butter
6 tbsp. brown sugar
6 tbsp. dry mustard
1 green pepper, shredded
Whole cloves (opt.)

Trim ham. Soak ham overnight in 4 cups milk. Combine butter, brown sugar and mustard. Spread on both sides of ham. Sprinkle green pepper over top. Stud with cloves. Place ham in baking pan; add remaining milk. Bake at 325 degrees for 3 to 4 hours. Yield: 10-12 servings.

*Mrs. H. W. Iverson*
*Pierre, South Dakota*

## Festive Baked Ham

1  3 to 7-lb. canned ham
¾ c. (firmly packed) brown sugar
¾ c. honey
1 No. 303 can red sour pitted cherries
2 tbsp. cornstarch
¼ c. sugar
¼ tsp. each allspice, ground cloves
Red food coloring

Place ham, fat-side up, in shallow baking dish. Combine brown sugar and honey in bowl. Spoon over ham. Bake at 325 degrees for 1½ to 2½ hours. Baste occasionally with pan drippings. Drain cherries, reserving juice. Combine cornstarch, sugar and spice in saucepan. Add reserved juice slowly. Cook until thick and clear, stirring constantly. Add cherries and red food coloring. Serve hot with ham.

*Mrs. Kathy Jepson*
*Hughson, California*

## Fresh Ham

1  4 to 5-lb. fresh ham
2 lg. onions

Salt and pepper
Monosodium glutamate to taste
2 tbsp. flour
Milk

Place ham and onions in shallow baking pan. Bake at 325 degrees for ½ hour per pound, seasoning after first hour. Place ham on serving platter. Blend flour and milk into pan drippings for gravy.

*Mrs. Hazel Jacobsen*
*Ault, Colorado*

## Baked Pork Roll-Ups

12 to 14 thin pork steaks
Salt and pepper
Prepared mustard
4 c. soft bread crumbs
½ c. raisins
½ c. chopped celery
½ c. chopped apple
2 tsp. sage
Flour

Trim and bone steaks. Render over very low heat in skillet. Remove steaks. Reserve pan drippings. Pound to ¼-inch thickness. Season with salt and pepper. Spread lightly with mustard. Combine next 5 ingredients and 1 teaspoon salt in bowl; mix lightly. Spread each steak with dressing. Roll as for jelly roll. Secure with toothpicks. Coat with flour. Brown in reserved pan drippings in Dutch oven. Add 1 cup hot water. Cover. Bake at 350 degrees for 1 hour or until tender. Yield: 12 servings.

*Mrs. Mann Nutt*
*Hohenwald, Tennessee*

## Barbecue Pork

½ c. each diced celery, onions
2 c. chopped cooked pork
½ c. catsup
1 tsp. chili powder
Salt to taste
8 sandwich buns

Cook celery and onions in ½ cup water in saucepan until tender. Remove from heat. Add pork, catsup and chili powder. Simmer for 10 minutes. Salt to taste. Serve on sandwich buns. Garnish with olive on toothpick.

*Phoebe Stout*
*Berlin, Maryland*

## Chow Mein

1 med. onion, chopped
¼ c. butter
2 c. diced celery
1 tsp. each salt, monosodium glutamate
Dash of pepper
1  1-lb. can bean sprouts, drained
2 c. cooked diced pork
2 tbsp. cornstarch
1 tbsp. soy sauce
1 tsp. sugar

Saute onion in butter in skillet for 3 minutes. Add celery, seasonings and 1½ cups hot water. Cover. Cook for 5 minutes. Add bean sprouts and pork; mix thoroughly. Cook for 5 minutes longer. Combine remaining ingredients with 2 tablespoons cold water in bowl; mix well. Add to meat mixture. Cook for 1 minute, stirring constantly. Serve with chow mein noodles. Garnish with sliced green onions or sliced hard-boiled eggs. Yield: 4-6 servings.

*Barbara Reynolds*
*Arco, Idaho*

## Chow Mein Casserole

½ lb. round steak, cubed
1 lb. pork, cubed
1½ c. diced onions
1½ tsp. each salt, pepper
1½ c. each bean sprouts, sliced celery
6 radishes peeled, sliced
4 tbsp. cornstarch
1 tbsp. soy sauce
1½ tsp. sugar

Saute steak and pork in skillet. Add onions; cook until transparent. Add salt, pepper, celery and 1½ cups hot water. Cook for 10 minutes. Add bean sprouts and radishes. Pour mixture into casserole. Combine remaining ingredients with ½ cup cold water in bowl. Mix well. Pour over meat mixture. Bake at 350 degrees for 10 minutes. Serve hot. Yield: 6 servings.

*LeNora Hudson*
*Sulphur, Oklahoma*

## Chop Suey

1 c. cubed lean pork
1 c. chopped celery
1 med. onion, chopped
2 No. 303 cans bean sprouts
1 c. chopped mushrooms
2 tbsp. soy sauce
1 tsp. salt
Cornstarch
3 c. cooked rice

Saute pork, celery and onion in skillet for 20 minutes. Add bean sprouts and a small amount of water; cover. Simmer for 15 to 20 minutes. Add mushrooms, soy sauce and salt; stir well. Mix a small amount of cornstarch and water together in bowl. Add to mixture. Cook until thick, stirring constantly. Remove from heat. Serve at once over rice. Yield: 6 servings.

*Charlotte K. Macy*
*Ottawa, Kansas*

## Island Chop Suey

1  8-oz. can mushrooms
1 sm. can bamboo shoots
1 can bean sprouts
1¼ lb. veal steak, cubed
½ lb. pork steak, cubed
3 c. finely chopped celery
2 c. finely chopped onions
1 sm. can water chestnuts, drained
4 tsp. flour
1 tsp. salt
3 tbsp. soy sauce

Drain liquid from mushrooms, bamboo shoots and bean sprouts, reserving liquid. Add enough water to reserved liquid to measure 1¾ cups. Saute veal and pork in skillet. Add celery, onions and reserved liquid. Cook over low heat for 35 minutes. Slice water chestnuts. Stir into meat mixture with remaining vegetables. Combine flour, salt, 2 tablespoons water and soy sauce in bowl. Stir to make smooth paste. Add to meat mixture, stirring until thick.

*Mrs. Cheryl Assenheimer*
*Avon Lake, Ohio*

## Mandarin Pork Balls

1 lb. lean ground pork
1 tbsp. minced pimento
Dash of hot pepper sauce
Pinch of pepper
1 clove of garlic, crushed
1 tbsp. minced onion tops
1 egg

6 tbsp. flour
1 tbsp. minced spring onion
3 tsp. salt
3 tbsp. soy sauce

Combine first 9 ingredients with 1 teaspoon salt and 1 tablespoon soy sauce in bowl; mix well. Shape mixture into walnut-sized balls with floured hands. Combine remaining salt and soy sauce with 1 quart water in saucepan. Bring to a boil. Drop meatballs into boiling liquid. Lower heat to medium; cook for 45 minutes. Serve with tender-crisp green peas or spinach. Yield: 6 servings.

*Mrs. Olive Weidman*
*Robesania, Pennsylvania*

## Pigs in Blanket

½ lb. rice
1 head cabbage
1 onion, chopped
1 tbsp. shortening
1½ lb. ground pork
Salt and pepper to taste
1 egg
1 lg. can sauerkraut
1 qt. tomatoes

Place rice in hot water in bowl. Soak until soft; drain. Cook cabbage until soft and limp. Drain; cool. Separate cabbage leaves; set aside. Saute onion in shortening in skillet until transparent. Combine ground pork, seasoning and rice. Add egg, onion and pan drippings; mix well. Place mixture on cabbage leaves. Fold sides in; roll up to enclose filling. Alternate layers of sauerkraut and cabbage rolls in Dutch oven. Spread with tomatoes. Bring to boil. Cover. Cook over medium heat for 1½ hours or until tender. Yield: 8-10 servings.

*Mary Barbara Hardy*
*Farrell, Pennsylvania*

## Pork Shanks and Beans with Dumplings

4 lg. pork shanks
1 lb. navy beans
2 med. onions, sliced
1½ tsp. salt
Pepper to taste
2 lg. potatoes, peeled, chopped
2 c. flour

3 tsp. baking powder
½ tsp. salt
2 tsp. butter
⅔ c. milk

Place pork shanks in cold water to cover in large stockpot. Bring to a boil. Skim. Reduce heat to low. Cook until tender. Remove skin and bones from shanks. Reserve broth and lean meat. Set aside. Soak beans in water to cover in large saucepan for several hours or overnight. Cook slowly until almost tender. Drain. Combine broth, lean pork, onions, 1 teaspoon salt, pepper and beans in large stockpot. Simmer over medium heat. Add potatoes to meat mixture. Cook for 10 minutes. Sift ½ teaspoon salt and dry ingredients together in bowl. Cut butter into flour until mixture is crumbly. Add milk gradually, stirring to make soft dough. Drop by spoonfuls over pork mixture. Cover. Steam for 12 minutes. Yield: 6-8 servings.

*Mrs. Mary K. Adams*
*New Troy, Michigan*

## Sweet and Sour Pork

1-lb. lean pork, cubed
¼ tsp. salt
1 c. diced celery
½ c. diced onion
1 No. 1 can mushrooms
4 tbsp. butter
1 No. 2 can crushed pineapple
3 tbsp. sugar
1 tbsp. cornstarch
3 tbsp. vinegar
1 tbsp. soy sauce

Parboil pork in 1 cup salted water in saucepan. Drain. Saute celery, onion and mushrooms in 2 tablespoons butter in Dutch oven for 5 minutes. Add pineapple. Bring to a boil. Combine sugar, cornstarch, vinegar and soy sauce in bowl; mix well. Add to pineapple mixture. Cook until thick, stirring constantly. Melt remaining butter in Dutch oven. Add pork. Cook for 5 minutes, stirring constantly. Pour pineapple mixture over pork. Cover. Bake at 350 degrees for 45 minutes. Serve with rice or baked potato.

*Mrs. Georgia Short*
*Dell City, Texas*

## Apple-Stuffed Pork Chops

4 double pork chops with pockets
Salt and pepper to taste
1 tart apple, sliced
2 tsp. brown sugar
1 egg
Soft bread crumbs

Season pork chops with salt and pepper. Toss apple with brown sugar. Stuff chops with apple mixture. Beat egg lightly with 1 tablespoon water. Dip chops in egg mixture. Coat with bread crumbs. Brown chops in small amount of shortening in Dutch oven. Add 1 cup water; cover tightly. Bake at 350 degrees for 45 minutes or until tender.

*Mrs. Emma Lou Schwagel*
*Boonsboro, Maryland*

## Arabian Pork Chops

4 shoulder pork chops
2 onions, sliced
2 tomatoes, sliced
2 tbsp. chopped green pepper
2 tbsp. flour
1 tsp. salt

Brown pork chops on both sides in skillet. Drain, reserving 2 tablespoons pan drippings. Place pork chops in shallow casserole. Arrange onion and tomato slices on each chop. Sprinkle with green pepper. Stir flour and salt into reserved pan drippings in skillet. Stir in 1 cup water gradually. Cook until thick, stirring constantly. Pour over chops. Cover. Bake at 350 degrees for 1¼ hours or until tender. Yield: 4 servings.

*Mrs. Joanne G. Thomas*
*Greencastle, Pennsylvania*

## Crispy Baked Pork Chops

4 to 6 lean pork chops, ½ to 1 in. thick
1 egg, beaten
Salt and pepper to taste
Corn flakes, crushed
Butter

Dip pork chops into egg seasoned with salt and pepper. Roll in corn flake crumbs. Melt 2 tablespoons butter in baking dish. Place pork chops in baking dish; dot with butter. Bake at 375 degrees for ½ hour, turning once to brown both sides. Cover baking dish with foil. Reduce temperature to 350 degrees. Bake for 1 hour longer. Yield: 4-6 servings.

*Mary Ann Watters*
*Herington, Kansas*

## Baked Pork Chops with Apples

6 thick pork shoulder chops
Salt to taste
6 tart apples
¼ c. sugar

Brown chops in skillet. Sprinkle with salt. Cut apples into 1 inch slices. Place chops in casserole. Top with apples. Add ¼ cup water. Sprinkle lightly with salt and sugar. Cover. Bake at 350 degrees for 45 minutes to 1 hour or until tender. Yield: 6 servings.

*Kathryn Woods*
*Beckley, West Virginia*

## Baked Pork Chops and Sauerkraut

1 can sauerkraut
4 thick pork chops
1 tsp. pepper
½ tsp. salt

Place sauerkraut in bottom of casserole. Top with pork chops, season with salt and pepper. Cover. Bake at 350 degrees for 1 hour. Remove cover. Bake for 20 minutes longer or until pork chops are brown. Yield: 4 servings.

*Barbara Ann Dunbury*
*Woburn, Massachusetts*

## Barbecued Pork Chops

6 lean pork chops
2 tbsp. shortening
Salt and pepper to taste
1 green pepper, sliced
1 onion, sliced
1 bottle chili sauce

Brown pork chops on both sides in shortening in skillet. Cook over medium heat for 15 minutes. Season. Place slice of green pepper on each pork chop. Place onion slice inside green pepper ring. Combine chili sauce with 1 cup water in bowl. Pour over chops. Cover. Reduce heat. Simmer for 25 to 30 minutes or until chops are tender. Yield: 6 servings.

*Sister M. Isabel, S.S.N.D.*
*Roxbury, Massachusetts*

## Braised Pork Chops with Grapefruit

Flour
4 pork chops, 1 in. thick
2 tbsp. unsalted butter
1 tbsp. oil
2 sm. onions, sliced, separated
2 fresh pears, quartered
1 tsp. dried leaf marjoram
¼ tsp. cinnamon
2 Florida grapefruits, sectioned

Flour pork chops liberally on both sides. Heat butter and oil in large skillet over medium heat. Brown pork chops on both sides. Remove from skillet. Saute onion rings in pan drippings in skillet. Return chops to skillet. Add pears and ½ cup water; sprinkle with marjoram and cinnamon. Cook over low heat for 1 hour and 15 minutes or until chops are tender and sauce is thick. Add grapefruit sections; heat briefly. Serve immediately. Yield: 4 servings.

*Photograph for this recipe on cover.*

## California Pork Chops

6 pork loin chops
Salt and pepper
1 tbsp. shortening
1 clove of garlic, slit
2 tbsp. cornstarch
½ tsp. rosemary
2 tbsp. lemon juice
6 lemon slices, ¼ in. thick

Sprinkle pork chops with salt and pepper to taste. Brown on each side in hot shortening in heavy skillet. Add garlic. Cook for 1 minute longer. Remove chops and garlic to warm serving platter. Reserve a small amount of pan drippings. Combine cornstarch, ½ teaspoon salt and rosemary with ¼ cup cold water; mix well. Add to pan drippings gradually, stirring constantly. Cook until thick and smooth. Add 1¼ cup hot water gradually, stirring constantly. Cook until smooth. Add lemon juice. Return pork chops to skillet. Add lemon slices to sauce. Cover. Simmer for 40 to 50 minutes or until tender. Yield: 6 servings.

*Ruby Jo Bonds*
*Killeen, Texas*

## Meadow Pork Casserole

6 pork chops
1 tsp. salt
Pepper to taste
Flour
2 tbsp. chopped onion
Chopped green pepper to taste
3 tbsp. shortening
1 c. rice
1 No. 2 can stewed tomatoes

Season pork chops with salt and pepper; coat with flour. Brown chops, onion and green pepper in shortening in skillet. Place rice in greased casserole; top with tomatoes. Arrange chops, onion and green pepper over tomatoes. Cover. Bake at 350 degrees for 1 hour or until liquid is absorbed. Yield: 6 servings.

*Patty Maxwell*
*Gadsden, Alabama*

## Pork Chop Scallop

6 pork chops
5 tbsp. butter
4 med. potatoes, pared, sliced
1 sm. onion, chopped
2 tbsp. flour
1 tsp. salt
¼ tsp. pepper
2 c. milk
1 tsp. soy sauce
½ c. sliced water chestnuts

Brown pork chops on both sides in 3 tablespoons butter in skillet. Drain. Cook potatoes in boiling salted water for 5 minutes. Drain. Saute onion in remaining butter, in skillet, until tender. Blend in flour, salt and pepper. Stir in milk and soy sauce gradually, stirring constantly. Cook until smooth & thickened, stirring constantly. Alternate layers of potatoes and water chestnuts in greased 2-quart casserole. Add sauce. Top with pork chops. Cover. Bake at 350 degrees for 25 to 30 minutes. Yield: 6 servings.

*Mrs. Eleanor Hatch*
*Joseph, Oregon*

## Fruited Pork Chops

*Salt and pepper to taste*
*6 pork chops*
*3 lg. sweet potatoes, peeled*
*Lemon juice*
*6 slices pineapple*
*12 whole cloves*
*12 large prunes, pitted*
*½ c. pineapple juice*

Season pork chops. Brown chops in a small amount of oil in skillet. Cut sweet potatoes into halves. Rub with lemon juice. Place one potato on each chop. Top each chop with pineapple slice. Insert clove into each prune. Add prunes and pineapple juice. Cover. Cook over high heat until steaming. Reduce heat. Cook over low heat for 45 minutes.

*Mrs. Nina Parker*
*Williamston, North Carolina*

## Pork Chops with Curry Stuffing

*¾ c. diced apple*
*2 tbsp. diced onion*
*¼ c. chopped celery*
*3 tbsp. shortening*
*1½ c. soft whole wheat bread crumbs*
*¼ c. milk*
*1 tsp. each curry powder, salt*
*4 1-in. pork chops with pockets*
*3 tbsp. flour*

Brown apple, onion and celery lightly in 1 tablespoon shortening in skillet. Combine bread crumbs with milk in bowl. Fold in apple mixture. Sprinkle with ½ teaspoon each curry powder and salt; toss to mix well. Stuff chops with mixture. Coat pork chops with flour seasoned with remaining curry powder and salt. Brown chops in remaining 2 tablespoons shortening in skillet. Arrange in casserole; cover. Bake at 325 degrees for 45 minutes. Remove cover. Bake for 15 minutes longer.

*Mrs. Patsy Steffensen*
*Lake Norden, South Dakota*

## Pork Chop-Sweet Potato Casserole

*6 whole canned sweet potatoes, drained*
*6 thin slices unpeeled orange*
*6 pork chops*
*1 tsp. salt*
*¼ tsp. pepper*
*⅓ c. (firmly packed) light brown sugar*

Place sweet potatoes in greased baking dish. Top with orange slices. Arrange pork chops on top. Season with salt and pepper. Sprinkle with brown sugar. Cover. Bake at 350 degrees for 1 hour. Remove cover. Bake ½ hour longer.

*Judith Shannon*
*Ft. Lauderdale, Florida*

## Smothered Pork Chops

*6 lean pork chops*
*2 tbsp. flour (opt.)*
*Salt and pepper to taste*
*1 can cream of mushroom soup*
*½ tsp. each thyme, ginger (opt.)*
*¼ tsp. crushed rosemary (opt.)*
*1 tsp. parsley flakes (opt.)*
*½ c. sour cream (opt.)*
*1 3½-oz. French-fried onions (opt.)*

Saute pork chops in skillet until brown. Arrange in baking dish. Sprinkle flour, salt and pepper over chops. Combine soup and seasonings with ½ cup water in saucepan; mix well. Heat through; add parsley, sour cream and half the onions; mix well. Pour over chops. Cover. Bake at 350 degrees for 1 hour or until tender. Uncover. Sprinkle remaining onions over chops. Bake for 5 minutes longer. Yield: 4-6 servings.

*Mary Elizabeth Burns*
*Mt. Gilead, North Carolina*

## Spanish Rice and Pork

*5 or 6 pork loin chops*
*Bread crumbs*
*1 c. rice*
*1 can condensed tomato soup*
*1 med. onion, chopped*
*1 sm. jar chopped pimento*
*½ c. chopped bell pepper*
*⅛ tsp. pepper*
*1 tsp. salt*

Coat pork chops with bread crumbs. Saute chops in skillet until brown. Combine remaining ingredients with 1 cup water in bowl; mix well. Pour into buttered casserole. Place pork chops over mixture. Cover. Bake at 350 degrees for 1 hour or until liquid is absorbed. Add additional water if needed to prevent dryness. Yield: 4-6 servings.

*Mrs. Rachel M. Pearce*
*Fort Worth, Texas*

## Stuffed Pork Chops

1 tbsp. each grated onion, chopped
    parsley
½ c. chopped celery
½ tsp. each salt, poultry seasoning
2 c. bread crumbs
½ c. diced apple
1 can chicken with rice soup
6 pork loin chops, butterflied

Combine all ingredients except chops in bowl;
mix well. Stuff chops with mixture. Place in
baking dish. Bake at 375 degrees for 1 hour to 1
hour and 15 minutes. Yield: 6 servings.

*Mrs. Helen Alders*
*Douglass, Texas*

## Tangy Barbecued Pork Chops

3 to 4 lb. pork chops
1 lg. onion, finely chopped
2 to 3 tsp. salt
2 tbsp. vinegar
4 tbsp. lemon juice
2 tbsp. brown sugar
1 c. catsup
2 tsp. dry mustard
½ c. chopped celery
1 tsp. paprika

Saute pork chops in skillet over lot heat.
Remove chops; saute onion. Pour off pan
drippings. Return chops to skillet. Combine
remaining ingredients with 1 cup water; pour
over chops; cover. Cook over low heat for 1½
hours or until tender. Yield: 6 servings.

*Betty Horn*
*Midland, Texas*

## Loin Roast with Apple Butter Glaze

1  4 to 6-lb. pork loin roast
Salt and pepper to taste
½ c. each apple butter, orange juice

Have butcher loosen back bone by cutting
across rib bones. Place roast, fat-side up, on
rack in shallow baking pan. Season with salt
and pepper. Bake at 325 degrees for 35
minutes per pound or to 170 degrees on meat
thermometer. Combine apple butter and orange juice; mix well. Spoon over roast 30
minutes before end of baking time. Run
carving knife along edge of roast to remove
back bone before serving.

*Photograph for this recipe below.*

## Orange-Glazed Pork Roast

1  5-lb. pork loin roast, trimmed, scored
Salt and pepper to taste
6 orange slices
12 whole cloves
1 c. orange juice
½ c. honey
2 sticks cinnamon
1 tsp. grated orange rind

Sprinkle roast with salt and pepper. Attach
orange slices to roast with cloves. Place on rack,
fat-side up, in roasting pan. Combine next 3
ingredients in saucepan. Bring to a boil.
Simmer, uncovered, for 15 minutes. Add
orange rind. Bake at 325 degrees for 3 to 3½
hours or until meat thermometer registers 185
degrees. Baste with orange mixture every 20
minutes during last hour of baking. Yield: 8-10
servings.

*Mrs. Jo Ann Albright*
*Lytton, Iowa*

## Pineapple-Stuffed Pork Roll

1 smoked boneless pork butt
1½ c. crushed, drained pineapple
½ c. chopped celery
1 c. bread crumbs
1 tsp. salt
Apricot juice
Apricot halves

Brown pork in heavy skillet. Cool. Combine pineapple, celery, bread crumbs and salt in bowl; mix well. Make slashes 2 inches deep and 2 inches apart in top of pork to form pockets. Fill pockets with stuffing mixture. Shape into roll. Tie with heavy string. Place in baking pan. Pour apricot juice over pork; cover. Bake at 325 degrees for ½ hour. Baste pork with apricot juice. Place apricot halves over pork. Bake for 1 hour longer or until tender. Yield: 8 servings.

*Mrs. Jack C. Montgomery*
*Fort Gibson, Oklahoma*

## Pork A La Pineapple

1 4 to 5-lb. pork loin
1 13½-oz. can crushed pineapple
2 cans cream of celery soup
1 8-oz. package herb stuffing mix
¼ c. chopped green pepper
2 tbsp. butter, melted
¼ tsp. ginger

Have butcher remove backbone from pork loin. Cut loin into thick chops almost to bottom of loin. Drain pineapple, reserving juice. Combine ¾ cup pineapple juice, 1 can soup and next 3 ingredients in bowl; mix well. Spoon between chops. Tie loin together lengthwise. Place rack in pan, fat-side up; cover. Bake at 325 degrees for 1½ hours or until tender. Combine remaining juice and soup with pineapple, ginger and 2 tablespoons pan drippings. Heat to boiling point. Serve over pork. Yield: 8-10 servings.

*Mrs. Rama Steen*
*Caldwell, Ohio*

## Southern Stuffed Pork Roll

1 smoked boneless pork butt
2 med. sweet potatoes, peeled, diced
½ c. chopped celery
1 c. bread crumbs

1 tsp. salt
1 1-lb. can apricot halves

Cook roast in Dutch oven over low heat to render fat. Increase heat. Brown roast quickly in pan drippings. Remove from Dutch oven. Cool. Combine next 4 ingredients in bowl. Make slashes 2 inches deep and 2 inches apart in top of roast to form pockets. Fill pockets with potato mixture. Insert metal skewer in each end of roast. Return roast to Dutch oven. Drain apricots; reserve syrup. Pour syrup over roast. Cover. Bake at 325 degrees for 2 hours or until tender. Remove cover. Baste roast with pan drippings. Place apricot halves around roast. Bake for ½ hour longer or until top is glazed. Remove skewers. Slice roast through stuffing. Arrange with apricot halves on serving platter. Serve with pan drippings.

*Norma Hillberry*
*Basin, Wyoming*

## Roast Pork with Tomato Sauce

1 5-lb. pork roast
Garlic
4 tsp. oregano
Olive oil
Juice of 3 lemons
Salt and pepper
Flour
½ c. chopped celery
1 lg. onion minced
1 bell pepper, finely chopped
1 lg. can tomatoes, mashed
1 lg. bay leaf

Place roast in large shallow dish. Mash one bulb of garlic. Combine with 1 tablespoon oregano, 2 to 3 tablespoons olive oil, ⅔ of the lemon juice, 1 tablespoon salt and 1 teaspoon pepper in bowl; mix well. Spread over roast. Cover with plastic wrap. Refrigerate overnight. Remove roast. Coat with seasoned flour. Place in baking pan. Mince 2 to 3 cloves of garlic. Saute with celery, onion and bell pepper in oil in skillet. Add tomatoes and 1 tomato can water; mix well. Add bay leaf, salt and pepper, remaining lemon juice, 1 teaspoon oregano and 4 tablespoons olive oil. Mix well. Pour over roast. Cover. Bake at 325 degrees for 3 to 3½ hours or until 185 degrees on meat thermometer.

*Josephine P. Clark*
*Fairview, Tennessee*

## Spicy Spareribs

1 med. onion, chopped
1 med. green pepper, chopped
½ c. chopped celery
2 tbsp. butter
4 tbsp. lemon juice
2 tbsp. vinegar
2 tbsp. brown sugar
½ tsp. cayenne pepper
3 tbsp. Worcestershire sauce
1 c. catsup
½ tbsp. dry mustard
1 tbsp. celery salt
4 lb. ribs
2 tbsp. shortening

Saute vegetables in butter in saucepan. Add next 8 ingredients; mix well. Cook over low heat for 10 to 12 minutes. Brown ribs in shortening in Dutch oven. Pour sauce over ribs. Bake at 350 degrees for 2 hours or until tender. Yield: 6 servings.

*Ruth Darnell*
*Neoga, Illinois*

## Barbecued Pork Ribs

4 lb. pork ribs
¼ c. vinegar
1 tsp. Lawry's seasoned salt
½ tsp. each garlic salt, Accent, pepper
¼ tsp. cayenne pepper

Dip ribs in vinegar. Sprinkle with seasonings. Cook over charcoal, bone-side down, for 3 to 4 hours or until tender. Add hickory chips soaked in water to charcoal. Turn ribs over to drain. Yield: 2 servings.

*Mrs. Mary R. Middleton*
*Waxahachie, Texas*

## Deluxe Barbecued Ribs

3 to 4-lb. spareribs
1 c. catsup
1 tbsp. grated onion
4 tbsp. (firmly packed) brown sugar
Juice of 1 lemon
1 tsp. salt
1 tbsp. each Worcestershire sauce, steak
    sauce
¼ tsp. Tabasco sauce
1 tsp. grated lemon rind

Arrange spareribs, meaty side up on broiler rack. Combine remaining ingredients in bowl; mix well. Spread sauce over ribs generously. Place ribs 5 inches from heat source in broiler. Broil until glazed. Bake at 325 degrees for 2 hours, basting with remaining sauce. Yield: 4-5 servings.

*Mrs. Thordis K. Danielson*
*New Rockford, North Dakota*

## Grilled Barbecued Spareribs

3 lb. spareribs
1 lg. onion, sliced
2 bay leaves
6 whole peppercorns
2½ tsp. salt
1 c. catsup
2 tbsp. vinegar
1 tbsp. Worcestershire sauce
½ tsp. pepper
2 tbsp. brown sugar

Place spareribs, onion, bay leaves, peppercorns and 2 teaspoons salt in large pan; add water to cover. Bring to a boil; reduce heat. Simmer for 30 minutes or until tender. Drain. Place spareribs in shallow dish. Combine remaining ingredients; and ¾ cup water in bowl; mix well. Pour over spareribs. Marinate overnight. Drain spareribs. Broil over hot charcoal. Yield: 6-8 servings.

*Mrs. Shelba Barnes*
*West Lafayette, Indiana*

## Italian Barbecued Spareribs

1 pkg. dry Italian salad dressing mix
3 to 3½ lb. pork ribs, cut in serving
    pieces
2 onions, chopped
2 tbsp. each vinegar, Worcestershire sauce
1 tbsp. salt
1 tsp. each paprika, chili powder

Prepare salad dressing using package directions. Place ribs in shallow dish; cover with dressing. Marinate for 4 hours or longer in refrigerator. Combine remaining ingredients in small bowl; mix well. Cook ribs over hot coals, basting frequently with sauce until tender. Yield: 8 servings.

*Mrs. Barbara Knowlton*
*Wellman, Texas*

## Rail Splitter's Roast

½ c. chopped onion
¼ c. butter
1 med. apple, pared, diced
2 c. soft bread crumbs
2 tsp. salt
1 tsp. celery seed
½ tsp. monosodium glutamate
¼ tsp. pepper
¼ c. apple cider
2 2-lb. sections spareribs
Applesauce (opt.)

Saute onion in butter in skillet. Combine apple, bread crumbs, 1 teaspoon salt, celery seed, ¼ teaspoon monosodium glutamate and ⅛ teaspoon pepper in bowl. Add onions and cider; toss lightly. Mix remaining seasonings in small bowl. Sprinkle over spareribs. Place 1 sparerib section on rack in roasting pan. Spread with apple mixture. Place remaining spareribs on top. Fasten with skewers. Spread thin layer of applesauce on top. Bake at 350 degrees for 1½ hours. Remove skewers. Cut into serving pieces. Garnish with crab apples. Yield: 4 servings.

Mrs. Ruth Romesberg
Rockwood, Pennsylvania

## Southern-Barbecued Spareribs

¼ c. oil
¼ c. vinegar
½ c. canned peach juice
½ c. catsup
2 tbsp. brown sugar
2 tbsp. onion juice
1½ tsp. Worcestershire sauce
2 tsp. salt
¼ tsp. oregano
Cayenne pepper to taste
Hot sauce to taste
4 lb. spareribs

Combine all ingredients except spareribs in saucepan. Blend well. Bring to a boil; lower heat. Simmer for 5 minutes. Arrange spareribs in single layer on greased grill. Cook slowly over low coals for almost 2 hours or until well done, turning frequently and basting with sauce.

Lillie Mae Holmes
Danville, Alabama

## Tenderloin-Cheese Bake

8 slices pork tenderloin
Flour
Salt and pepper to taste
1 tbsp. shortening
¼ c. minced green pepper
1 pimento, chopped
1 can mushroom soup
½ c. light cream
¼ tsp. pepper
1 tsp. Worcestershire sauce
½ c. crumbled bleu cheese

Brown pork coated with seasoned flour in shortening in skillet. Remove pork. Saute green peppers in pan drippings. Stir in remaining ingredients. Bring to a boil. Pour into shallow baking dish. Arrange pork over mixture. Bake at 350 degrees for ½ hour. Yield: 4 servings.

Mrs. Mary Ann Sewalt
Richardson, Texas

## Tenderloin Filets In Milk Gravy

2 lb. pork tenderloin, cut into ¾ in. slices
Flour
Salt and pepper to taste
2 tbsp. butter
2 c. milk

Trim fat from tenderloin. Dredge in flour; season with salt and pepper. Brown in butter over medium heat in heavy skillet. Cover. Cook over low heat for ½ to 1 hour or until tender. Add milk; heat until bubbly. Serve immediately. Yield: 6-8 servings.

Mrs. A. F. Burnett
Eminence, Indiana

## Tenderloin Treat

6 slices pork tenderloin
1 tbsp. shortening
1¼ tsp. salt
Pepper
3 tbsp. butter
3 tbsp. flour
1 c. milk
3 oz. bleu cheese, crumbled
6 oz. noodles, cooked

Brown pork in hot shortening in skillet. Season with ½ teaspoon salt and pepper to taste. Melt butter in saucepan. Blend in flour, ¾ teaspoon salt and pepper to taste. Add milk gradually. Cook until thickened, stirring constantly. Add bleu cheese. Stir until melted. Add noodles; mix well. Pour into casserole. Top with pork. Bake at 350 degrees for 30 minutes. Yield: 6 servings.

Mrs. Norma Raffo
Winter Park, Florida

## Breakfast Hot Dish

2½ c. herbed croutons
2 c. shredded sharp cheese
2 lb. sausage
4 eggs, beaten
¾ tsp. dry mustard
2½ c. milk
1 c. mushroom soup
1 sm. can mushrooms

Place croutons in greased 8 × 8 × 2-inch casserole. Top with cheese. Brown sausage in skillet, stirring until crumbly. Drain. Spoon sausage over cheese. Combine remaining ingredients in bowl; mix well. Pour over sausage. Bake in preheated 300-degree oven for 1½ hours. May be reheated. Casserole may be refrigerated overnight before baking.

Mrs. Jean McOmber
Spring Lake, Michigan

## Cheese-Sausage Balls

1  10-oz. package Cheddar cheese, cubed
1 lb. hot sausage
2½ c. Bisquick

Place cheese in top of double boiler. Melt over hot water. Place sausage, Bisquick and melted cheese in large mixing bowl; mix well. Shape into small balls. Place on cookie sheet. Bake in 350-degree oven for 15 minutes. May be frozen before baking.

Mrs. Ruth Irwin
Wolf Lake, Illinois

## Gourmet Sausage Casserole

½ to ¾ lb. pork sausage
1 med. onion, chopped
1 med. green pepper, chopped
½ c. chopped celery
1 c. wild rice

1 can cream of chicken soup
1 can cream of mushroom soup
1 2-oz. can mushroom pieces, drained
1 sm. can pimento, drained, chopped
1 c. grated American cheese

Brown sausage in skillet, stirring until crumbly. Add next 3 ingredients. Saute until vegetables are tender. Drain. Add remaining ingredients; mix well. Pour into 2-quart casserole; cover. Bake at 325 degrees for 1½ hours. Yield: 8 servings.

Mrs. M. A. Hawley, Jr.
Start, Louisiana

## Homemade Sausage with Sage

2 lb. lean ground pork
1 tsp. salt
½ tsp. each sage, cumin, pepper
¼ tsp. ginger
1 bay leaf

Combine all ingredients in large bowl; mix well. Shape into 12 or 15 patties. Brown for 8 minutes on each side in skillet. May wrap patties in foil and broil over charcoal. Yield: 8-12 servings.

Mrs. Vivian Steinbauer
Hanover, Illinois

## Macaroni-Sausage Casserole

1 lb. sausage
1 c. chopped onions
1 pkg. macaroni, cooked
3 eggs, beaten
⅔ c. milk
1 c. celery soup
2 c. grated sharp cheese

Brown sausage in skillet stirring until crumbly. Add onion; cook until transparent. Place sausage mixture in greased casserole. Add macaroni. Combine eggs, milk and soup in saucepan; mix well. Cook until thick, stirring constantly. Add cheese; stir until melted. Pour cheese sauce over sausage mixture in casserole. Bake at 350 degrees until bubbly and brown. Yield: 6 servings.

Mrs. Ruby S. Willimon
Greenville, South Carolina

## Quick Sausage Pie

1 lb. sausage
1 lb. ground beef
2 lg. onions, chopped
1 green pepper, chopped
1 recipe corn bread batter

Brown sausage, ground beef, onions and green pepper in skillet, stirring until crumbly. Spread mixture in 11 × 13-inch baking pan. Top with cornbread batter. Bake at 375 degrees for 20 minutes or until tender. Yield: 12 servings.

*Mrs. Dorothy Bent*
*Bethel, Vermont*

## Sausage Balls

2 lb. sausage
1 med. onion, diced
1 46-oz. can tomato juice
1 lg. package noodles

Shape sausage into 1-inch balls. Combine onion and 2 quarts water in large saucepan. Bring to a boil. Drop in sausage balls. Cover. Reduce heat. Simmer for 15 minutes. Chill for several hours. Skim. Add tomato juice. Bring to a boil. Add noodles. Cook until noodles are tender. Yield: 8 servings.

*Mrs. Mary Kathryn Lands*
*Amanda, Ohio*

## Sausage-Corn Casserole

4 eggs, beaten
1 No. 2 can cream-style corn
1 c. bread crumbs
1 lb. sausage
1 t. salt
⅛ tsp. pepper
Catsup

Combine first 6 ingredients in bowl; mix well. Pour into well-greased 1½-quart casserole. Pour catsup over mixture. Bake at 350 degrees for 1 hour. Yield: 6-8 servings.

*Mrs. Lois R. Springer*
*Oakboro, North Carolina*

## Succotash With Sausage

½ to ¾ -lb. sausage
2 tbsp. onion, chopped
1 pkg. frozen corn

1 pkg. frozen lima beans
½ c. light cream

Shape sausage into small balls. Saute sausage balls in skillet. Drain, reserving 1 tablespoon pan drippings. Saute onion in reserved pan drippings in skillet. Cook corn and lima beans using package directions. Combine with onion in casserole; mix well. Arrange sausage balls on top. Pour cream over mixture; cover. Bake at 350 degrees for ½ hour. Yield: 6-8 servings.

*Mrs. Wyatt D. Lipscomb*
*Odessa, Texas*

## Thrifty Sausage Casserole

½ lb. sausage
1½ c. rice, cooked
1½ tbsp. minced onion
½ can cream of tomato soup
Salt and pepper to taste
2 tbsp. grated cheese

Brown sausage in skillet, stirring until crumbly. Drain. Arrange layers of rice, sausage and onion in greased casserole, ending with rice. Cover with soup. Season with salt and pepper. Top with cheese. Bake at 375 degrees for 20 minutes. Yield: 3 servings.

*Mrs. Judy C. Hall*
*Seagoville, Texas*

## Scalloped Potatoes With Vienna Sausages

3 c. sliced potatoes
8 Vienna sausages, diced
1 8-oz. can sliced mushrooms, drained
¼ c. flour
1 tsp. salt
⅛ tsp. pepper
3 tbsp. minced onion
1 c. milk
1 tomato, sliced
¼ c. grated American cheese
Parsley

Arrange half the potatoes, sausages, and mushrooms in greased casserole. Sprinkle with half the flour, salt, pepper and onion. Repeat layers. Pour milk over top. Cover. Bake at 350 degrees for 45 minutes. Top with tomato and cheese. Bake uncovered for 30 minutes longer. Sprinkle with parsley. Yield: 3-4 servings.

*Dorothy Marie Salter*
*Midlothian, Texas*

# Poultry

# POULTRY

Versatile, appetizing, nutritious and economical, poultry is a favorite main dish for all occasions.

Chicken is the most popular of all, and with good reason. Serve it for the most elegant meals—boned and simmered in a creamy rich sauce—or heaped high on a paper plate outdoors.

Turkey, next in popularity among American cooks, is emerging from a strictly "holiday-only" bird into a year-round cooking delight.

The following recipes explore new ways to serve all types of poultry, including a great number of savory chicken dishes, recipes for turkey, duck and Cornish Game Hens.

# TYPES OF POULTRY

When buying, look for birds with short legs, plump bodies and unbruised skin. A good fatty layer indicates tender meat.

Broiler/Fryer..........................Younger tender bird (about 9 weeks old) weighing 1½ to 3½ pounds. Cut up, they're excellent for frying, sauteing, baking or broiling. Use whole birds for roasting or barbecuing.

Capon................................Young male chicken especially bred for white, flavorful meat. Weighing 4 to 8 pounds, capons are usually roasted.

Cornish Game Hen.............The smallest, youngest and most expensive member of the chicken family. Allow a whole bird for each serving since they weigh 1½ pounds or less.

Duck...................................Sold frozen at grocery stores, labeled "Duckling" or "Young Duck". These fatty birds are usually roasted, but can be broiled or barbecued.

Goose................................Many gourmets consider it to be the best tasting poultry. A fatty bird, its creamy-white flesh cooks to a light brown color and has a slightly gamey flavor.

Hen or Stewing Chicken....Mature, less tender bird weighing 2½ to 5 pounds. Cook these fatty birds in a large amount of liquid. One stewing chicken usually yields enough meat for a chicken casserole or a salad with plenty of rich broth left over.

Roasters..............................Tender, 3½ to 5 pound birds. Ideal for roasting, barbecuing or frying.

Turkey................................The best buy for the most meat per pound is 16 to 24 pounds. To test for doneness, prick skin of thigh with fork. If juice runs clear, it's done. Or, jiggle drumsticks to see if joint is loose. Allow to cool before carving.

# BUYING POULTRY

| Chicken | One Serving |
|---|---|
| Broiler/Fryer | ¼ to ½ bird |
| Capon | About ½ pound |
| Cornish Game Hen | 1 bird |
| Roaster | ½ pound |
| Stewing | ½ pound |

| Duck | |
|---|---|
| Domestic | ¾ to 1 pound<br>(1 duckling halved or quartered serves 2 to 4 people) |

| Goose | |
|---|---|
| Domestic | 1 to 1½ pounds |

| Turkey | |
|---|---|
| 5 to 12 pounds | ¾ to 1 pound |
| 12 to 24 pounds | ½ to ¾ pounds |
| Boneless roast | ⅓ pound |

## Chicken Mushroom Pie

1 c. sliced carrots
6 tiny white onions
½ c. peas
1 can cream of mushroom soup
½ c. milk
3 c. diced cooked chicken
2 tsp. chooped parsley
1 pkg. refrigerator biscuits

Cook vegetables in a small amount of boiling salted water until tender; drain. Combine soup and milk in saucepan; heat to boiling. Add vegetables, chicken and parsley. Pour into 1½ quart casserole. Top with biscuits. Bake at 450 degrees for 15 minutes or until biscuits are browned. Canned mixed vegetables may be substituted for carrots and peas.

*Mrs. Alice M. Blakely*
*Cheshire, Connecticut*

## Asparagus Chicken Delight

2 c. diced cooked chicken
1½ c. cooked asparagus, cut up
½ c. sliced water chestnuts
1½ c. chicken consomme
1½ tbsp. flour
½ tsp. each salt, pepper

Combine chicken, asparagus and water, chestnuts in greased casserole. Heat consomme, in saucepan; blend in flour and seasoning. Pour over chicken mixture. Bake in 325-degree oven for 20 minutes. Yield: 4-6 servings.

*Mrs. Mary Pinkston Whaley*
*Northport, Alabama*

## Chicken Fricassee

1 4-lb. chicken, disjointed
½ c. flour
2 tsp. salt
½ tsp. paprika
1 can cream of chicken soup
1¼ c. milk

Coat chicken in flour seasoned with salt and paprika. Brown in hot shortening in skillet over low heat. Fransfer chicken to casserole. Blend soup and milk in bowl; pour over chicken. Bake at 325 degrees for 1 hour or until tender. Serve with soup mixture for gravy.

*Mrs. Mavis Tom*
*Saline, Louisana*

## Baked Chicken Loaf

1 4-lb. cooked hen, chopped
1 tbsp. minced parsley
1 pimento, chopped
½ tsp. salt
¼ tsp. pepper
1 c. milk
2 eggs
2 tbsp butter, melted
2 c. soft bread crumbs

Combine first 8 ingredients in bowl. Add 1¾ cups bread crumbs; mix well. Spoon into loaf pan. Sprinkle with remaining bread crumbs. Bake at 325 degrees for 45 minutes. Cut into squares. Serve with hot mushroom sauce.

*Mrs. R. S. Clark*
*La Grange, Georgia*

## Philippine Chicken

1 fryer, cut up
Garlic salt
Salt
1½ tbsp. white corn syrup
¼ c. soy sauce
¼ c. vinegar

Lay chicken flat in casserole. Add salts to taste. Mix corn syrup, soy sauce and vinegar; pour over chicken. Cover. Bake at 350 degrees for 1 hour.

*Marcia F. Swanson*
*McDonough, Ga.*

## Chicken-Broccoli Casserole

2 cans cream of chicken soup
1 can mushroom soup
¼ c. butter, melted
½ c. mayonnaise
2 tbsp. lemon juice
¾ tsp. curry powder
½ can water chestnuts, sliced
1 4-lb. cooked chicken, skinned, boned
2 pkg. frozen broccoli, cooked
slivered almonds

Combine first 7 ingredients in large bowl; mix well. Alternate layers of chicken, broccoli and soup mixture in casserole until all ingredients are used. Sprinkle with slivered almonds. Bake in 350-degree oven for ½ hour or until heated through. Serve over cooked rice.

*Broxie C. Stuckey*
*Gordo, Alabama*

## Chicken Cacciatore

2 broilers, cut in quarters
½ c. flour
4 tbsp. olive oil
¾ c. onion, chopped
¾ c. green pepper, chopped
2 cloves garlic, chopped
2 tbsp. parsley, chopped
2½ c. tomatoes
1 8-oz. can tomato paste
1 bay leaf
½ tsp. salt
¼ tsp. each pepper
ginger
1 tsp. oregano

Coat chicken with flour. Brown in oil in Dutch oven. Remove chicken; set aside. Saute onion, green pepper and garlic in drippings until brown. Blend in remaining ingredients. Return chicken to Dutch oven, spooning sauce to cover. Bake at 350 degrees for 1 hour to 1½ hours or until chicken is tender. Yield: 8 servings.

D. Armond
Columbus, New Jersey

## Chicken-Corn Pie

Pastry for 2-crust pie
2. c. cooked rice
¼ lb. crisp cooked bacon, crumbled
2 c. canned chicken, drained, sliced
1 No. 303 can cream-style corn
½ tsp. salt
¼ tsp. pepper
Cream

Roll out half the pastry on lightly floured surface. Fit pastry into fluted 9-inch pie plate. Arrange ½ of the rice, bacon, chicken and corn in layers in pastry. Repeat layers; sprinkle with salt and pepper. Roll out remaining pastry to 9-inch circle. Place over layers; press edges to seal. Slash top in several places. Brush with cream. Bake at 400 degrees for ½ hour or until golden brown. Yield: 6 servings.

Mrs. Kay Sandoz
Sargent, Nebraska

## Chicken Diable

4 tbsp. butter
½ c. honey
¼ c. prepared mustard
1 tsp. each salt, curry powder
1 3-lb broiler-fryer, cut in serving pieces, skinned

Melt butter in shallow baking dish; stir in remaining ingredients except chicken. Dip chicken pieces into butter mixture. Arrange in single layer over butter mixture. Bake at 375 degrees for 1 hour, basting once during baking. Yield: 4 servings

Wilma Brereton Gross
Tuscon, Arizona

## Chicken Normandy

1 3-lb. broiler-fryer, cut up
1 tsp. salt
4 tbsp. butter, melted
3 apples, peeled, cut into 9 pieces
1 c. heavy cream
1½ tsp. lemon juice
1 pkg. scallopini sauce mix

Sprinkle chicken with salt. Brown in butter in skillet. Remove chicken to casserole. Brown apples lightly in pan drippings. Add apples to chicken. Blend cream with lemon juice in bowl. Mix scallopini sauce with ¼ cup water. Stir into cream mixture. Bake at 350 degrees for 45 minutes. Sprinkle with chopped parsley. Yield: 4-5 servings.

Mrs. Juanita Finlayson
Inglewood, California

## Chicken with Onion Rice

1 c. rice
1 can mushrooms, drained (opt.)
1 pkg. dry onion soup mix
Margarine
1 chicken, disjointed

Combine rice and mushrooms with 2½ cups water in bowl. Pour into greased baking dish. Sprinkle soup mix over rice. Dot with margarine. Arrange chicken pieces over top. Cover. Bake in 350-degree oven for 1½ hours.

Denise Kalmus
Middletown, Ohio

## Chicken in Foil

1 2½ to 3-lb. fryer, cut-up
1 stick margarine
1 can mushrooms
½ c. chopped onions
Dash each of parsley, paprika
2 tbsp. light cream
1 tbsp. Sherry
3 c. cooked rice

Brown chicken in margarine in skillet. Remove chicken; set aside. Drain mushrooms, reserving liquid. Brown onions and mushrooms in margarine in same skillet. Place chicken on heavy-duty foil; add next 3 ingredients. Add liquid from mushrooms. Add onions and mushrooms. Fold foil tightly around chicken. Place on baking sheet. Bake at 425 degrees for 1 hour. Serve with rice. Yield: 6 servings.

Frances Stewart
Bowie, Texas

## Chicken Paprika

1 2 to 2½-lb. chicken, quartered
½ c. oil
½ c. flour
1½ tsp. salt
¼ tsp. pepper
1 tbsp. paprika

Cut chicken into 4 pieces. Combine remaining ingredients in bowl. Dip chicken into flour mixture. Place in baking dish. Bake at 400 degrees for 1 hour. Yield: 4 servings.

Frances H. Judy
Richwood, West Virginia

## Almond Chicken Pie

1 4 to 5-lb. hen stewed, chopped
2 c. rich white sauce
1 can cream of mushroom soup
1 can mushrooms
1 sm. can pimento, chopped
1 c. almonds
6 hard boiled eggs, diced
½ c. each diced celery, onion
1 recipe pastry for 2-crust pie

Stir chicken into white sauce in large saucepan. Add remaining ingredients except pastry; mix well. Cook for 10 minutes, stirring occasionally. Line baking dish with half the pastry. Spoon chicken mixture over pastry. Place remaining pastry over chicken mixture. Seal edges. Bake at 300 degrees until golden brown.

Mrs. Anne Devon
Provo, Utah

## Chicken-Tamale Pie

1 can tomales, sliced
Cheese
1 c. tomato puree
1 c. corn
¼ c. raisins
1 tsp. salt
2 tsp. chili powder
2 c. cooked chopped chicken
1 c. broth

Line casserole with tamales. Combine ½ cup cheese with remaining ingredients in bowl. Stir to blend well. Add to casserole. Sprinkle with additional cheese. Bake at 350 degrees for about 1 hour.

Mrs. Byron Jacobsen
Ault, Colorado

## Chicken Tetrazzini

3 tbsp. butter
2 tbsp. flour
2 c. chicken broth
⅓ c. minced onion
½ c. minced green pepper
2 c. grated American cheese
¼ c. slivered almonds, toasted
¼ c. chopped pimento
1¾ c. cooked green peas
3 c. cooked chopped chicken
1 c. macaroni, cooked
1 c. sauted mushrooms (opt.)

Melt butter over low heat in saucepan. Blend in flour. Add chicken broth gradually. Cook until thick, stirring constantly. Saute onion and green pepper in skillet. Add to sauce. Add remaining ingredients; mix well. Cook until heated through.

Mrs. Janice Watson
Florence, Mississippi

## Chicken Sopa

12 corn tortillas
1 5-oz. can boned chicken
1 sm. can chopped green chilies

1 lb. Velveeta cheese grated
1 can chicken soup

Place 4 tortillas in greased casserole. Alternate layers of chicken, chilies, cheese and tortillas until all ingredients are used. Spread soup over top; cover. Bake at 350 degrees for 20 minutes.

Billye Slaton
Marfa, Texas

## Chicken Vermouth with Rice

3 lb. fryer pieces
3 tsp. salt
½ tsp. pepper
3 med. carrots, sliced
2 stalks, celery, thinly sliced
1 med. onion, thinly sliced
4 cloves of garlic
2 tbsp. chopped parsley
⅓ c. dry vermouth
1 c. rice
2 c. chicken broth
¼ c. sour cream

Place chicken in greased 2-quart casserole. Sprinkle with 2½ teaspoons salt and pepper. Add next 6 ingredients; cover. Bake in 375-degree oven for 1½ hours. Combine rice, chicken broth and remaining salt in greased casserole. Cover. Bake for 30 minutes. Remove casserole from oven. Remove garlic from chicken mixture. Stir in sour cream. Serve chicken mixture over rice. Yield: 6 servings.

Martha W. Good
West Virginia

## Chinese New Year's Chicken

1 fryer, cut into sm. pieces
Garlic salt to taste
Cornstarch
2 eggs, beaten
1 tsp. monosodium glutamate
¾ c. sugar
¼ c. chicken broth
½ c. wine vinegar
1 tsp. salt
1 tbsp. soy sauce
¼ c. catsup

Sprinkle chicken with garlic salt. Roll in cornstarch. Dip into eggs. Brown in a small amount of oil in skillet. Place in shallow casserole. Mix remaining ingredients in small bowl. Pour over chicken. Bake in 350-degree oven for 1 hour and 15 minutes or until chicken is tender.

Kay Caskey
Reno, Nevada

## Country Captain

2 frying chickens, cut up
Salt and pepper to taste
Flour
2 onions, finely chopped
2 green peppers, chopped
2 tsp. curry powder
2 cans tomatoes
½ tsp. each chopped parsley, thyme,
    white pepper
2 c. hot cooked rice
2 tbsp. currants
¼ lb. almonds, roasted

Season chicken with salt and pepper. Roll in flour. Brown in shortening in Dutch oven. Drain, reserving a small amount of pan drippings. Saute onions and green peppers in reserved pan drippings in skillet, stirring constantly. Add tomatoes and spices; mix well. Pour over chicken; cover. Bake at 350 degrees for 45 minutes or until chicken is tender. Place chicken in center of platter. Surround with rice. Add currants to tomato sauce. Spoon sauce over rice and chicken. Sprinkle almonds over rice. Garnish with parsley if desired.

Mrs. Jean Morris
Florence, Alabama

## Easy Chicken Curry

1 can cream of chicken soup
¼ c. milk
1 to 2 tsp. curry powder
1 6-oz. can boned chicken
1 5-oz. can shrimp, drained
1 5-oz. package precooked rice, cooked
1 tbsp. butter
¼ tsp. salt
2 tbsp. parsley, chopped

Blend soup, milk and curry powder in saucepan. Add chicken and shrimp. Heat thoroughly. Stir butter and salt into rice. Spread rice in casserole. Top with chicken and shrimp. Bake at 275 degrees for 10 minutes. Sprinkle with parsley before serving. Yield: 4-6 servings.

Mrs. Nancy W. Darden
Durham, North Carolina

## Crusty Herbed Chicken

1 3 to 3½-lb. chicken, cut-up
½ tsp each thyme, marjoram
¾ to 1 c. flour
¾ c oil
½ tsp. rosemary
1 tbsp. minced parsley
½ tsp. salt
½ tsp. pepper

Sprinkle chicken with thyme and marjoram. Let stand for ½ hour to 1 hour. Roll chicken in flour. Brown in hot oil in skillet on both sides. Transfer to baking pan. Sprinkle with next 4 ingredients. Drain pan drippings; add ¾ cup water to skillet; stir well. Pour over chicken. Bake at 375 degrees for 40 to 45 minutes or until tender.

*Mrs. Richard Comtois*
*Bellows Falls, Vermont*

## Honey Chicken

½ tsp. garlic powder
2 tsp. salt
¼ tsp. pepper
1 2½ to 3-lb. fryer, cut up
1 egg yolk
1½ tbsp. honey
4 tbsp. butter, melted

Combine garlic powder, salt and pepper; rub chicken with mixture. Beat egg yolk with honey and 2 tablespoons butter in small bowl. Brush chicken with honey mixture. Place, skin-side up, in greased baking dish. Bake at 325 degrees for 45 minutes to 1 hour, basting with remaining butter. Turn. Bake for 10 to 15 minutes longer until brown.

*Mrs. Irene J. Hodges*
*Cullowhee, North Carolina*

## Hot Chicken Salad

4 whole chicken breasts
⅛ tsp. ginger
½ tsp. nutmeg
¼ tsp. garlic powder
Pepper to taste
⅓ c. white cooking wine
3 tbsp. lemon juice
9 hard-boiled eggs, chopped
½ c. chopped onion
¼ tsp. each basil, rosemary
¾ c. slivered almonds

2 cans cream of celery soup
1 can cream of chicken soup
1½ c. mayonnaise
1⅓ c. finely-crushed potato chips

Season chicken with ginger, ¼ teaspoon nutmeg, garlic powder and pepper. Place in baking pan. Pour wine and lemon juice over top. Bake at 325 degrees or until tender. Cool in pan juices. Bone and dice. Place in bowl; add next 7 ingredients and ⅔ cup potato chips. Mix well. Place in baking dish; sprinkle remaining potato chips over top. Bake at 350 degrees for ½ hour. May be served as a hot dip by heating after mixing and omitting ⅔ potato chip crumbs.

*Mrs. Linda Bailey*
*Powhatan, Virginia*

## Italian Baked Chicken

¼ c. flour
1 tsp. salt
¼ tsp. garlic salt
⅛ tsp. pepper
4 chicken drumsticks
2 whole chicken breasts, cut in half
¼ c. oil
1 chicken bouillon cube
1 tsp. vinegar
1 med. onion, sliced
¼ c. chopped celery
1 8-oz. can tomato sauce
¾ cup pizza-flavored catsup

Combine flour, salt, garlic salt and pepper in bowl. Coat chicken in flour mixture. Brown in oil in skillet. Place chicken in 1½-quart baking dish. Dissolve chicken bouillon cube in ½ cup water in saucepan over low heat. Add bouillon and remaining ingredients. Simmer for 5 minutes. Pour over chicken. Bake at 350 degrees for 1 hour. Yield: 4 servings.

*Sister St. Anita Marie, C.N.D.*
*Mabou, Nova Scotia, Canada*

## Spicy Chicken-Rice Loaf

1 4-lb. chicken, cooked chopped
3 c. bread crumbs
1 c. cooked rice
3 c. broth
4 eggs, beaten
1 sm. can pimento
1½ tbsp. Worcestershire sauce
¼ tsp. Tabasco sauce

*Salt and red pepper to taste*
*1 sm. onion, chopped*

Combine chicken and remaining ingredients in large bowl; mix well. Spoon mixture into buttered loaf pan. Place in pan of hot water in oven. Bake at 325 degrees for 1½ hours. Serve with mushroom sauce. Yield: 12 servings.

*Sheron Ann Weinbirg*
*Ramer, Tennessee*

## A New Casserole

*1 lg. hen, cooked, boned*
*1 c. each chopped onion, bell pepper,*
   *celery*
*6 lg. green olives, chopped*
*2 sm. jars pimento*
*1 sm. can mushrooms*
*1 stick butter*
*Chicken broth*
*1 can mushroom soup*
*Juice of 3 lemons*
*½ lb. cheese, grated*
*2 pkg. noodles*

Cut chicken into large pieces. Brown vegetables in butter in large skillet. Add ½ cup chicken broth and remaining ingredients except noodles; mix well. Simmer for 20 minutes. Add chicken. Cook noodles according to package directions, using chicken broth. Add noodles to mixture.

*Mrs. John Y. Smith*
*Greenwood, Mississippi*

## Plantation Chicken

*1 c. diced celery*
*1 med. onion, chopped*
*2 t. green pepper*
*5 tbsp butter*
*6 tsp. flour*
*3 c. milk*
*1 can mushroom soup*
*2 c. each diced cooked ham, chicken*
*2 tbsp. pimentos*
*Salt and pepper to taste*
*1 c. grated cheese*
*Bread crumbs*

Saute celery until tender. Combine onion, green pepper and butter in top of double boiler. Cook over hot water until tender. Add flour; blend well. Add milk gradually; cook, stirring constantly, until smooth and thick. Stir in soup, ham, chicken, pimento and seasoning.

Spoon in greased casserole. Combine cheese and bread crumbs. Top casserole with crumb mixture. Bake in 375-degree oven for ½ hour.

*Mrs. Frances Detmer*
*Weeping Water, Nebraska*

## Polynesian Packages

*6 pieces broiler chicken*
*2 tbsp. flour*
*½ tsp. garlic salt*
*1 tsp. paprika*
*3 tbsp. shortening*
*½ c. pineapple juice*
*2 tbsp. vinegar*
*1 tbsp. sugar*
*1 tsp. soy sauce*
*2 tbsp. cornstarch*
*2 tbsp. thinly sliced green onion*
*6 med. sweet potatoes, cooked*
*6 slices canned pineapple, drained*

Coat chicken with flour seasoned with garlic salt and paprika. Brown in shortening in skillet. Remove from skillet; drain on absorbent paper. Combine next 4 ingredients in saucepan. Bring to a boil. Stir in cornstarch. Cook until thick and clear, stirring constantly. Add onion. Place chicken piece, sweet potato, pineapple slice and 2 tablespoons sauce on 12-inch square of foil. Repeat with remaining chicken. Seal foil. Bake in 450-degree oven for 30 minutes.

*Mrs. Doris Rhodebeck*
*Sparta, Ohio*

## Quick Chicken Casserole

*1 6-oz. can boned chicken*
*1 can cream of chicken soup*
*1 c. diced celery*
*2 tsp. minced onion*
*½ c. chopped pecans*
*½ tsp. salt*
*¼ tsp. pepper*
*1 tbsp. lemon juice*
*¾ c. mayonnaise*
*3 hard-boiled eggs, thinly sliced*
*2 c. crushed potato chips*

Drain chicken, reserving broth. Dice. Combine all ingredients except potato chips in large bowl; mix well. Spoon into 1-quart baking dish. Sprinkle with potato chips. Bake at 450 degrees for 15 minutes or until lightly browned.

*Mrs. Helen S. Underwood*
*Shepherdsville, Kentucky*

### Wild Rice and Chicken Casserole

1 6-oz. can sliced mushrooms
1 c. long grain and wild rice
½ c. chopped onion
½ c. butter
½ c. flour
1½ c. each chicken broth, cream
3 c. diced cooked chicken
½ c. diced pimento
2 tbsp. minced parsley
¼ tsp. pepper
½ c. slivered blanched almonds

Drain mushrooms; reserve liquid. Prepare rice according to package directions. Saute onion in butter in skillet until transparent. Blend in flour. Stir in chicken broth and reserved mushroom liquid gradually. Add cream. Cook until thick, stirring constantly. Add remaining ingredients except almonds; mix well. Place in baking dish. Sprinkle almonds over top. Bake in 350-degree oven for 25 minutes.

Mrs. Virginia O. Savedge
Eastville, Virginia

### Oven-Baked Chicken

1⅓ c. Minute rice
1 2 to 2½-lb. fryer, cut up
1 10½-oz. can condensed cream of
    mushroom soup.

Sprinkle rice in lightly buttered shallow baking pan. Lay chicken pieces, skin-side up, over rice. Spread soup evenly over all; cover. Bake in 350-degree oven for 1 hour or until tender. May remove cover after ½ hour for crispy chicken. Yield: 4-5 servings.

Mrs. Marijean Gissel
Kenmare, North Dakota

### Scalloped Chicken Au Gratin

2 c. chopped cooked chicken
½ c. slivered almonds
2 c. giblet gravy
1 c. crushed potato chips
1 c. grated cheese

Combine chicken and almonds in bowl; mix well. Layer chicken mixture, gravy, potato chips and ½ cup cheese in greased casserole. Bake at 350 degrees for 20 minutes. Sprinkle

with remaining cheese. Bake for 10 minutes longer. Yield: 4-6 servings.

Mrs. Dorothy M. Grace
York, Alabama

### Chicken Breasts in Sour Cream

4 whole breasts of chicken
Flour
Salt and pepper to taste
1 can mushroom soup
⅔ c. mushrooms
1 c. sour cream
½ c. cooking Sherry

Coat chicken with flour seasoned with salt and pepper. Brown in skillet in small amount of shortening. Place in baking dish. Combine remaining ingredients. Pour over chicken. Bake at 350 degrees for 1 hour or until tender.

Mrs. Ruth T. Hanegan
Hope, Arkansas

### Chicken and Orange Burgundy

2 whole chicken breasts
3 tbsp. oil
⅓ c. each, Burgundy, orange juice
1 tsp. lemon juice
3 tbsp. each orange marmalade, brown
    sugar
¼ tsp. salt
1 orange, sliced

Brown chicken breasts in oil in skillet. Combine next 6 ingredients in saucepan. Bring to a boil. Place chicken in flat casserole. Pour marmalade mixture over chicken. Place orange slices over chicken. Bake at 350 degrees for 45 minutes to 1 hour, basting occasionally. Yield: 4 servings.

Mrs. Mildred Rivers
Charlotte, North Carolina

### Orange Chicken

4 chicken breasts
Juice of 1 orange
1 tbsp. orange rind
½ tsp. each salt, paprika, mustard
¼ tsp. Worcestershire sauce
3 tbsp. oil
1 can broken mushroom pieces, drained

Place chicken breasts in baking pan, skin-side down. Combine remaining ingredients except mushrooms in bowl. Pour over chicken, coating each piece well. Bake at 375 degrees for 1 hour, basting occasionally. Turn chicken; sprinkle with mushrooms. Baste again. Bake for 15 to 30 minutes longer or until tender. Yield: 4 servings.

*Mrs. Florence N. Jackson*
*Belchertown, Massachusetts*

## Pecan-Stuffed Chicken Breasts

*6 tbsp. butter, melted*
*3 c. toasted bread crumbs*
*⅓ c. chopped onion*
*½ c. chopped celery*
*2 tsp. parsley flakes*
*¾ c. chopped pecans*
*¼ tsp. Accent*
*4 sm. chicken breasts*
*Lemon juice*
*Salt and pepper to taste*

Mix 3 tbsp. butter and next 6 ingredients in bowl. Add enough water to moisten; mix lightly. Shape into 4 mounds on double-thick foil squares. Place on baking sheet. Brush both sides of chicken breasts with lemon juice and remaining 3 tbsp. butter. Season with salt and pepper. Place chicken breasts over stuffing mounds. Seal foil. Bake at 350 degrees for 40 minutes. Fold foil back. Bake at 400 degrees for 20 minutes longer or until brown.

*Mrs. T. Juett*
*Union City, Indiana*

## Rolled Chicken Breasts

*6 boned, skinned, chicken breasts*
*Salt to taste*
*1 6-oz. package sliced Swiss cheese*
*6 thin slices ham*
*Flour*
*2 tbsp. butter*
*1 tsp. instant chicken bouillon*
*1 3-oz. can sliced mushrooms*
*⅓ c. Sauterne*
*Toasted almonds*

Pound chicken breasts lightly to ¼-inch thickness with wooden mallet. Sprinkle with salt. Place cheese slice and ham slice on each piece of chicken. Fold sides in; roll up to enclose filling. Press to seal. Coat with ¼ cup flour. Brown chicken in butter in skillet. Remove to

11 × 7 × 1½-inch baking dish. Stir ½ cup water, bouillon, mushrooms and Sauterne into pan drippings, mixing well. Pour over chicken; cover. Bake in 350-degree oven for 1 to 1½ hours or until tender. Transfer chicken to warm serving platter. Blend 2 tablespoons flour with ½ cup water. Pour liquid from baking pan into saucepan. Stir flour mixture into liquid. Cook until thick, stirring constantly. Pour a small amount over chicken. Garnish with almonds. Serve chicken with remaining gravy.

*Vicki Ann Sommers*
*Coffeyville, Kansas*

## Russian Chicken Bake

*2 lg. chicken breasts, cut in half, skinned*
*Salt and pepper to taste*
*4 tbsp. butter*
*1 lemon, cut in half*
*1 c. Russian dressing*

Season chicken with salt and pepper. Arrange in 9 × 6 × 2-inch baking dish, skin side up. Place 1 tablespoon butter on each chicken breast. Squeeze lemon juice over chicken. Pour Russian dressing over top. Cover with foil. Bake at 350 degrees for 1 hour and 50 minutes. Remove foil. Bake 10 minutes longer. Yield: 4 servings.

*Susan E. Connell*
*Panama City, Florida*

## Baked Chicken Breasts with Almonds

*Salt and pepper to taste*
*4 or 5 chicken breasts*
*4 tbsp oil*
*1 can cream of mushroom soup*
*½ c. cooking Sherry*
*¼ c. sharp Cheddar Cheese*
*3 tbsp. grated onion*
*2 tbsp. Worcestershire sauce*
*½ c. slivered almonds*

Season chicken. Brown in oil in large skillet. Place in baking dish. Combine next 5 ingredients in bowl; mix well. Pour over chicken. Sprinkle with almonds. Cover with foil. Bake at 350 degrees for 45 minutes. Yield: 4-5 servings.

*Patricia Allen*
*Smyrna, Tennessee*

## Best Barbecued Chicken

1 3-lb. fryer, cut up
Flour (opt.)
1 or 2 med. onions, chopped
½ to 1 c. catsup
2 or 3 tbsp. Worcestershire sauce
Salt and pepper to taste
1½ tbsp. prepared mustard
½ c. chopped celery (opt.)
2 tbsp. vinegar
3 to 4 tbsp. brown sugar
¼ c. lemon juice
2 tbsp. light corn syrup (opt.)

Coat chicken with flour. Brown in hot shortening in large skillet. Add onion. Saute until transparent. Add remaining ingredients and 1 cup water. Simmer for ½ hour. Place chicken in shallow baking pan. Pour sauce over chicken. Bake at 325 degrees for 1½ hours or until tender. Yield 6 servings.

*Mrs. Luana Hutchings*
*Overton, Nevada*

## Grilled Barbecued Chicken

4 chicken quarters
Salt
2 c. red wine vinegar
1 c. oil
1 tbsp. Tabasco sauce
Dash of garlic salt

Sprinkle chicken generously with salt. Combine 3 tablespoons salt and remaining ingredients in bowl; mix well. Place chicken on grill, skin-side down; brush with sauce. Grill Chicken, turning every 10 minutes until tender; baste with sauce frequently.

*Mrs. Claude L. Fox, Jr.*
*Oxford, Mississippi*

## Oven-Barbecued Chicken

1 frying chicken, quartered
¼ c. seasoned flour
¼ c. shortening
½ c. each sliced onion, green pepper
1 c. mushrooms
3 tbsp. butter
¼ tsp. salt
1 c. catsup
2 tbsp. Worcestershire sauce
2 drops of hot sauce

1 tbsp. brown sugar
½ tsp. paprika

Coat chicken with seasoned flour. Brown in shortening in skillet. Saute onion, green pepper and mushrooms in butter in saucepan until tender. Add ⅔ cup water and remaining ingredients. Bring to a boil. Place chicken in 2-quart casserole. Pour sauce over chicken. Cover. Bake at 350 degrees for 45 minutes or until tender. Yield: 6 servings.

*Margaret Whitley*
*Caney, Oklahoma*

## Broiled Ginger Chicken

2½ lb. chicken, split for broiling
1 tsp. onion salt
¼ c. melted butter
¾ c. apple juice
1 tsp. cinnamon
Ground ginger

Season chicken with onion salt. Place in broiler pan, cut side up. Brush with half the melted butter. Combine apple juice, cinnamon and remaining melted butter. Broil 6 to 7 inches from heat source for 40 minutes or until tender. Baste with sauce and turn every 10 minutes. Sprinkle lightly with ginger after 20 minutes. Yield: 2 servings.

*Harriet J. Harless*
*Logan, West Virginia*

## Lemon-Fried Chicken

1 broiler-fryer, cut up
¼ c. lemon juice
½ c. corn oil
¼ tsp. each garlic salt, ground thyme,
    ground marjoram
¾ tsp. salt
⅛ tsp. pepper
½ tsp. grated lemon rind
½ c. flour
½ tsp. paprika

Place chicken in large, shallow dish. Mix lemon juice, ¼ cup corn oil, garlic salt, salt, thyme, majoram, pepper and lemon rind in small bowl. Pour over chicken. Marinate in refrigerator for at least 3 hours, turning occasionally. Drain chicken on absorbent paper. Mix flour and paprika. Coat chicken pieces with flour mixture. Shake off excess. Heat remaining corn oil in heavy skillet over medium heat for about 3 minutes. Add chicken carefully. Cook for about 15 minutes or until golden brown, turning once. Cover. Cook over low heat for 20 minutes longer. Remove cover. Cook until tender. Yield: 4 servings.

*Susan Ashton*
*Roanoke Falls, North Carolina*

## Alabama-Fried Chicken

*1 lg. fryer, cut-up*
*Salt and pepper to taste*
*1 tsp. garlic salt*
*1 c. buttermilk*
*1 c. flour*
*2 c. corn oil*

Sprinkle chicken with salt, pepper and garlic salt. Dip into buttermilk, coat with flour. Fry chicken in oil at 275 to 350 degrees in electric frypan until golden brown. Drain on paper towel. Arrange on platter. Garnish with parsley.

*Mary Y. Thompson*
*Ashland, Alabama*

## Chinese-Fried Chicken in Sweet-Sour Sauce

*4 chicken breasts, boned*
*⅝ tsp. salt*
*2 cloves of garlic, minced*
*½ tsp. powdered ginger*
*¾ tsp. pepper*
*1 egg, beaten*
*¾ c. flour*
*1 c. oil*
*2 stalks celery*
*2 lg. carrots*
*1 green pepper, sliced into strips*
*1 c. (firmly packed) brown sugar*
*1 c. vinegar*
*1 1-lb. can stewed tomatoes*
*½ c. cornstarch*
*⅛ tsp. salt*

Pound chicken breasts until thin between sheets of waxed paper. Slice into 1 × 1½-inch strips. Combine ½ teaspoon salt, garlic, ginger, pepper, egg and flour in bowl; mix well. Coat chicken slices in mixture. Heat oil to 350 degrees in electric fry pan. Cook chicken in 350-degree oil in electric frypan for 10 minutes or until golden brown on both sides. Drain on paper towels. Slice celery and carrots ¼ inch wide. Combine with green pepper in 1 quart boiling water in large saucepan. Boil for 10 minutes or until carrots are tender. Drain. Set aside. Bring 1½ cups water to a boil in saucepan. Add brown sugar. Cook for 1 minute. Add vinegar and stewed tomatoes. Cook for 1 minute. Combine cornstarch with 1 cup water in small bowl; mix well. Bring tomato mixture to a boil. Add cornstarch mixture gradually. Boil for 3 minutes, stirring constantly. Stir in salt and vegetables. Add chicken. Cook for 15 minutes on medium heat until sauce is heated through. Serve over hot rice.

*Mrs. Janet Trigg*
*Wauwatosa, Wisconsin*

## Chicken Russe

*2 c. sour cream*
*2 tbsp. lemon juice*
*2 tsp. salt*
*½ tsp. pepper*
*Garlic powder to taste*
*6 chicken breasts*
*Bread crumbs*
*½ c. butter, melted*

Combine sour cream, lemon juice and seasonings in plastic bag. Add chicken pieces. Seal bag. Marinate chicken in refrigerator overnight. Remove chicken. Shake with bread crumbs in plastic bag. Fry chicken in butter in skillet for 25 to 30 minutes or until golden brown and tender. Add water to pan drippings to make gravy. Yield: 6 servings.

*Mrs. Delores Weir*
*Comfrey, Minnesota*

## Garlic-Fried Chicken

*1 fryer, cut up*
*Powdered garlic*
*Monosodium glutamate*
*Salt and pepper*
*Seasoned flour*
*Oil for deep frying*

Sprinkle chicken with seasonings. Drop into seasoned flour in paper bag one piece at a time. Shake to coat thoroughly. Fry in hot deep oil until golden brown. Yield: 8 servings.

*Bonnie O'Neal*
*New Summerfield, Texas*

## Hotchkiss Herb Chicken

4 tbsp. each marjoram, rosemary,
     oregano, thyme, instant minced
     parsley, paprika
2 tbsp. each dried mint, basil, sage, chervil
1 c. flour
¼ tsp. pepper
1 tsp. salt
1  2½ to 3-lb. fryer, cut up

Combine first 10 ingredients in airtight container. Shake to blend thoroughly. Combine 2 tablespoons herb mixture with flour, pepper and salt in paper bag. Shake chicken pieces in flour mixture to coat well, one at a time. Pour oil into large skillet to ¼ inch depth. Brown chicken on all sides over medium heat. Reduce heat. Cover. Cook until chicken is tender. Remove cover. Cook for 10 minutes longer. Remaining herb blend may be used in spaghetti sauce, meat loaf, salads and egg dishes. Yield 4-6 servings.

*Mary Woodruff*
*Hotchkiss, Colorado*

## Mabel's Fried Chicken

½ c. each cornmeal, flour
½ tsp. each salt, seasoned salt
¼ tsp. pepper
1  4-lb. chicken, cut up
2 eggs, well beaten

Combine cornmeal, flour, salt, pepper and seasoned salt in shallow bowl; mix well. Dip chicken into eggs. Coat with cornmeal mixture. Cook chicken in hot oil in skillet over medium heat until tender and golden brown.

*Maria Campo*
*Glenrock High School*
*Glenrock, Wyoming*

## Chicken Parmesan

1 pkg. saltine crackers, crushed
¾ c. grated Parmesan cheese
6 chicken breasts halves
1 stick butter, melted

Combine cracker crumbs and Parmesan cheese. Dip chicken in melted butter; coat with cracker mixture. Place chicken in baking pan. Bake at 325 degrees for 1 hour. Yield: 6 servings.

*Louise R. Clark*
*Jacksonville, Alabama*

## Oven-Fried Chicken Parmesan

1 c. crushed package herb stuffing
⅔ c. grated Parmesan cheese
¼ c. chopped parsley
1 clove of garlic, minced
1  2½ to 3-lb. frying chicken, cut up
¼ c. butter, melted

Combine first 4 ingredients in bowl. Dip chicken into butter; coat with crumb mixture. Place chicken, skin-side up, in shallow baking pan. Sprinkle with remaining butter and crumb mixture. Bake at 375 degrees for 45 minutes or until tender. Yield: 4 servings.

*Carolyn Baldwin*
*Pontiac, Michigan*

## Easy Oven-Fried Chicken

1 c. biscuit mix
2 tsp. salt
1 tsp. each paprika, oregano
1  3 to 4-lb. chicken, cut up
¼ c. butter

Combine biscuit mix, and seasonings in bowl. Coat chicken pieces with dry mixture. Melt butter in shallow baking pan. Add chicken. Bake at 350 degrees for 1½ hours or until tender, basting frequently. Yield: 4 servings.

*Helen McSparrin*
*Quakertown, Pennsylvania*

## Oven-Fried Pecan Chicken

1 c. biscuit mix
1½ tsp. salt
2 tsp. paprika
2 tbsp. sesame seed (opt.)
½ tsp. poultry seasoning (opt.)
¼ to ½ c. finely chopped pecans
1  2½ to 4-lb. fryer, cut up
½ c. evaporated milk
¼ to ½ c. butter melted

Combine biscuit mix, seasonings and pecans. Dip chicken pieces into evaporated milk. Coat well with dry mixture. Place in 13 × 9 × 2-inch baking pan. Pour butter over chicken pieces, covering as completely as possible. Bake, uncovered, at 375 degrees for 1 hour or until tender. Yield: 4-6 servings.

*Betty Jo Hill*
*Cartersville, Illinois*

## Oven-Fried Herb Chicken

*½ env. garlic salad dressing mix*
*2 tbsp. flour*
*¼ tsp. salt*
*¼ c. butter, softened*
*1 tbsp. lemon, juice*
*1 2½ to 3-lb. broiler*

Combine salad dressing mix, flour and salt in bowl. Blend in butter and lemon juice. Spread mixture evenly over top of chicken. Place skin-side up in shallow baking dish. Bake at 350 degrees for 1¼ hours or until tender. Yield: 4 servings.

*Jane Cole*
*Geneva, Illinois*

## Chicken Breast in Lemon Sauce

*3 chicken breasts, split, boned, skinned*
*butter*
*2 tbsp. Sherry*
*2 tsp. grated lemon peel*
*2 tbsp. lemon juice*
*Salt and pepper to taste*
*1 c. whipping cream*
*Grated Parmesan cheese*

Pound chicken breasts until thin. Saute on both sides in ¼ pound butter in large skillet for 5 to 8 minutes. Remove to overproof serving platter. Stir Sherry, lemon peel and lemon juice into pan drippings. Cook for 1 minute, stirring constantly. Add seasoning. Add cream gradually, stirring constantly. Pour sauce over chicken breasts. Dot with butter, it desired. Sprinkle with cheese. Brown under moderate broiler. Yield: 6 servings.

*Mrs. James Pfeil*
*Milwaukee, Wisconsin*

## Chicken with Herbs

*1 broiler-fryer, cut into serving pieces*
*⅓ c. flour*
*1 tbsp. salt*
*1 tsp. salad herbs*
*¼ tsp. pepper*

Dip chicken in flour seasoned with salt, herbs, and pepper. Brown on all sides in hot oil in skillet. Reduce heat. Cook for 45 minutes or until tender. Yield: 4 servings.

*Gwladys Jeanneret*
*Kettle Falls, Washington*

## Oriental Chicken

*1 lb. skinned, boned, chicken breasts*
*2 tbsp. butter*
*1 c. sliced celery*
*1 bunch scallions, sliced*
*1 6-oz. can sliced mushrooms, drained*
*1 8-oz. can water chestnuts, drained, sliced*
*1 4-oz. jar pimento, drained, diced*
*1 10¾-oz. can condensed golden*
*    mushroom soup*
*1 tbsp. angostura bitters*
*2 tbsp. soy sauce*

Cut chicken into strips. Brown in butter in large skillet. Add remaining ingredients; mix well. Simmer for 15 minutes, stirring occasionally. Serve over rice. Yield: 4 servings.

*Photograph for this recipe below.*

## Chicken Kiev

5 chicken breasts, boned, cut into halves
Salt and pepper to taste
1 onion, finely chopped
10 pats butter
3 eggs
⅓ c. milk
Fine bread crumbs
2 c. oil

Pound chicken breasts between waxed paper until flat. Sprinkle with salt and pepper. Spread each piece with onion and 1 pat butter. Fold sides in; roll up to enclose filling. Secure with toothpicks. Beat eggs with milk in bowl. Coat each chicken roll with bread crumbs. Dip in egg mixture. Roll again in bread crumbs. Refrigerate for 6 to 8 hours or overnight. Fry rolls in hot oil at 350 degrees for 8 minutes per side or until golden brown. Yield: 10 servings.

Amelie B. Sheffield
Eagle Springs, North Carolina

## Chicken Spaghetti

1½ c. chopped onions
1 sm. clove of garlic
1 lg. bell pepper, chopped
3 stalks celery, sliced
2 lg. cans tomatoes
2 sm. cans tomato paste
Juice and rind of 1 lemon
1 c. chicken fat
1 lg. chicken, cooked, boned
1 lb. spaghetti, cooked, drained
2 cans mushroom soup
1 sm. bottle stuffed olives, chopped
Salt, pepper, garlic salt to taste
Chicken broth

Saute onions and garlic in large skillet. Add bell pepper and celery. Cook until tender. Stir in next 6 ingredients. Simmer for 10 minutes. Add spaghetti, soup and olives; mix well. Add seasonings. Simmer until ready to serve. Add chicken broth as needed to increase liquid. Sprinkle with cheese before serving.

Mrs. Carolyn C. Burton
Doyline Louisiana

## Chicken Kiev with Mushroom Sauce

8 chicken breasts halves, boned, skinned
Salt to taste

1 tbsp. each chopped parsley, green onion
Butter
Flour
2 eggs, beaten
1 c. fine bread crumbs
Oil for deep-frying
½ lb. mushrooms, sliced
1 tsp. soy sauce
¾ c. light cream

Pound chicken breasts to ¼-inch thickness with mallet. Sprinkle with salt, parsley and onion. Cut 1 stick of butter into 8 small sticks. Place stick of butter at long end of each cutlet. Fold sides in; roll up to enclose butter. Press ends to seal. Coat rolls with flour; dip into eggs. Roll in bread crumbs. Chill for 1 hour. Fry in deep hot oil for 5 minutes or until golden. Melt 3 tablespoons butter in saucepan. Add mushrooms. Sprinkle with 1 tablespoon flour; toss to coat mushrooms. Cook over medium heat for 8 to 10 minutes or until tender, stirring occasionally. Add soy sauce. Stir in cream gradually. Cook until mixure bubbles and thickens, stirring constantly. Season to taste. Serve over chicken. Yield: 4-6 servings.

Linda Berson
Batavia, Illinois
Elaine Armburgeg
Union City, Ohio

## Chicken Chow Mein

1 c. each chopped onions, celery
1 13 ¾-oz. can chicken broth
2 cans cream of mushroom soup
1 14-oz. can chicken, diced
½ tsp. salt
¼ tsp. pepper
2 tbsp. chopped pimento
1 pkg. frozen peas
2 No. 2½ cans chow mein noodles

Combine onions, celery and broth in large saucepan. Simmer until celery is tender. Stir in next 5 ingredients. Simmer for 30 minutes. Add peas. Cook until peas are tender. Serve over chow mein noodles. Yield: 10 servings.

Mrs. Thelma Terrell
Sullivan, Indiana

## Chicken Croquettes

4 hard-boiled eggs
1 sm. can mushrooms, cut into pieces
6 tbsp. butter

6 tbsp. flour
1 c. each milk, chicken broth
Salt and red pepper to taste
2 c. bread crumbs
2 eggs, beaten

Sieve eggs. Combine with mushrooms in large bowl. Melt butter in saucepan; stir in flour gradually. Add milk, chicken broth and 1 teaspoon salt. Cook until thickened, stirring constantly. Add cream sauce and chicken to mushroom mixture. Season with salt and pepper. Shape into croquettes. Dip in bread crumbs, beaten eggs, and bread crumbs again. Brown in deep hot shortening.

*Mrs. Floy C. Poston*
*Blue Ridge, Georgia*

## Chicken Fritters

2 eggs, separated
2 c. chopped cooked chicken
½ c. minced celery stalks and leaves
1 tsp. grated onion
¼ c. flour
½ tsp. salt
2 tbsp. oil
Chicken gravy

Mix egg yolks with next 5 ingredients in large bowl. Beat egg whites until soft peaks form; fold gently into chicken mixture. Heat oil in skillet. Drop mixture from large spoon into hot oil; brown on both sides. Serve with gravy.

*Mrs. R. Gale Manley*
*Bristol, Virginia*

## Quick Chicken with Dumplings

1 can chicken with rice soup
1 egg, beaten
½ c. milk
1 c. flour
½ tsp. salt
1 tsp. baking powder

Heat soup in 1½-quart saucepan. Add 1 soup can water; mix well. Combine egg and milk in bowl. Combine dry ingredients. Add to egg mixture; mix well. Drop from tablespoon into hot soup mixture. Cover. Cook for 8 to 10 minutes. Do not remove cover during cooking. Serve immediately. Yield: 2-4 servings.

*Marlene K. Lien*
*Minneota, Minnesota*

## Chicken with Dumplings

1 stewing chicken, cut up
Flour
Salt and pepper
2½ tsp. baking powder
1 egg, beaten
⅓ c. milk

Cook chicken in boiling salted water in large saucepan until tender. Remove chicken reserving 4 cups broth. Bone chicken. Set aside. Skim broth, reserving 6 tablespoons chicken fat. Combine 6 tablespoons flour with reserved fat in bowl; blend well. Add a small amount of reserved broth, stirring until smooth. Stir flour mixture into remaining reserved broth in saucepan. Cook over low heat until slightly thickened, stirring constantly. Season with salt and pepper. Sift ¾ cup flour, ½ teaspoon salt and baking powder together into bowl. Combine eggs and milk in separate bowl. Stir into dry ingredients; mix well. Drop by spoonfuls into boiling gravy. Cover. Cook for 15 minutes. Do not remove cover during cooking. Serve dumplings and gravy over chicken.

*Mrs. Nell Inez Lawless*
*Jackson, Mississippi*

## Chicken Paprika

4 chicken breasts, cut in half, boned
4 tbsp. butter
1 tbsp. paprika
1 tsp. salt
Flour
2 tbsp. shortening
1 med. onion, minced
¾ c. finely diced celery
½ c. cream

Brown chicken in 2 tablespoons butter in large frypan. Cream remaining butter, paprika, salt and ¼ cup flour in bowl. Spread over chicken. Cover. Cook over low heat for 30 minutes. Saute onion in shortening in skillet. Add celery and ⅔ cup water. Cover. Cook for 8 to 10 minutes. Pour onion mixture over chicken. Cover. Cook for 15 minutes. Stir 2 tablespoons flour into cream. Add to pan drippings with chicken. Cover. Cook for 5 or 6 minutes longer. Yield: 4 servings.

*Elizabeth Heard*
*Jackson, Mississippi*

## Chicken in White Wine

½ lb. small onions, peeled
1 clove of garlic, finely chopped
¼ c. oil
1 3-lb. fryer, cut up
2 tbsp. flour
1 c. dry white wine
1 tsp. each salt, thyme
⅛ tsp. pepper
2 tbsp. chopped parsley
1 3-oz. can mushrooms, sliced, drained

Saute onions and garlic in oil in heavy skillet, until golden. Remove; set aside. Saute chicken in pan drippings. Remove chicken to warm platter. Drain all but 2 tablespoons pan drippings. Blend in flour; cook until bubbly. Add wine gradually, cook until smooth, stirring constantly. Add remaining ingredients except mushrooms. Cover; simmer for ½ hour or until almost tender. Add mushrooms, cover. Simmer for 10 minutes longer. Garnish with additional parsley.

Ruth B. Rayer
Turbotville, Pennsylvania

## Special Southern Chicken

6 tbsp. flour
3 tsp. baking powder
1½ tsp. salt
1 tsp. thyme
½ tsp. soda
2 c. cornmeal
2 eggs, slightly beaten
1 c. buttermilk
2 tbsp. finely chopped parsley
4 tbsp. chicken fat
1 c. each chicken broth, milk
2 c. chopped cooked chicken
¼ c. chopped pimento

Sift 2 tablespoons flour, 1 teaspoon salt, and dry ingredients into bowl. Combine eggs and buttermilk; mix well. Blend into dry ingredients. Add parsley; mix well. Pat into greased ring mold. Bake at 400 degrees for 30 minutes or until brown. Unmold on heated serving platter. Blend chicken fat and 4 tbsp. flour in saucepan. Add milk and chicken broth gradually, stirring until smooth. Fold in chicken and pimento. Add ½ teaspoon salt. Pour over corn bread ring to serve. Yield: 10 servings.

Mrs. Eileen Wilson
Poolville, Texas

## Shamrock Chicken

2 chickens, disjointed
1 onion, sliced
4 celery tops
2 bay leaves
2 tsp. each monosodium glutamate, salt
½ tsp. peppercorns
¼ c. butter
¼ c. flour
3 egg yolks
4 tbsp. lemon juice
½ c. finely chopped parsley

Place chicken in Dutch oven; add next 6 ingredients and 3 cups water. Bring to a boil. Reduce heat. Simmer for 1 hour or until tender. Place chicken on serving platter. Strain broth reserving 3 cups. Melt butter in saucepan; blend in flour until smooth. Add reserved broth gradually. Cook until mixture thickens, stirring constantly. Blend egg yolks and lemon juice in bowl. Add to broth, stirring rapidly. Bring to a boil. Remove from heat source. Stir in parsley. Spoon part of sauce over chicken; serve remaining sauce separately.

Mrs. Brenda Hurm
Jasper, Indiana

## Creamed Chicken Livers

4 slices bacon
2 tbsp. all-purpose flour
Dash of pepper
½ lb. chicken livers
1 tbsp. chopped onion
1 can cream of mushroom soup
1 c. hot cooked rice

Cook bacon in skillet until crisp. Remove from skillet. Drain, reserving drippings. Combine flour and pepper. Coat livers with flour mixture. Brown livers and onion in 2 tablespoons reserved bacon drippings.Cover.Cook over low heat for 8 to 10 minutes. Blend soup with ¼ cup water; stir into liver mixture. Heat through. Spoon over rice; top with bacon strips.

Kathryn G. Motsinger
Winston-Salem, North Carolina

## Epicurean Chicken Livers

1 lb. chicken livers, cut into bite-sized pieces
½ c. each chopped celery, onion
½ tsp. rubbed sage

4 tbsp. butter
1 4-oz. can sliced mushrooms, drained
1 10½-oz. can giblet gravy
¼ tsp. salt
Curried rice

Cook livers, celery, onion and sage in butter in 10-inch skillet over low heat until tender. Stir in mushrooms, gravy and salt. Cook over medium heat until heated through, stirring occasionally. Serve over curried rice. Yield: 4 servings.

June D. Mikrut
Fords, New Jersey

## Chicken Livers and Mushrooms Gourmet

½ lb. chicken livers
2 tbsp. butter
1 16-oz. can sliced mushrooms, drained
¼ c. chopped green onion
½ c. sour cream
1 1½ tsp. soy sauce
1 tbsp. chili sauce
Dash of pepper

Cook chicken livers in butter in covered skillet over medium heat for 5 minutes or until almost tender, stirring occasionally. Add mushrooms and onions. Cook until tender. Combine remaining ingredients in bowl; mix well. Add to liver mixture. Heat through, stirring constantly. Serve on toast points, pancakes or with omelet. Yield: 4 servings.

Lula Smith
Sand Springs, Oklahoma

## Chicken Livers Baked with Rice

¾ lb. chicken livers
Salt and pepper to taste
Flour
4 tbsp. butter
3 tbsp. each minced onion, chopped
    celery
1 c. rice
2 c. chicken broth
1 tsp. minced parsley

Sprinkle chicken livers with salt and pepper. Coat with small amount of flour. Brown quickly in butter in hot skillet. Place in 6-cup casserole. Saute onion, celery and rice in pan drippings until slightly brown. Add chicken broth; stir well. Add parsley. Pour sauce over chicken livers. Cover. Bake at 350 degrees for ½ hour or until rice is tender. Yield: 6 servings.

Imogene Brashear
Palatka, Florida

## Cornish Hens in Sour Cream

2 Rock Cornish hens
½ c. flour
3 tbsp. butter
¾ c. sliced onions
1½ tsp. salt
1 tsp. paprika
¾ tsp. sweet basil leaves
½ tsp. pepper
1 3-oz. can sliced mushrooms, undrained
1½ c. sour cream

Coat hens with flour. Saute in butter in deep skillet for 10 to 15 minutes or until golden. Add onions. Cook for 5 minutes, stirring constantly. Combine remaining ingredients except sour cream in bowl; mix well. Pour over hens. Bring to a boil; reduce heat. Cover. Simmer for 30 to 45 minutes are until tender. Blend sour cream into pan drippings gradually, stirring constantly. Heat; pour over hens. Yield: 2 servings.

Louise A. Hall
Sutter Creek, California

## Rock Cornish Hens with Wild Rice Stuffing

¾ c. wild rice
1½ c. chicken broth
Butter
1½ c. each chopped celery, onions
2 tsp. seasoned salt
¼ c. Sherry
6 Rock Cornish hens

Place rice in bowl with water to cover. Soak for 2 hours. Drain. Place in 2-quart saucepan. Add chicken broth and 1 tablespoon butter. Bring to a boil. Reduce heat. Cover. Simmer for 30 minutes or until rice is tender. Saute celery and onions in 2 tablespoons butter in skillet until tender-crisp. Add to rice. Add 1 teaspoon seasoned salt and Sherry; mix lightly. Stuff each hen loosely with ½ cup rice mixture. Truss hens. Place in shallow baking dish. Blend remaining 1 teaspoon seasoned salt into ¼ cup melted butter. Brush on hens. Bake at 350 degrees for 1½ hours. Yield: 6 servings.

Dorothy Maynard
Knoxville, Tennessee

## Stuffed Cornish Hens Orlando

¼ c. finely chopped celery
½ c. finely chopped onion
1 clove of garlic, mashed
1 tsp. dried leaf tarragon
3 tsp. unsalted butter
2 c. whole wheat bread cubes, toasted
    (opt.)
1 tsp. grated orange rind
3 Florida oranges, peeled, sectioned,
    chopped
1 8-oz. can water chestnuts, drained,
    chopped
4 Cornish game hens
½ c. Florida orange juice

Saute first 4 ingredients in butter in skillet until onions are transparent. Combine onion mixture, bread cubes, orange rind, orange pieces and water chestnuts in large bowl; mix well. Stuff each game hen lightly with 1 cup stuffing. Place game hens in shallow baking dish. Bake in 350-degree oven for 1 hour or until tender. Baste game hens with orange juice every 15 minutes during baking. Yield: 4 servings.

Photograph for this recipe on cover.

## Grilled Barbecued Turkey

¼ c. vinegar
1 tbsp. salt
¼ tsp. pepper
⅛ tsp. cayenne pepper
1 thick slice lemon
1 onion, sliced
¼ c. butter or margarine
1 tbsp. Worcestershire sauce
1½ tsp. Liquid Smoke
1 3 to 5-lb. turkey, quartered

Combine first 8 ingredients and ½ cup water in saucepan; mix well. Simmer for 20 minutes. Stir in Liquid Smoke. Bring to a boil. Brush turkey generously with sauce. Arrange, skin-side up, on grill 5 to 8 inches above coals. Cook for 1 hour or until tender, turning and brushing with sauce every 15 minutes.

Linda Voga
Ankeny, Iowa

## Turkey-Olive Enchiladas

2 c. sliced mushrooms
½ c. finely chopped onion
3 tbsp. butter
2 to 3 c. diced cooked turkey
1 10¾-oz. can cream of chicken soup
½ c. sliced pimento-stuffed olives
1 c. sour cream
½ c. slivered almonds, toasted
1½ to 2 tsp. chili powder
12 corn tortillas
½ c. grated Cheddar cheese

Saute mushrooms and onion in butter in skillet until onion is tender. Remove from heat. Stir in next 6 ingredients, mixing well. Prepare tortillas according to package directions. Place ⅓ cup turkey mixture in center of each tortilla. Roll up to enclose filling. Arrange seam-side down in 13 × 9-inch baking dish. Spoon remaining turkey mixture down center of each enchilada. Sprinkle with cheese. Bake, uncovered, in 400-degree oven for 25 minutes or until cheese is bubbly.

Photograph for this recipe above.

## Crusty Turkey Casserole

1 env. dry cream of mushroom soup mix
2 c. fine noodles, cooked, drained
1 c. milk

1 c. chopped cooked turkey
⅛ tsp. curry powder
¼ tsp. pepper
¼ tsp. hot sauce
½ tsp. salt
2 tbsp. oil
2 cloves of garlic, sliced
1 c. bread crumbs
¼ c. chopped parsley

Combine soup mix and 2 cups water in saucepan. Bring to a boil. Remove from heat; let stand for about 10 minutes. Combine noodles, soup, milk, turkey and seasonings in large bowl; mix well. Turn into casserole. Saute garlic lightly in oil in skillet. Remove garlic. Stir in bread crumbs and parsley. Spread over turkey mixture. Cover baking dish with foil. Refrigerate overnight. Remove foil. Bake at 375 degrees for ½ hour. Yield: 6 servings.

*Mrs. Martha J. Barr*
*Fluvanna, Texas*

## Turkey Charade Casserole

2 tbsp. minced onion
¼ c. butter
¼ c. flour
1 c. chicken broth
1 c. milk
2 chicken bouillon cubes
2 eggs, slightly beaten
½ c. mayonnaise
2 c. diced turkey
¼ c. slivered almonds, toasted
2 tbsp. minced pimento
1 can chow mein noodles

Cook onion in butter in large covered saucepan over low heat until tender. Blend in flour. Add broth and milk gradually, stirring constantly. Add bouillon cubes. Cook over medium heat until mixture thickens, stirring constantly. Stir a small amount of hot mixture into egg yolks; stir egg yolks into hot mixture. Cook for 1 minute. Remove from heat. Fold in remaining ingredients. Pour into greased 1½-quart casserole. Bake in 350-degree oven for 35 minutes. Do not overcook. Yield: 6 servings.

*Majorie Mouser*
*Grant, Michigan*

## Turkey-Cranberry Squares

2 tbsp. butter
¾ c. sugar
1 tsp. grated orange rind
2 c. fresh cranberries
5 c. diced cooked turkey
1 c. turkey gravy
1 c. milk
1 tsp. salt
¼ tsp. pepper
2 tbsp. minced onion
2 c. soft bread crumbs
2 eggs, slightly beaten

Melt butter in 8×8-inch baking dish. Stir in sugar and orange rind, blending well. Spoon cranberries over sugar mixture. Combine remaining ingredients in large bowl; mix well. Pack turkey mixture firmly over cranberries. Bake at 400 degrees for 45 minutes. Invert immediately onto serving platter. Cut into squares to serve. May substitute cranberry sauce for cranberries, reducing sugar to ¼ cup.

*M. Christiana Gates*
*Middleboro, Massachusetts*

## Turkey Tetrazzini

4 oz. spaghetti
1 can cream of celery soup
½ c. milk
2 c. shredded sharp Cheddar cheese
2 c. diced cooked turkey
1 3-oz. can sliced mushrooms, drained
⅓ c. chopped onion
½ tsp. salt
¼ tsp. pepper
¼ c. each chopped pimento, sliced black
  olives

Break spaghetti into 2-inch pieces. Cook according to package directions. Rinse with hot water. Drain. Combine soup and milk in large bowl; mix well. Add spaghetti, 1½ cups cheese, and remaining ingredients except reserved cheese; toss gently. Pour spaghetti mixture into lightly greased 1½-quart casserole. Bake at 350 degrees for 45 minutes. Remove from oven. Sprinkle remaining cheese over top. Bake for several minutes longer until cheese melts. Yield: 6 servings.

*Mrs. Jama K. Montgomery*
*Alexandria, Indiana*

# Lamb, Game and Variety Meats

## Casserole Catsarola

*1 lb. ground lean lamb*
*1 c. chopped onions*
*½ c. margarine*
*2 tbsp. tomato paste*
*¼ c. chopped parsley*
*¼ tsp. each cinnamon, salt*
*¼ c. Claret*
*Dash of pepper*
*1 lg. eggplant, peeled, sliced ½ inch thick*
*¼ c. olive oil*
*3 tbsp. flour*
*2 c. milk*
*2 eggs, beaten*
*½ tsp. nutmeg.*
*1 c. ricotta cheese*
*½ c. bread crumbs*
*½ c. grated Romano cheese*

Brown lamb and onions in ¼ cup margarine in skillet. Add next 6 ingredients; mix well. Simmer for 5 minutes. Cool; set aside. Soak eggplant in hot water for 5 minutes. Drain on absorbent paper. Brown eggplant in olive oil in skillet. Set aside. Melt remaining margarine in saucepan. Stir in flour until smooth. Blend in milk. Bring to a boil, stirring constantly. Cool slightly. Add eggs, nutmeg and ricotta to milk mixture; blend well. Alternate layers of meat sauce, eggplant, ¼ cup bread crumbs and ¼ cup Romano cheese in 1½-quart greased casserole. Pour cheese sauce over last layer. Sprinkle with remaining cheese and bread crumbs. Bake at 325 degrees for 35 minutes. Reduce heat to 250 degrees; bake 5 minutes longer or until golden brown. Yield: 4-6 servings.

*Margaret Jordan*
*White Plains, New York*

## Lamb Casserole

*¼ c. corn oil*
*2 c. chopped onions*
*2 c. cubed cooked lamb*
*1 10-oz. package frozen French-style*
 *green beans, thawed, drained*
*2 c. canned tomatoes*
*1 tbsp. Worcestershire sauce*
*½ tsp. salt.*

Heat oil in skillet. Saute onions until golden. Add lamb. Saute for 2 minutes. Arrange green beans in single layer over lamb mixture.

Combine tomatoes, Worcestershire sauce and salt in bowl; mix well. Pour over green beans, cover. Cook over low heat for 15 minutes or until green beans are tender. Yield: 6 servings.

*Mrs. Marion Tover*
*Mellen, Wisconsin*

## Lamb Curry

*3 lg. apples, pared, cored, sliced*
*1 onion, sliced*
*1 clove of garlic*
*2 to 3 tbsp. flour*
*1 tbsp. curry powder*
*1 tbsp. lemon juice*
*2 c. meat stock*
*1 tsp. gravy flavoring*
*Grated rind of ½ lemon*
*½ c. raisins*
*3 cloves*
*2 c. cubed cooked lamb*

Saute apples, onion and garlic in skillet until golden. Remove garlic. Add flour and curry powder to apple mixture; mix well. Combine lemon juice, meat stock and gravy flavoring in bowl. Stir into mixture gradually. Add lemon rind, raisins and cloves; cover. Simmer ½ hour. Add lamb. Heat thoroughly. Serve with rice on hot platter. Yield: 6 servings.

*Mrs. Dortha Cooper*
*Spencer, Tennessee*

## Shish Kabobs

*1 bottle of French dressing*
*2 lb. lamb shoulder, cut into 1-inch cubes*
*4 lg. sweet pickles*
*4 lg. cherry tomatoes*
*12 sm. onions*
*1 13½-oz. can pineapple chunks, drained*

Pour French dressing over lamb in shallow baking dish; coat thoroughly. Marinate for several hours. Remove lamb; reserve French dressing. Thread lamb, pickles, tomatoes, onions, and pineapple onto skewers. Place on foil-lined baking pan. Brush with French dressing. Broil for 10 minutes. Turn; brush with French dressing. Broil for 10 minutes. Serve immediately. Yield: 4 servings.

*Mrs. Susan Richman*
*Freeport, New York*

## Lamb Chops in Tomato Sauce

6 thick lamb chops
Salt and pepper
1 green pepper, cut in rings
1 lg. onion, sliced
1 lemon, sliced
2 c. tomato juice

Brown chops in hot shortening in skillet. Season with salt and pepper. Place in baking dish. Top each with green pepper ring, onion slice and lemon slice. Pour tomato juice over chops; cover. Bake in 325-degree oven for 1½ hours. Yield: 6 servings.

Pruda Caudill Prather
Carter City, Kentucky

## Lamb Chops Deluxe

6 lamb chops, ¾ in. thick
3 tbsp. shortening
1½ tsp. salt
¼ tsp. pepper
1 tsp. each salt, paprika
½ tsp. nutmeg

Brown chops on both sides in shortening in skillet. Combine seasonings. Sprinkle on both sides of chops. Pour off pan drippings; cover. Cook over low heat until tender, adding water if needed to prevent sticking. Yield: 6 servings.

Mrs. Sally A. Kmon
Manchester, New Hampshire

## Barbecued Breast of Lamb

1 2-lb. breast of lamb, boned, quartered
1 tsp. salt
⅛ tsp. pepper
1 med. onion, peeled, sliced
½ c. chili sauce
¼ tsp. paprika
1 tbsp. vinegar

Season lamb with salt and pepper. Arrange lamb in large skillet. Add 1 cup water and remaining ingredients; cover. Simmer for 1½ hours. Skim. Simmer for 20 minutes longer or until tender. Yield: 4 servings.

Swanie Smoot
Madison, West Virginia

## Barbecued Leg of Lamb

4 to 5-lb. leg of lamb
Salt and pepper to taste
Flour
2 onions, chopped
¼ c. vinegar
½ tsp. dry mustard
4 tbsp. catsup
2 tbsp. sugar
2 tbsp. Worcestershire sauce

Season lamb with salt and pepper. Roll in flour to coat. Place in roaster. Surround with onions. Combine remaining ingredients in bowl; mix well. Pour over lamb. Cover roaster. Bake in 350-degree oven for 3 to 4 hours or until tender, turning and basting lamb every 30 minutes. Remove cover during last 30 minutes to permit browning. Serve with sauce.

Mrs. Patricia Nixon
St. Louis, Oklahoma

## Roast Lamb Shoulder

½ tsp. salt
¼ tsp. pepper
1 tbsp. mustard
3 tbsp. flour
1 4-5 lb. lamb shoulder, boned and
   rolled
1 c. currant jelly

Mix seasonings and flour in bowl. Blend in ½ cup water. Place lamb shoulder in baking dish. Spread with flour mixture. Bake at 300 degrees for 3½ hours or until tender. Baste every 15 minutes. Spread with jelly the last hour.

Mrs. Mary G. Meyer
Griggsville, Illinois

## South of the Border Leg of Lamb

1 clove of garlic, crushed
½ tsp. each marjoram, salt
2 tbsp. lemon juice
¼ tsp. Tabasco sauce
1 8-lb. leg of lamb, trimmed
1 bottle of stuffed green olives
2 strips bacon, cut into ½ inch pieces

Combine first 5 ingredients in small bowl; mix well. Make 10 holes about 1½ inches deep in lamb using handle of wooden spoon. Fill each hole with: 1 olive, bacon piece, ½ teaspoon garlic mixture, another olive. Place lamb in backing dish. Bake at 325 degrees for 30 to 35 minutes per pound or to 175 degrees on meat thermometer. Yield: 12 servings.

*Mrs. Martha Foster*
*Marshall, Michigan*

## Wild Duck with Apple-Raisin Stuffing

*6 c. dry bread cubes*
*1 c. chopped apple*
*½ c. raisins*
*¾ c. butter, melted*
*2 tsp. salt*
*½ tsp. pepper*
*¼ tsp. cinnamon*
*⅛ tsp. ginger*
*3 ducks*

Combine first 8 ingredients in large bowl; mix well. Stuff cavity of each duck with mixture. Close opening of duck with skewers or string Place ducks breast-side up in baking pan. Bake at 450 degrees for 15 minutes. Reduce temperature to 325 degrees. Cover. Bake for 2 hours or until tender. Yield: 6 servings.

*Helen Myers*
*Mountain Home, Idaho*

## Wine-Spiced Wild Duck

*1 c. white wine*
*1 clove of garlic*
*1 tsp. each thyme, oregano, seasoned salt,*
*    pepper*
*1 c. oil*
*2 duck breasts*
*Bacon strips*

Combine first 4 ingredients in bowl; mix well. Place duck breast in mixture. Refrigerate for several days. Place marinade and duck breast in saucepan; cover. Simmer for 2 hours or until tender. Add water if necessary to prevent sticking. Place duck breast on broiler rack; top with bacon. Broil for 3 to 5 minutes.

*Mrs. Carol Frazee*
*Burlington, New Jersey*

## Roast Pheasant with Wild Rice

*1 pheasant*
*Salt*
*Pepper*

*1 c. wild rice*
*1 c. apricot juice*

Place pheasant on foil in large baking pan. Rub interior with salt and pepper; cover with uncooked rice. Pour apricot juice over all. Wrap tightly in foil. Bake at 325 degrees for 1 hour or until tender. Yield: 4 servings.

*Mrs. Floyd King*
*Malden, Illinois*

## Roast Pheasant

*Salt*
*1 whole young pheasant*
*1 bay leaf*
*3 to 4 celery leaves*
*4 slices bacon*
*⅓ c. oil*
*½ c. mushroom pieces*
*1 lg. onion, sliced*

Rub inside and outside of pheasant with salt. Place bay leaf and celery leaves in cavity. Wrap pheasant breast with bacon. Secure with string. Place pheasant in baking pan. Pour oil over pheasant. Add mushrooms and onion slices. Bake at 350 degrees for 1½ hours. Turn pheasant at 30 minute intervals basting with pan drippings. Place on platter; remove string, celery leaves and bay leaf. Garnish with special apples and parsley if desired.

*Mrs. Lonnie Disterhaupt*
*Lyons, Nebraska*

## Quail with Mushrooms

*6 quail*
*6 slices bacon*
*Salt and pepper to taste*
*½ lb. mushroom caps*
*1 bunch green onions, chopped*
*3 tbsp. butter, melted*
*2 tbsp. prepared mustard*
*½ tsp. dry ginger*
*1 c. orange marmalade*

Wrap each quail with bacon slice. Arrange in rows on large sheet of heavy foil. Season with salt and pepper. Saute mushroom caps and onions in butter in skillet. Pour over quail. Seal foil well. Place on baking sheet. Bake at 325 degrees for 1 hour or until tender. Combine remaining ingredients; mix well. Serve with quail.

*Mrs. Elizabeth W. Knape*
*Douglas, Arizona*

## Quail in Wine

2 shallots, chopped
2 cloves of garlic, finely chopped
½ bay leaf
1 tsp. peppercorn
2 cloves
¾ c. butter
6 quail
1 pt. white wine
4 tbsp. flour
½ tsp. salt
⅛ tsp. pepper
1 tsp. finely cut chives

Combine shallots and next 4 ingredients in small bowl; mix well. Saute in ½ cup butter in skillet for 8 minutes, stirring constantly. Saute quail until well-browned. Add white wine; simmer for ½ hour or until tender. Remove quail. Strain; reserving sauce. Melt remaining butter in saucepan; blend in flour. Stir in reserved sauce; cook until thick. Add remaining ingredients, mixing thoroughly. Add quail; cover. Heat to boiling point. Yield: 8 servings.

Mrs. Mary P. Light
Kingsville, Texas

## Onion Smothered Venison Steak

4 venison steaks
Flour
Seasoning salt and pepper to taste
Shortening
1 pkg. dry onion soup mix
1 tbsp. Worcestershire sauce

Pound steaks. Combine flour with seasonings. Coat steaks with flour mixture. Brown steaks in shortening in skillet. Add dry onion soup mix, 1½ cups water and Worcestershire sauce. Simmer for 1 hour or until tender. Serve with rice. Yield: 4-6 servings.

Mrs. Martha Jo Bredemeyer
Lancaster, Texas

## Braised Venison

2 c. flour
1 tsp. salt
½ tsp. pepper
8 venison steaks
2 tbsp. shortening
¾ c. onion rings
Garlic salt to taste

Sift together dry ingredients except garlic salt. Coat venison with mixture. Brown steaks in shortening in large skillet. Top with onion rings; sprinkle with garlic salt. Add 2 cups water. Simmer for 1 hour over medium heat or until tender. Yield: 8 servings.

Mrs. Brooksie Rentz
Cayce, South Carolina

## Graustark Venison

1 6-lb. leg of venison
Salt to taste
2 c. dry red wine
2 med. onions, quartered
2 med. carrots, sliced
4 sprigs of parsley
2 bay leaves
10 peppercorns
4 whole cloves
Dash of thyme
6 strips salt pork
¾ c. butter, melted
2 tbsp. flour
1 c. beef broth
3 lb. small potatoes, peeled, cut into halves
White pepper to taste
Snipped parsley to taste
2 10-oz. packages frozen Brussels sprouts, thawed
¼ c. chopped walnuts

Season venison with salt. Place in shallow pan. Combine next 8 ingredients in bowl. Pour over venison. Refrigerate for 24 hours, turning occasionally. Remove venison from marinade. Strain, reserving marinade. Place venison on rack in shallow baking pan. Place salt pork across venison. Bake in 450-degree oven for 25 minutes. Reduce oven temperature to 325 degrees. Bake for about 2 hours longer or until venison is medium rare, basting frequently with half the reserved marinade. Remove venison to hot platter. Combine remaining marinade with pan drippings in saucepan. Bring to a boil. Blend 2 tablespoons butter with flour; stir into marinade. Stir in broth slowly. Bring to a boil, stirring constantly. Cook for 1 minute longer. Cook potatoes in boiling, salted water in saucepan for 15 to 20 minutes

## Braised Kidney on Toast

1 kidney, cubed
Flour
Salt and pepper to taste
1 to 2 tbsp. shortening

Coat kidney in flour. Season to taste. Brown in shortening in heavy skillet. Cover. Cook until tender. Add enough water to thicken for gravy. Serve over toast. Yield: 2 servings.

*Mrs. Margaret Swigart*
*Bainville, Montana*

## Sauteed Kidney

1 beef kidney
3 tbsp. vinegar
1 c. flour
3 tbsp. butter
1 med. onion, chopped
¼ lb. mushrooms, sliced
1 bouillon cube
½ tsp. salt
⅛ tsp. pepper
½ tbsp. Worcestershire sauce
2 tbsp. pimento
¼ c. red cooking wine
2 tbsp. chopped parsley

Soak kidney in vinegar and 1 quart water for 2 hours. Rinse. Slice thinly. Coat slices thoroughly with flour. Melt butter in skillet. Saute onion and mushrooms. Remove; set aside. Brown kidney quickly on both sides in pan drippings. Dissolve bouillon cube in 1½ cups boiling water; pour over kidney. Add all ingredients except parsley; mix well. Cover. Reduce heat. Simmer 10 minutes or until tender. Sprinkle with parsley before serving. Yield: 4 servings.

*Mrs. Mari Hurley*
*El Centro, California*

or until tender. Drain. Toss with 6 tablespoons butter, white pepper, salt and parsley. Saute Brussels sprouts in remaining butter in skillet for 10 minutes. Add walnuts. Cook for 5 minutes. Arrange potatoes and Brussels sprouts around venison. Serve with gravy. Yield: 6-8 servings.

*Photograph for this recipe on page 83.*

## Smothered Venison

1  1 lb. venison steak, cut ½-inch thick
Flour
¼ c. oil
2 c. milk
Salt and pepper to taste
Garlic salt
1 lg. onion, sliced

Tenderize venison; cut into serving pieces. Dip steaks in 1 cup flour. Brown in hot oil in skillet. Remove steaks. Stir 3 tablespoons flour into pan drippings. Add milk gradually, stirring constantly, until thickened. Add seasonings and steak. Place onion slices over steak. Gravy should cover steak and onions. Cover. Bake at 275 degrees for 2 hours. Yield: 4 servings.

*Rosanne Looney*
*Texarkana, Texas*

## Fried Liver

1 lb. beef liver, sliced ¼ to ½-in. thick
½ c. flour
½ tsp. salt
⅛ tsp. pepper
1 c. oil

Cut liver into serving pieces. Combine flour, salt and pepper. Coat liver with flour mixture. Brown in oil in heavy skillet for 25 minutes or until tender. Yield: 4 servings.

*Lessie Oaks*
*Memphis, Tennessee*

## Baked Beef Liver

¼ c. milk
1 egg, slightly beaten
4 slices liver
Flour
Bread crumbs
Salt and pepper to taste
8 bacon strips

Combine milk and egg in bowl; mix well. Dip liver in flour, egg mixture, and bread crumbs. Place liver in greased baking pan. Season with salt and pepper. Cover with bacon strips. Bake at 350 degrees for 20 minutes or until bacon is browned. Yield: 4 servings.

*Mrs. Carolyn Fredrick*
*Pinkney, Michigan*

## Creole Beef Liver

1½ lb. beef liver, thinly sliced
Flour
3 tbsp. butter, melted
1¾ c. sliced onions
2 c. canned tomatoes, heated
¾ c. diced celery
1½ c. thinly sliced green pepper
¾ tsp. salt
Dash of cayenne

Coat liver with flour. Brown liver in butter in skillet. Add remaining ingredients. Cover. Simmer for 20 minutes. Drain. Add 2 tablespoons flour to small amount of water; blend with pan drippings. Add liver and vegetables. Simmer for 2 minutes longer. Yield: 6 servings.

*Mrs. Patsy Steagald*
*Starke, Florida*

## Liver with Sour Cream Sauce

1 lb. beef liver, cut into ½ inch cubes
Flour
3 tbsp. bacon drippings
2 tbsp. chopped onion
2 4-oz. cans mushrooms
1 beef bouillon cube
Salt and pepper to taste
½ c. sour cream

Dip liver in flour. Brown in bacon drippings with onion in skillet. Cook for 8 minutes. Add mushrooms. Dissolve beef bouillon cube in small amount of water. Pour over liver. Simmer until tender. Season with salt and pepper. Add sour cream before serving. Yield: 4 servings.

*Mrs. Rosetta Bartels*
*Inman, Kansas*

## Liver in White Wine

1 lb. liver, sliced
Flour
4 tbsp. olive oil
2 cloves of garlic, split into halves
1 sm. onion, minced
Salt and pepper to taste
1 tsp. basil
½ c. white wine

Coat liver with flour. Brown slowly in olive oil in skillet. Add garlic and onion. Saute until tender. Spoon over liver. Add seasonings. Pour wine over top; cover. Cook slowly for ½ hour, basting every 10 minutes. Discard garlic before serving. Yield: 4 servings.

*Leila Steckelberg*
*Mount Vernon, Washington*

## Sweet and Sour Luncheon Meat

1 12-oz. can luncheon meat, ground
¼ lb. cheese, ground
½ c. oats
1 egg, beaten
1 tbsp. shortening
1 tbsp. each brown sugar, cornstarch
1 c. undrained pineapple chunks
1 tbsp. vinegar
¼ tsp. ginger

Combine first 4 ingredients in medium bowl; mix well. Form into 8 large balls; place in shallow baking pan. Bake at 400 degrees for 20 minutes. Heat shortening in saucepan; blend in brown sugar and cornstarch. Stir in 1 cup water and remaining ingredients. Cook until thick, stirring constantly. Drain off grease from meatballs. Pour sauce over meatballs. Bake for 10 minutes longer. Yield: 6-8 servings.

*Mrs. Ruth Eleazer*
*Columbia, South Carolina*

## Wagon Wheel Pie

½ c. chopped onion
2 tbsp. butter
1 12-oz. can luncheon meat
1½ pkg. frozen mixed vegetables
½ c. grated Cheddar cheese
1 c. evaporated milk
2 eggs, beaten
2 tbsp. flour
½ tsp. salt
¼ tsp. paprika
1 unbaked pastry shell

Steam onion in butter in covered saucepan over low heat for 10 minutes. Set aside. Cut meat lengthwise into ¼-inch slices. Reserve 5 slices. Cut remaining slices into bite-sized pieces. Partially cook frozen vegetables; drain. Combine vegetables with next 6 ingredients; mix well. Pour into pastry shell. Cut reserved luncheon meat slices into halves diagonally. Arrange over filling. Bake at 400 degrees for 30 to 35 minutes.

*Mrs. Greta Litchfield*
*Taunton, Massachusetts*

## Sweetbreads a la King

½ lb. sweetbreads
1 c. chopped celery
½ c. chopped green pepper
4 tbsp. butter
2 c. flour
2 c. milk
½ c. chopped red pepper
4 hard-boiled eggs
Salt and pepper to taste

Cook sweetbreads in boiling water in saucepan over low heat until tender. Cool. Cut into small pieces. Boil celery and green pepper in salted water in saucepan until tender. Drain. Melt butter in saucepan. Blend in flour; cook until bubbly. Add milk gradually, stirring until thick. Add sweetbreads, celery peppers and eggs. Season with salt and pepper. Serve hot over toast.

*Kathryn Davis*
*Pickneyville, Illinois*

## Cumberland Tongues

1 beef tongue
1 c. currant jelly

2 tbsp. prepared mustard
1 tbsp. lemon juice
1 tbsp. grated orange rind

Place tongue in pressure cooker. Cook for 1 hour at 10 pounds pressure. Cut into thin slices. Place in skillet. Combine jelly, mustard and lemon juice in saucepan. Cook until heated. Add orange rind. Spoon sauce over sliced tongue; cover. Cook over low heat for 10 to 20 minutes. Yield: 6 servings.

*Jean Collins*
*Sauk Rapids, Minnesota*

## Barbecued Frankfurters

1 onion, chopped
3 tbsp. shortening
1 tbsp. sugar
1 tsp. each salt, dry mustard, paprika
½ c. catsup
¼ c. vinegar
1 tbsp. Worcestershire sauce
¼ tsp. Tabasco sauce
12 frankfurters, split

Saute onion lightly in shortening in skillet. Combine ½ cup water and remaining ingredients except frankfurters in bowl; mix well. Stir mixture into onion. Simmer for 15 minutes. Arrange frankfurters in 8½ × 11-inch baking dish. Pour sauce over frankfurters. Bake in 350-degree oven for ½ hour, basting frequently. Yield: 6 servings.

*Mary Kay Pearson*
*Waupaca, Wisconsin*

## Carolina Corn Dogs

¾ c. self-rising flour
¼ c. self-rising cornmeal
1 tbsp. sugar
1 tsp. dry mustard
2 tbsp. minced onion
1 egg, beaten
½ c. milk
1 lb. frankfurters
Oil for frying

Combine first 5 ingredients in bowl; mix well. Combine egg and milk in small bowl. Add to dry ingredients; mix well. Dip frankfurters into batter, coating completely. Fry in deep hot oil in skillet until golden brown.

*Mrs. Elizabeth M. Culbreth*
*Inman, South Carolina*

## Cheese Puppies

6 frankfurters
6 4 × ½ × ¼-in. cheese strips
3 bacon slices, cut into halves

Slit frankfurters lengthwise to within ½-inch of end. Place cheese strip in each frankfurter. Place bacon over cheese. Secure bacon with toothpicks. Arrange frankfurters in shallow baking pan. Broil until bacon is crisp and cheese is melted. Yield: 8 servings.

Mrs. Evia C. Arnold
Rio Vista, Texas

## Cowboy Supper

½ c. each chopped onion, green pepper
2 tbsp. butter
12 frankfurters, quartered
2 c. chopped tomatoes
½ tsp. each caraway seed, salt
1 bay leaf
¼ tsp. paprika
4 hard-boiled eggs, quartered

Saute onion and green pepper in butter in skillet until transparent. Stir in remaining ingredients except eggs. Simmer for 15 minutes. Top with eggs. Simmer for 10 minutes longer. Serve on thin slices of corn bread or crisp toast.

Marble Henderson
Tahlequah, Oklahoma

## Barbecued Frankfurters

1 onion, chopped
3 tbsp. shortening
1 tbsp. sugar
1 tsp. each dry mustard, salt, paprika
½ tsp. pepper
½ c. catsup
¼ c. vinegar
1 tbsp. Worcestershire sauce
¼ tsp. Tabasco sauce
12 frankfurters

Brown onion lightly in shortening in skillet. Combine ½ cup water and remaining ingredients except frankfurters. Add to onions; simmer for 15 minutes. Split frankfurters lengthwise. Place in 8½ × 11-inch baking dish. Cover with sauce. Bake at 350 degrees for 30 minutes, basting several times.

Mary Kay Pearson
Waupaca, Wisconsin

## Hot Dog Chili

3 lb. ground beef
3 tbsp. paprika
2½ tbsp. chili powder
2 tbsp. salt
1 tbsp. celery salt
1 tsp. pepper
1 clove of garlic
Tomato juice

Mix first 7 ingredients in large skillet. Add 1 cup tomato juice. Bring to a boil, stirring occasionally until crumbly. Cover with additional tomato juice. Simmer for 3 hours or until liquid is absorbed. Yield: 1 quart.

G. Sue Lacy
Kermit, West Virginia

## Frankfurters with Two-Bean Succotash

1 lb. frankfurters
1 12-oz. can whole kernal corn
1 pkg. frozen cut green beans
1 pkg. frozen fordhook lima beans
Salt and pepper to taste
2 tbsp. butter
Chopped green onion

Score frankfurters diagonally several times with sharp knife; brown lightly in small amount of shortening in skillet. Remove from heat; keep hot. Drain liquid from corn into skillet; add green beans and limas. Season with salt and pepper. Cook for 10 minutes, breaking up blocks with fork. Add a small amount water, if needed. Add corn; heat. Mix vegetables well; add butter. Top with frankfurters; sprinkle with onion.

Mrs. Elizabeth H. Kneesha
Goldsboro, North Carolina

## Gourmet Hot Dogs

4 tbsp. butter
1 lg. can sliced mushrooms, drained
3 tbsp. flour
½ tsp. salt
Wieners

Brown butter in frypan. Coat mushrooms with flour; add to butter. Saute until brown. Add salt and 2 tablespoons water. Cover. Cook until tender. Arrange wieners over mushrooms. Cover. Steam for 7 to 10 minutes or until wieners are puffed. Garnish with parsley.

Mrs. Marjorie C. Vickery
Holland, Texas

# Seafood

# SEAFOOD

Americans are blessed with a wealth of fish—in staggering quantities and variety. Considering our bounty, it's surprising we didn't learn to prepare it properly until the twentieth century. Until then, it was generally overcooked, smothered in fat, or fried in crumbs—ruining the texture and taste.

No longer! As you'll discover from the assortment of Home Economics teachers' fish recipes included in this chapter, there are many new ways to prepare fillets, seafood casseroles, quiches, even barbecued fish.

## BUYING FISH

There are three basic types of fish to look for: Saltwater, Freshwater and Shellfish. All are nutritious and lower in calories than many meats.

*Saltwater Fish*
- Normal serving is ⅓ to ½ pound of eatable fish.
- To provide for this, allow 1 pound of whole fish per serving; ½ pound dressed fish; ⅓ to ½ pound fillet or sticks.
- Fish is extremely perishable. Cook immediately or remove from the wrapper and re-wrap in aluminum foil, plastic wrap or place in a tightly covered dish. Store in the coldest part of the refrigerator.

*Freshwater Fish*
- Make sure fish smells fresh and clean, not fishy; eyes are bright and bulging, not sunken or cloudy.
- As fish becomes stale, gills fade from light pink to gray to a greenish-brown color.
- Frozen fish should be solid without a brownish tinge or other skin discolorations.
- Frozen fish should be well centered in package. If not, it's probably been thawed out and re-frozen.

*Shellfish*
- Less expensive when bought in shells
- Make sure fresh shrimp has a mild odor and firm meat.
- Purchase only live crabs and lobsters. The tails will curl under when picked up.
- Fresh scallops should have a sweet odor, firm white flesh; free of liquid when bought in packages.
- Shells of live clams, mussels and oysters should be tightly closed. Or, if slightly open, should close immediately when lightly tapped.
- Gapping shells indicate the shellfish is dead and shouldn't be eaten.
- Shucked oysters should be plump, naturally creamy in color, and in a small amount of clear liquid.

# COOKING FISH

A simple rule of thumb that's foolproof:
1. Measure the thickness of the fish at its biggest point.
2. Whatever the cooking method, estimate 10 minutes per inch.
3. Double cooking time for frozen fish.

For example, if you're poaching salmon that measures 4 inches at its thickest point, poach for 40 minutes. Saute a fillet that's ½ inch thick for 5 minutes. Broil a 1½-inch salmon steak for 7½ minutes on each side. It's as simple as that.

*Broiling.............................* This is the fastest way to cook fish, so be sure and watch your oven. Place fish in broiler pan and broil under full heat for the entire cooking time. Turn steaks or whole fish one time. Fillets and split fish don't need any turning, but be sure and place them skin down. If fish is lean, baste with olive oil or melted butter.

*Frying..................................* It's America's most popular way of preparing fish. Place fish, flesh side down, to prevent curling but don't crowd in the pan. Heat vegetable oil (peanut and corn oil are also satisfactory) until it's hot, but not smoking. Drain fried fish thoroughly on paper towels before serving.

*Steaming and Broiling........* Here's an excellent way to prepare fish for salads or special diets. Salt the fish and wrap in cheesecloth, leaving long enough ends to hang outside saucepan for handles. Place in a colander, steamer, or rack over rapidly boiling water. Make sure the water doesn't touch the fish. Cover tightly and steam until fish flakes easily.

## Baked Fish Fillets

1 lb. fish fillets
Pepper
½ can mushroom soup
¼ c. milk
¼ tsp. each salt, onion salt
1 tbsp. dried parsley flakes
2 tbsp. butter

Cut fish into 5 or 6 serving pieces. Arrange in baking dish. Combine ¼ teaspoon pepper and next 4 ingredients in bowl. Pour around fish. Sprinkle with additional pepper and parsley flakes. Dot with butter. Bake at 350 degrees for 20 to 25 minutes or until fish flakes easily.

*Mrs. Marguerite Darnall*
*Campo, California*

## Barbecued Fish

1 med. onion, chopped
2 tbsp. butter
1 c. catsup
2 bay leaves
½ tsp. garlic salt
¼ tsp. salt
Dash of pepper
1½ to 2 lb. fish fillets

Saute onion in butter in skillet until tender. Stir in catsup, bay leaves and seasonings. Place half the sauce on large square of foil. Place fish on sauce. Cover with remaining sauce. Seal foil tightly. Place on rack over hot coals. Cook for 10 minutes. Turn. Cook for 10 minutes longer or until tender. Yield: 6 servings.

*Mrs. Louise Hudson*
*Yuma, Arizona*

## Fish En Coquilles

1 c. leftover fish
8 mussels
½ c. bread crumbs
10 tbsp. milk
1 clove of garlic
Parsley to taste
1 med. onion, chopped
Salt and pepper to taste
3 tbsp. butter
Buttered crumbs

Flake fish into bowl; add mussels. Soak crumbs in 2 tablespoons milk; combine with fish mixture. Add garlic, parsley, onion, salt and pepper; mix well. Melt butter in saucepan; add fish mixture. Cook for 5 minutes. Stir in ½ cup milk. Spoon into small ramekins. Cover each ramekin with buttered crumbs. Bake at 350 degrees for 15 minutes. Yield: 6 servings.

*Mrs. Lucy Jonsson*
*Massapequa, New York*

## New Orleans Baked Fish

2 tbsp. butter
2 tbsp. flour
2 c. milk
Salt and pepper to taste
1 lb. cooked shrimp, cut into small pieces
½ lb. canned crab meat, cut into small pieces
Dried parsley
6 fish fillet

Melt butter in saucepan. Add flour; mix well. Cook until bubbly. Add milk gradually. Cook until thick, stirring constantly. Add salt and pepper. Add shrimp, crabmeat and parsley; mix well. Place each fillet on piece of heavy foil. Spread shrimp mixture over each. Seal foil. Place on cookie sheet. Bake at 450 degrees for 15 minutes. Yield: 6 servings.

*Mrs. Hobert Keller*
*Clayton, Georgia*

## Southern Panfried Fish

2 to 3 lb. fish
1 c. shortening
2 tbsp. salt
½ c. cornmeal

Cut fish into serving pieces. Heat shortening in frypan over medium heat. Combine salt and cornmeal. Roll fish in mixture. Fry in hot shortening for 3 minutes or until delicately browned. Yield: 4 servings.

*Glendola Pinson*
*Hermitage, Arkansas*

## Bass Pinecone Magic

3 lb. stripped bass fillets with skins
Salt, pepper, Accent, marjoram, paprika to taste
½ lb. butter

Sprinkle fillets with seasonings. Grill over hot coals, skin-side down. Dot fillets with butter. Grill for 10 to 12 minutes; turn. Add several days pinecones to hot charcoal to flavor fish. Turn fillets skin-side down when pinecones begin to brown. Add butter as needed to keep fillets moist. Grill until fish flakes easily. Remove to serving platter; garnish with parsley and lemon wedges. Yield: 4 servings.

*Mrs. Esther Sigmund*
*Larado, Texas*

## Codfish Quickie

*1 lb. codfish*
*2 tbsp. dried green and red pepper flakes*
*4 tbsp. shortening*
*1 sm. can mushrooms, chopped*
*1 can cream of mushroom soup*
*½ tsp. salt*
*4 potatoes, cooked*

Cut codfish into 1-inch cubes. Saute peppers in shortening in skillet for 10 minutes; add cod-fish. Cook for 10 minutes or until fish flakes easily. Add mushrooms, soup and salt. Heat through. Let stand for 5 minutes. Serve over potatoes.

*Mrs. Ella Adair*
*Tropic, Utah*

## Baked Flounder Fillets

*1 lb. fillet of flounder*
*½ tsp. salt*
*2 tbsp. lemon juice*
*3 tbsp. butter*

Sprinkle flounder with salt and lemon juice; dot with butter. Place in foil-lined baking pan. Bake at 350 degrees for 20 minutes or until brown.

*Mrs. Clarinda A. Britt*
*Maiden, North Carolina*

## Lemon-Buttered Haddock

*4 haddock fillets*
*Salt and pepper to taste*
*¾ c. butter, softened*
*3 lemons, sliced*
*3 med. onions, sliced*

Place fillets on individual sheets of foil. Season with salt and pepper. Spread 3 tablespoons butter over each fillet. Place lemon and onion slices alternately on each fillet. Seal foil tightly. Place over hot coals. Cook for 15 minutes on each side.

*Rosemarie Burns*
*Saugerties, New York*

## Elegant Halibut Fillets

*1 1-lb. package frozen halibut fillets, thawed*
*Pepper to taste*
*2 tbsp. butter*
*1 can frozen cream of shrimp soup, thawed*
*¼ c. grated Parmesan cheese*
*Paprika to taste*

Arrange fillets in buttered 9-inch pie plate. Sprinkle with pepper. Dot with butter. Spread soup over fillets. Sprinkle with cheese and paprika. Bake at 400 degrees for 25 minutes. Serve with lemon wedges. Yield: 3-4 servings.

*Mrs. Joann Ketterer*
*Shippensburg, Pennsylvania*

## Fisherman's Luck

*1 ¾ lb. halibut fillets, 1 in thick*
*Salt and pepper to taste*
*½ c. chopped green pepper*
*½ c. chopped onions*
*2 tbsp. butter*
*½ c. catsup*
*½ tsp. garlic salt*
*2 sm. bay leaves*

Divide fish into 4 serving portions. Arrange on squares of foil. Season with salt and pepper. Mix remaining ingredients in saucepan. Simmer for 10 to 15 minutes. Pour ¼ of the sauce over each portion of fish. Seal foil tightly. Grill over hot coals for 15 to 20 minutes or until fish flakes easily.

*Mrs. Marjorie Browning*
*Pensacola, Florida*

## Charcoal-Grilled Snapper

*1 red snapper*
*Garlic salt and pepper to taste*
*Butter, melted*
*2 tsp. lemon juice*

Season snapper with garlic salt and pepper. Brush sides and cavity with butter. Cook over low coals for 5 minutes per side. Combine ½ cup butter with lemon juice. Brush lemon butter over snapper. Wrap in foil. Grill for 15 to 20 minutes longer. Yield: 4-6 servings.

*Mrs. Tommie Mouser*
*Richardson, Texas*

## Baked Red Snapper

8 red snapper, cleaned, boned
6 slices bread, toasted, cubed
Milk
1 egg, beaten
1 med. onion, grated
½ c. whole kernel corn
¼ c. grated cheese (opt.)
1 sm. tomato, cubed
½ c. each mayonnaise, Thousand Island
    dressing
1 med. onion, chopped
3 tbsp. each Worcestershire sauce, lemon
    juice
3 tbsp. butter, melted

Slash cavity in side of each snapper for stuffing. Set aside. Place bread in bowl with enough milk to cover. Let stand to soften. Drain. Add egg, grated onion, corn, cheese and tomato; mix well. Spoon into cavity of each snapper. Place in shallow baking dish. Combine mayonnaise, Thousand Island dressing, chopped onion, Worcestershire sauce, lemon juice and butter; mix well. Spoon over snapper. Bake at 350 degrees for 50 minutes.

*Gayle Scott*
*Alton, Texas*

## Baked Stuffed Red Snapper

1 2½ to 3-lb. red snapper
Salt
2 c. corn bread crumbs
2 slices white bread, crumbled
1 egg, beaten
1 onion, chopped
½ tsp. poultry seasoning
¼ c. margarine, melted
2 slices bacon

Rub snapper cavity with salt. Combine 1 teaspoon salt and next 5 ingredients in bowl; mix well. Add enough hot water to bind mixture together. Spoon stuffing into snapper cavity. Secure with toothpicks. Pour margarine over top of snapper. Place bacon on top. Bake at 325 degrees for ½ hour per pound. Serve with tartar sauce. Yield: 6-8 servings.

*Ruth D. Jordan*
*Alexander City, Alabama*

## Baked Salmon

1 salmon steak
Salt and pepper to taste
¼ c. sour cream
4 thin lemon slices
1 tsp. minced parsley

Place salmon in buttered dish. Sprinkle with salt and pepper. Top with sour cream and lemon slices. Sprinkle with parsley. Bake in 350-degree oven for 35 to 40 minutes. Yield: 2 servings.

*Mrs. Nancy Roop*
*Dodge City, Kansas*

## Barbecued Salmon Steaks

3 lb. salmon steaks, ¾ in. thick
¼ c. oil
Juice of 1 lemon
¼ c. barbecue sauce

Place salmon steaks in shallow dish. Combine oil and lemon juice. Pour over salmon. Chill for ½ hour, turning once. Arrange salmon in folding wire broiler. Brush well with heated barbecue sauce, cook close to coals for about 3 minutes or until golden brown. Brush with sauce; turn. Cook for 2 to 3 minutes longer. Brush with sauce before serving. Yield: 8 servings.

*Sister Tabitha Kaup*
*Omaha, Nebraska*

## Salmon-Cheese Puff

3 eggs, separated
2¼ c. milk
1 c. each soft bread crumbs, shredded
    cheddar cheese
1 tsp. instant minced onion
1 1-lb. can flaked salmon, drained,
    boned
⅛ tsp. pepper
1¼ tsp. salt
Lemon juice
3 tbsp. butter
3 tbsp. flour
1½ tbsp. chopped parsley

Beat egg yolks with ¾ c. milk in mixing bowl. Add next 5 ingredients, ½ teaspoon salt and 2 teaspoons lemon juice. Beat egg whites in bowl until stiff peaks form. Fold into salmon mixture. Turn into shallow 1-quart baking dish.

Bake in 350-degree oven for 30 to 35 minutes or until knife inserted in center comes out clean. Melt butter in 1-quart saucepan. Stir in flour and ¾ teaspoon salt. Remove from heat. Stir in 1½ cups milk gradually. Cook over medium heat until thick, stirring constantly. Cook for 2 minutes longer. Stir in 1 tablespoon lemon juice and parsley. Serve over salmon. Yield: 6 servings.

*Agnes Huffman*
*Modesto, California*

## Salmon Puff

4 eggs, lightly beaten
½ c. milk
1 can mushroom soup
1 medium can salmon
2 c. soft bread crumbs
1 tbsp. minced parsley
2 tbsp. butter

Combine eggs, milk and soup in bowl; mix well. Blend in remaining ingredients. Place in buttered casserole. Bake at 350 degrees for 45 to 50 minutes. Yield: 6 servings.

*Mildred L. Callahan*
*Miami, Florida*

## Salmon Souffle

1½ c. canned pink salmon, drained
1 tbsp. minced parsley
1 tsp. lemon juice
½ tsp. salt
⅛ tsp. each pepper, paprika
1½ c. medium white sauce
3 eggs, separated

Combine salmon with all ingredients except egg whites in large bowl; mix well. Beat egg whites until stiff peaks form. Fold gently into salmon mixure. Turn into greased baking dish. Place dish in pan of hot water. Bake at 350 degrees until center is firm. Serve immediately. Yield: 6 servings.

*Mrs. Berline Baldwin*
*Clarkton, North Carolina*

## Salmon Croquettes

1 can salmon
2 med. potatoes, cooked, mashed

Salt and pepper to taste
1 egg, beaten
Cornmeal

Combine salmon and potatoes in bowl. Add salt and pepper; mix well. Shape into croquettes. Dip in egg. Coat with cornmeal. Brown in hot shortening in skillet. Yield: 6 servings.

*Mrs. Lucile Horton*
*Del Rio, Texas*

## Salmon Croquettes Deluxe

4 tbsp. flour
2 tbsp. butter, melted
Salt and pepper to taste
1 c. milk
1 can salmon, drained, flaked
1 tsp. lemon juice
Cracker crumbs
2 eggs, beaten
Oil for frying

Combine flour, butter and ½ tsp. salt in saucepan. Cook over low heat until bubbly. Add milk gradually, stirring constantly. Cook over low heat for 15 to 20 minutes until thick, stirring constantly. Remove from heat. Combine salmon and lemon juice in bowl. Season with salt and pepper. Add white sauce; mix well. Shape mixture into croquettes. Coat with cracker crumbs. Dip into egg. Roll in crumbs again. Fry in deep hot fat until golden brown.

*Mary Frances C. Boyd*
*Stovall, North Carolina*

## Fillet of Sole in Sherry

4 fillets of sole
12 shrimp, cooked, chopeed
4 green onions, chopped
2 tbsp. butter
2 tbsp. flour
⅓ c. Sherry

Stuff fillets with shrimp and onions. Arrange in single layer in 8-inch baking dish. Combine butter, flour and Sherry in bowl; mix well. Pour sauce over fillets. Cover. Bake at 350 degrees for 45 minutes. Yield: 4 servings.

*Mrs. Robert A. Still*
*Olympia, Washington*

## Sole Marguery

12 fillet of sole
2 eggs, beaten
1 can mushroom soup
1 pt. half and half
3 drops Tabasco sauce
½ c. small shrimp

Arrange fillets in shallow, buttered baking dish. Combine next 4 ingredients in bowl; mix well. Pour over sole. Top with shrimp. Bake at 450 degrees for 30 minutes.

*Laura Belle Carmany*
*Carmel, California*

## Tuna-Stuffed Baked Potato

6 med. potatoes, baked
6 tbsp. butter
Milk
1 tsp. salt
⅛ tsp. pepper
2 tbsp. grated onion
1 can white tuna
1 c. grated American cheese

Cut potatoes in half lengthwise. Scope out centers into a bowl; reserve shells. Mash potatoes until smooth. Add butter, a small amount of milk, salt and pepper. Whip until fluffy. Add grated onion and tuna; mix well. Fill shells. Sprinkle with cheese. Bake at 400 degrees until cheese melts and potatoes are heated through.

*Mrs. Martha L. Matthews*
*Colorada City, Texas*

## Chopstick Tuna

1 c. mushroom soup
2 c. chow mein noodles
1 can chunk-style tuna
1 c. sliced celery
½ c. salted cashews
¼ c. chopped onion

Combine soup and ¼ cup water in bowl. Add 1½ cup chow mein noodles and remaining ingredients. Toss lightly. Place in ungreased baking dish. Sprinkle remaining noodles over top. Bake at 325 degrees for 20 minutes. Serve immediately. Yield: 4 servings.

*Mrs. Sue Gray*
*Kansas City, Kansas*

## Tuna Pie with Cheese Roll Crust

½ c. chopped bell pepper
¼ c. chopped onion
3 tbsp. butter
Flour
1 tsp. salt
3½ c. milk
1 tbsp. lemon juice
1 lg. can tuna
3 tsp. baking powder
Pinch of cayenne
3 tbsp. shortening
¾ c. grated cheese
2 pimentos, chopped

Saute bell pepper and onion in butter in skillet until soft. Add 6 tablespoons flour and ½ teaspoon salt; blend well. Add 3 cups milk gradually, stirring constantly until thick. Boil for 2 minutes. Add lemon juice and tuna. Pour into baking dish. Sift 1½ cups flour and ½ teaspoon salt with next 2 ingredients into bowl. Cut shortening into dry ingredients until crumbly. Stir in ½ cup milk to make soft dough. Roll out on floured surface as for biscuits. Sprinkle with cheese and pimento. Roll as for jelly roll. Slice. Place over pie. Bake in 425-degree oven for ½ hour. Yield: 6 servings.

*Nelle H. Woodward*
*Holt, Alabama*

## Whitefish Amandine

2 lb. whitefish fillets
2 tbsp. lemon juice
2 tsp. salt
Dash of pepper
½ c. flour
½ c. oil
½ c. slivered blanched almonds
2 tbsp. chopped parsley

Cut whitefish into serving pieces. Sprinkle with lemon juice, salt and pepper. Coat with flour. Brown both sides in oil in skillet over medium heat. Cook for 10 to 12 minutes or until tender. Remove whitefish to hot platter. Saute almonds until lightly brown. Add parsley. Spoon over whitefish. Yield: 6 servings.

*Mrs. Irma B. Morley*
*Allegan, Michigan*

## Barbecued Clams

*36 clams*
*⅓ c. catsup*
*¼ lb. sharp cheese, sliced*
*4 strips lean bacon*

Shuck clams; loosen from shells. Leave clams on larger half shells. Place in 2-inch deep baking pan. Cut bacon into ½-inch pieces. Place ¼ teaspoon catsup on each clam. Add ½-inch slice cheese. Top with bacon. Broil for about 5 minutes or until bacon is crisp.

*Ellen Morgan Schenck*
*West Lawn, Pennsylvania*

## Deviled Clams

*12 lg. clams, scrubbed*
*1 egg*
*2 med. potatoes, cooked, mashed*
*¼ c. chopped celery*
*1 med. onion, chopped*
*1 sprig of parsley, chopped*
*½ tsp. dry mustard*
*⅛ tsp. pepper*
*1 tsp. salt*
*Fine dry bread crumbs*

Steam clams in a small amount of boiling water in saucepan until clams open. Remove from shells. Force through food grinder using medium blade. Separate shells. Combine remaining ingredients except bread crumbs in bowl; mix well. Add clams; mix well. Fill shells ½ full mixture. Sprinkle with bread crumbs. Place on baking sheet. Bake at 350 degrees for 15 to 20 minutes or until light brown, but not dry. Yield: 4-6 servings.

*Mrs. Carol N. Hall*
*Columbia, Pennsylvania*

## Crab Imperial

*¾ c. milk*
*1 slice bread, crumbled*
*2 tbsp. butter*
*2 tbsp. (heaping) flour*
*½ tsp. each salt, dry mustard*
*1 tsp. vinegar*
*½ tsp. Worcestershire sauce*
*2 tbsp. (heaping) mayonnaise*
*1 lb. crab meat*

Pour ¼ cup milk over bread in bowl. Set aside. Melt butter in saucepan; blend in flour. Add remaining milk gradually, stirring constantly. Cook until thick, stirring constantly. Stir in next 4 ingredients. Cool. Stir in mayonnaise, bread mixture and crab meat. Spoon into 8 ramekins. Bake at 350 degrees for 15 minutes. Yield: 8 servings.

*Elizabeth L. Hudson*
*Richmond, Virginia*

## Egg Foo Yung with Crab

*½ c. chopped onion*
*Oil*
*½ c. chopped tomatoes*
*1 pkg. frozen crab meat, thawed*
*3 eggs, beaten*
*Salt and pepper to taste*
*Monosodium glutamate to taste*
*2 tbsp. soy sauce*
*1 c. broth*
*1 tbsp. cornstarch*

Saute onion lightly in 1 tablespoon oil in skillet. Add tomatoes. Simmer for 2 minutes. Add crab meat. Heat through. Stir in next 4 ingredients; mix well. Shape crab meat mixture into patties. Fry in oil in skillet until brown. Combine soy sauce and broth in saucepan. Bring to a boil. Blend cornstarch with 1 tablespoon water. Add to hot mixture. Cook until thick, stirring constantly. Serve over crab meat patties.

*Mrs. Wilma C. Mitchell*
*Smithville, Ohio*

## Crab Pilaf

*1 7-oz. can crab meat, drained, flaked*
*1 sm. onion, sliced*
*½ c. celery, diced*
*1 pkg. frozen mixed vegetables, thawed*
*6 tbsp. oil*
*3 c. cooked rice*
*¼ c. salted peanuts*
*soy sauce*

Remove bone from crab meat. Set aside. Saute vegetables in 4 tablespoon oil in skillet. Saute rice in remaining oil in separate skillet for 10 minutes. Add crab meat, vegetables and peanuts to rice. Cook until hot, stirring occasionally. Serve immediately with soy sauce. Yield: 6 servings.

*Ella Metzler*
*Topeka, Indiana*

## Maryland Crab Cakes

1 lb. crab meat, shredded
3 slices bread, cubed
3 tbsp. mayonnaise
1 tsp. each mustard, vinegar, salt
⅛ tsp. red pepper
1 egg, beaten
Butter

Combine all ingredients except butter in bowl; mix well. Shape mixture into 6 cakes. Brown lightly in butter in heavy skillet for about 5 minutes on each side. Serve hot. Yield: 6 servings.

Mary S. Briscoe
Prince Frederick, Maryland

## Seafood Supreme

1  1½-oz. can crab meat
2 cans cream of mushroom soup
2 cans shrimp, drained
1  10½-oz. can minced clams
1  4-oz. can sliced mushrooms
¼ tsp. Worcestershire sauce
Cream (opt.)

Remove bone from crab meat. Combine crab meat with remaining ingredients except cream in saucepan; mix well. Add a small amount of cream, if needed. Bring to a boil. Serve hot over curried rice. Yield: 4-6 servings.

Mrs. Howard Pierce
Trimble, Tennessee

## Southern Crab Cakes

3 c. flaked crab meat
1½ tsp. salt
1 tsp. dry mustard
½ tsp. pepper
1 egg yolk
2 tsp. Worcestershire sauce
1 tbsp. mayonnaise
2 tsp. snipped parsley
1 egg, slightly beaten
Flour
Packaged bread crumbs
Butter

Combine first 8 ingredients in bowl; mix well. Shape mixture into 8 small cakes. Chill for several hours. Combine egg with 2 tablespoons water in bowl. Coat crab cakes with flour. Dip into egg mixture. Coat with bread crumbs.

Saute over high heat in butter in skillet until golden brown. Yield: 4 servings.

Janice Ann Schuster
Grand Rapids, Ohio

## Spanish Crab Meat

1 green pepper, finely shredded
2 tbsp. butter
2 tbsp. flour
½ tsp. salt
¼ tsp. mustard
¾ c. milk, scalded
1 egg, beaten
1 c. grated cheese
1 can tomato soup
1  7-oz. can crab meat, flaked
Crackers

Saute green pepper in butter in saucepan over low heat. Combine flour and seasonings. Stir into butter. Cook until smooth, stirring constantly. Add scalded milk gradually. Stir until thick. Remove from heat. Stir a small amount of hot mixture into egg; stir egg into hot mixture. Add cheese; mix well. Heat soup in separate saucepan. Bring to a boil. Pour into cheese sauce. Add crab meat; mix throughly. Cook until just heated. Do not allow to boil. Serve at once over crackers. Yield: 6-8 servings.

Magdalene Beehler
Crookston, Minnesota

## West Coast Crab Au Gratin

1 sm. onion, diced
4 tbsp. butter
2 tbsp. (rounded) flour
1½ c. milk
2 cans crab meat, drained
1 sm. can pimento, diced
Salt and pepper to taste
1 c. grated sharp cheese
1½ c. buttered bread crumbs

Saute onion in butter in saucepan until soft; blend in flour. Add milk; cook until thick, stirring constantly. Add crab meat, pimento, salt, pepper and cheese, stirring until cheese is melted. Place half the crab mixture in greased casserole. Cover with half the bread crumbs; add remaining crab mixture. Top with remaining bread crumbs. Bake in 350-degree oven for 20 minutes. Yield: 6 servings.

Caroline J. Ebell
Baker, Oregon

## Baked Crab Yummy

*2 onions, finely chopped*
*½ c. butter*
*2 tomatoes, chopped*
*2 green peppers, chopped*
*1 clove of garlic, minced*
*2 tbsp. chopped parsley*
*2 cans King crab meat*
*1½ tsp. salt*
*½ tsp. pepper*
*2 eggs, beaten*
*1 c. buttered crumbs*
*6 stuffed green olives, sliced*

Saute onions in butter in saucepan for 10 minutes, stirring occasionally. Add next 4 ingredients. Cook over low heat for 10 minutes. Add crab meat and seasoning. Cook for 5 minutes longer. Pour eggs over crab mixture. Cook for 3 minutes, stirring constantly. Spoon into individual ramekins; sprinkle with crumbs. Bake at 375 degrees for 15 minutes or until lightly brown. Garnish with olives.

*Dorothy Farst*
*Akron, Ohio*

## Broiled Crab Sandwiches

*1 6½-oz. can crab*
*¼ c. minced onion*
*1 c. shredded American cheese*
*1 c. mayonnaise*
*French bread slices*

Combine first 4 ingredients; mix well. Spread crab mixture on bread slices. Broil until brown and bubbly. Yield: 6 servings.

*Eleanor V. Harmon*
*Scobey, Montana*

## Crab Delight

*2 tbsp. chopped green pepper*
*2 tbsp. butter*
*2 tbsp. flour*
*½ tsp. mustard*
*½ tsp. Worcestershire sauce*
*¼ tsp. salt*
*1 c. tomato juice*
*1 c. grated cheese*
*1 egg, beaten*
*¼ c. milk, scalded*
*1 c. flaked crab meat*

Saute green pepper in butter in large skillet for 3 minutes or until soft. Blend in flour. Add next 6 ingredients. Cook over low heat, stirring constantly until cheese is melted. Add milk and crab meat; heat through. Serve in pattie shells or on toast rounds, sprinkled with additional grated cheese. Yield: 6 servings.

*Mrs. Ethel B. Miles*
*Westfield, Massachusetts*

## Creamed Mushrooms and Crab

*⅓ c. butter*
*⅓ c. flour*
*2 c. sour cream*
*1 tbsp. dried onion flakes*
*1 tbsp. dried parsley flakes*
*¼ tsp. nutmeg*
*1 lb. crab meat, drained*
*2 4-oz. cans mushrooms, drained*
*3 tbsp. Sherry*

Melt butter in saucepan over low heat; blend in flour until smooth. Stir in sour cream and remaining ingredients. Cover; cook for 25 to 30 minutes. Serve in rice ring.

*Mrs. Mildred R. Buck*
*Linden, Alabama*

## Stuffed Lobster Tails

*4 6-oz. frozen lobster tails*
*¼ c. butter*
*2 onions, chopped*
*1 sm. clove of garlic, minced*
*1 sm. can mushrooms*
*1 tbsp. flour*
*¾ c. Sherry*
*1 tsp. paprika*
*1 tsp. salt*
*¼ tsp. pepper*
*½ c. grated Parmesan cheese*

Cook lobster tails in boiling water in saucepan; cool. Remove lobster from shells, reserving shells. Cut lobster into cubes. Melt 2 tablespoon butter in heavy skillet; add onions, garlic and mushrooms. Cook over low heat for 5 minutes. Sprinkle with flour. Add Sherry gradually. Cook for 5 minutes longer; stirring constantly. Add lobster, paprika, salt and pepper. Cover; cook over low heat for 10 minutes. Place lobster shells in shallow baking pan; spoon lobster mixture into shells. Sprinkle with cheese; dot with remaining butter. Bake at 400 degrees for 10 minutes.

*Joan Farley*
*Waldron, Michigan*

## Barbecued Lobster Tails

4 lobster tails
¼ c. lemon juice
½ c. butter, melted
Salt to taste

Cut underside membrane of lobster tails, remove. Grasp tail in both hands; bend backwards toward shell side to crack. Grill tails over charcoal for 5 minutes, flesh-side down. Combine lemon juice, butter and salt in bowl. Turn lobster tails. Brush liberally with lemon-butter mixture. Grill, flesh-side up, until meat has lost opaque appearance. Yield: 4 servings.

Sue Daye
Mastic Beach, New York

## Lobster Cantonese

6 sm. lobster tails
1 clove of garlic, minced
¼ c. oil
½ lb. ground pork
3 tbsp. soy sauce
1 tsp. sugar
½ tsp. pepper
1 tbsp. salt
1½ c. chicken broth
½ tsp. monosodium glutamate
1 tbsp. cornstarch
1 egg, beaten slightly
2 green onions, chopped

Cut lobster tails into 1-inch pieces. Saute garlic in hot oil in large skillet until golden brown. Add pork; cook until brown. Add next 6 ingredients. Bring to a boil. Add lobster. Cover. Cook for 8 minutes. Combine cornstarch and ½ cup water. Stir into lobster mixture. Cook until slightly thick, stirring constantly. Drizzle egg over hot mixture. Cook over low heat until egg sets. Sprinkle with onions. Serve over rice.

Mrs. Jeanne Clark
Flint, Michigan

## Lobster Dainties

24 miniature lobsters, butterflied
¼ c. butter, melted
2 tbsp. paprika
1 c. cornmeal
2 tbsp. vermouth

Place lobsters tails in ¼-inch water in shallow baking pan. Brush with butter. Mix paprika and cornmeal in small bowl. Spread over lobster tails. Sprinkle with vermouth. Bake at 450 degrees for 10 to 15 minutes or until tender. Brown under broiler. Yield: 4 servings.

Mrs. Sandra Weidling
Mauston, Wisconsin

## Rock Lobster Tails

6 4-oz. frozen rock lobster tails
1 3-oz. package cream cheese, softened
4 tbsp. heavy cream
4 tbsp. butter
3 tbsp. flour
1½ c. milk
1 tsp. salt
¼ tsp. curry powder
¼ tsp. paprika

Drop lobster tails into boiling salted water. Boil for 1 minute. Drain; rinse with cold water. Remove meat from shells, reserving shells. Cut lobster into bite-sized pieces. Blend cream cheese with cream. Melt butter in saucepan; stir in flour. Add milk gradually, stirring constantly. Cook until thick. Add remaining ingredients and cream cheese mixture, stirring until smooth. Add lobster; simmer until heated through. Refill empty shells with lobster mixture. Serve immediately.

Mrs. Frances Bode
Greenfield, Oklahoma

## Deviled Oysters

1 pt. oysters
½ c. chopped celery
1 sm. onion, diced
¼ lb. butter
1 c. cracker crumbs
1 beaten egg
Juice of ½ lemon
Salt and cayenne pepper to taste
Buttered crumbs

Heat oysters in saucepan until edges curl. Chop. Cook celery and onion in skillet until tender. Add chopped oysters, crackers crumbs, egg and seasoning. Spoon into individual ramekins. Cover with buttered crumbs. Bake at 350 degrees until brown. Yield: 8 servings.

Ruth Huey
Austin, Texas

## Fried Oysters

*1 pt. oysters*
*1 c. fine cracker crumbs*
*2 eggs, well beaten*
*oil*

Drain oysters on absorbent paper. Roll oysters in cracker crumbs. Dip into beaten eggs. Roll in cracker crumbs. Place in wire deep fry basket. Fry in deep hot oil until golden brown and crisp.

*Mrs. Augusta Peacock*
*Merigold, Mississippi*

## Fried Oysters with Bernaise Sauce

*Milk*
*1 egg*
*1 egg yolk*
*1 tsp. baking powder*
*1 tbsp. oil*
*3 doz. oysters*
*oil for deep frying*

Combine 4 tablespoons milk and next 4 ingredients in bowl. Beat until smooth. Add additional milk until consistency of thick cream. Chill for 30 minutes. Dip oysters into batter. Fry in deep hot oil until golden brown.

### Bernaise Sauce

*2 egg yolks*
*1 tbsp. tarragon vinegar*
*2 tbsp. light cream*
*Cayenne pepper and salt to taste*
*Garlic to taste*
*2 tbsp. fresh herbs*
*4 tbsp. butter*

Combine first 5 ingredients in top of double boiler. Cook over hot water, beating constantly, until sauce begins to thicken. Add remaining ingredients; mix well. Serve with fried oysters. Yield: 9-12 servings.

*Elva Gloria Ruiz*
*Buckholts, Texas*

## Oyster Pie

*Pastry for 2-crust 9-in. pie*
*1½ qt. medium oysters*
*Salt to taste*
*2 tbsp. flour*
*¼ c. butter*
*½ tsp. hot sauce*

Line 9-inch pie plate with half the pastry. Drain oysters, reserving ¼ cup liquor. Turn oysters into pie pastry; sprinkle with salt and flour. Dot with butter. Combine reserved oyster liquor and hot sauce; pour over oysters. Top pie with remaining pastry; flute edges to seal. Cut slits in top crust for steam vents. Bake at 450 degrees for 30 minutes. Yield: 6-8 servings.

*Brownie Brooks*
*Orangeburg, North Carolina*

## Oysters Bienville

*Ice cream salt*
*1 doz. oysters on the half shell*
*1 bunch shallots, chopped*
*1 tbsp. butter*
*1 tbsp. flour*
*½ c. chicken broth*
*½ c. shrimp, minced*
*⅓ c. mushrooms, minced*
*⅓ c. gloss white wine*
*1 egg yolk, beaten*
*Salt and pepper to taste*
*Tabasco sauce (opt.)*
*Bread crumbs*
*Paprika*
*Grated cheese*

Spread ice cream salt in large shallow baking pan. Place oysters over salt. Bake at 350 degrees for 6 to 8 minutes or until thoroughly heated. Saute shallots in butter in skillet until brown. Stir in flour. Cook until brown. Add chicken broth gradually, stirring constantly, until smooth. Add shrimp and mushrooms; mix well. Beat wine into egg yolk gradually. Stir a small amount of hot mixture into egg yolk; stir egg yolk into hot mixture, stirring constantly. Season with salt and pepper. Add Tabasco sauce. Simmer for 10 to 15 minutes, stirring constantly. Spoon sauce over each oyster. Sprinkle bread crumbs, paprika and grated cheese over each. Bake at 350 degrees for 12 minutes or until brown.

*Virginia L. Langston*
*Baton Rouge, Louisiana*

## Scalloped Oysters

3 c. cracker crumbs
2 c. cream
¼ c. butter
1 pt. oysters
¼ tsp. salt
Pinch of pepper

Spread 1½ cups cracker crumbs in 11 × 8 × 2-inch baking pan. Drizzle with ¼ cup cream. Dot with half the butter. Add oysters. Sprinkle with salt and pepper. Top with remaining crumbs. Dot with remaining butter. Pour remaining cream over top. Bake at 350 degrees for 45 minutes.

*Mrs. Alice Applegate*
*Knoxville, Ohio*

## Baked Scallops on the Shell

1 lb. scallops
½ c. heavy cream
Salt and pepper
4 tbsp. bread crumbs
4 tbsp. butter

Place 4 or 5 scallops on each buttered scallop shell. Top with 2 tablespoons cream. Sprinkle with salt, pepper and bread crumbs. Place 1 tablespoon butter on each. Place on cookie sheet. Bake at 450 degrees for 20 minutes.

*Ann C. Lowe*
*Saint John, New Brunswick, Canada*

## Peachy Scallop

1 lb. fresh or frozen scallops
2 tbsp. melted butter
2 tbsp. lemon juice
½ tsp. salt
Dash of pepper
¼ tsp. cinnamon
¼ tsp. cloves
¼ tsp. mace
12 canned peach halves
3 slices bacon, quartered

Cut scallops into ½-inch pieces. Combine scallop pieces, butter, lemon juice, ¼ teaspoon salt and pepper in bowl; mix well. Combine spices with remaining salt. Place peach halves in 11 × 7 × 1-inch baking dish. Sprinkle with spice mixture. Place 2 tablespoons scallop mixture in center of each peach. Cover with 1 bacon piece. Broil 4 inches from heat source for 8 to 10 minutes or until bacon is crips.

*Lucille Reid Marker*
*Robertsdale, Alabama*

## Savory Scallops

½ c. chopped bacon
¼ c. minced onion
1 tsp. salt
¼ c. flour
⅛ tsp. hot sauce
¾ lb. scallops
2 tbsp. Worcestershire sauce
¼ c. lemon juice
½ c. minced parsley

Fry bacon slowly in heavy skillet. Add onion; saute lightly. Sprinkle salt, flour and hot sauce over onion; add scallops. Stir only to mix; cover. Cook for 5 minutes. Remove cover; cook for 10 minutes longer, stirring occasionally. Stir in remaining ingredients; remove from heat. Mix well, serve immediately.

*Christine Stage*
*New Lexington, Ohio*

## Seafood Scallop

1 lb. haddock fillet
1 lb. scallops
1 can shrimp
1 can shrimp soup
1 c. cracker crumbs
1 stick butter or margarine

Break haddock fillet into chunk-sized pieces; mix with scallops, shrimp and shrimp soup. Place in 2-quart casserole. Brown cracker crumbs lightly in butter; sprinkle tover top of casserole. Bake at 350 degrees for 45 minutes.

*Mrs. Gilberta W. Percival*
*Waterville, Maine*

## Marinated Shrimp

1 12-oz. bottle cocktail sauce
1½ c. mayonnaise
1 tbsp. Worcestershire sauce
¼ tsp. hot sauce
2 tsp. celery seed
¼ tsp. garlic salt
1 onion, thinly sliced
Salt and pepper to taste
2 lb. boiled shrimp, peeled

Combine all ingredients except shrimp in bowl; mix well. Pour into shallow dish; add shrimp. Cover. Refrigerate for 6 to 8 hours.

*Mrs. Johnnie Broome*
*Blackshear, Georgia*

½ c. sliced mushrooms
4 c. cooked rice
2 tbsp. soy sauce
½ tsp. sugar

Place oil, salt, and pepper in heavy skillet. Add eggs. Fry until firm. Cut fried egg into small strips. Add shrimp, onions and mushrooms. Stir-fry over moderate heat for 5 minutes. Add rice, soy sauce and sugar. Cook over moderate heat, stirring constantly, until rice is hot.

*Mrs. Ruth S. Riale*
*Bloomsburg, Pennsylvania*

## Savory Buttered Shrimp

1 clove of garlic, minced
2 tbsp. lemon juice
Basil and rosemary to taste
½ tsp. salt
¼ tsp. pepper
Tabasco sauce to taste
1 c. butter, melted
2 lb. peeled deveined shrimp

Mix seasoning with butter. Place shrimp in shallow baking pan. Broil for 5 minutes. Spoon sauce over shrimp. Broil for 5 to 8 minutes longer. Serve immediately. Yield: 8 servings.

*Mrs. Susan McAlexander*
*Abernathy, Texas*

## Shrimp Gumbo

2 tbsp. oil
2 tbsp. flour
1 c. chopped onion
⅓ c. each chopped green onion, shallots
2 cloves of garlic, minced
1 1-lb. 12-oz. can tomatoes
2 10-oz. packages frozen cut okra
1 sm. lemon, sliced
2 bay leaves
½ tsp. salt
½ tsp. Tabasco sauce
2 lb. shrimp

Heat oil in large skillet; blend in flour. Cook over low heat until dark brown, stirring constantly. Add next 4 ingredients. Cook until tender. Stir in remaining ingredients except shrimp; mix well. Bring to a boil; reduce heat. Simmer for 35 to 40 minutes. Stir in shrimp. Cook for 10 minutes longer. Serve over rice in soup bowls.

*Photograph for this recipe above.*

## Fried Rice and Shrimp

3 tbsp. oil
1 tsp. salt
Dash of pepper
2 eggs, beaten
1 lb. shrimp, shelled, cleaned, cut into thirds
⅓ c. finely diced onion

## Shrimp in Batter

1½ c. flour
1 tsp. baking powder
¾ tsp. salt
1 egg, beaten
1 c. milk
2 lb. shrimp
Oil for frying
1 c. catsup
2 tbsp. each lemon juice, chili sauce
1 tbsp. Worcestershire sauce
Dash of Tabasco sauce
2 tsp. prepared horseradish

Sift together flour, baking powder and ¼ teaspoon salt in bowl. Combine egg and milk in bowl. Add to dry ingredients, stirring until smooth. Dip shrimp in batter. Fry in 375-degree oil in skillet for 2 to 3 minutes or until brown. Drain on absorbent paper. Combine ½ teaspoon salt with remaining ingredients; mix well. Chill thoroughly. Serve with shrimp.

*Elizabeth Stokes*
*Sulligent, Alabama*

## Paella

Olive oil
½ to 1 clove of garlic
½ c. chopped onion
1 to 2 green peppers, chopped
2 tomatoes
1 pkg. frozen peas, thawed
1 pkg. frozen green beans, thawed
6 pieces broiled chicken
1 to 2 c. chopped cooked picnic ham
12 large shrimp
1½ c. rice
⅓ c. saffron
Salt to taste
1 sm. can pimento

Cover bottom of large cast iron skillet with ⅛-inch olive oil. Add next 3 ingredients. Cook until tender. Add tomatoes, peas and beans at 1 minute intervals, stirring constantly. Stir in chicken, ham and shrimp gradually. Add rice. Cook for 5 minutes. Add 3¼ cup water. Increase heat. Boil for 5 to 10 minutes. Reduce heat to low. Cook for ½ hour longer. Add saffron and salt last 10 minutes of cooking. Garnish with pimento. Yield: 6 servings.

*Mrs Helen Borton Parker*
*Downington, Pennsylvania*

## Shrimp Creole

1½ lb. cleaned shrimp
Salt
1 med. onion, chopped fine
1 green pepper, chopped fine
4 stalks celery, chopped fine
4 tbsp. butter
2 tbsp. flour
⅛ tsp. pepper
2 sm. cans tomato sauce
1 tbsp. vinegar

Sprinkle shrimp with salt. Brown onion, green pepper and celery in butter in large skillet. Blend in flour, 1 teaspoon salt and pepper. Add tomato sauce and vinegar. Cover. Simmer for 10 minutes. Add shrimp. Bring to a boil. Cover. Simmer for 5 minutes. Serve over fluffy rice. Yield: 6-8 servings.

*Gayle D. Lee*
*Forest Hill, Louisiana*

## Shrimp Au Gratin

3 tbsp. onion
Butter
¼ c. flour
½ tsp. salt
¼ tsp. dry mustard
Dash of pepper
1½ c. milk
1 c. grated cheese
¾ lb. large cooked shrimp, cut in half
¼ c. dry bread crumbs

Saute onion in 3 tablespoons butter in skillet until tender. Blend in flour and seasonings; add milk gradually. Cook until thick, stirring constantly. Add ¾ cup cheese; stir until melted. Stir in shrimp. Pour into individual casseroles. Mix crumbs with butter and remaining cheese. Sprinkle over casseroles. Bake at 400 degrees for 10 minutes. Yield: 6 servings.

*Kathleen Garrett*
*Albertville, Alabama*

## Shrimp Jambalaya

3 tbsp. butter
½ c. each chopped onion, green onions, celery
¾ c. green pepper
¼ lb. cooked ham, diced
2 cloves of garlic, minced
2 c. chicken broth
3 lg. tomatoes, chopped
¼ c. chopped parsley (opt.)
½ tsp. salt
⅛ tsp. each pepper, cayenne pepper
¼ tsp. thyme
1 bay leaf
1 c. rice
3 4½-oz. cans shrimp

Heat butter in large heavy skillet over low heat. Stir in onions, celery, ½ cup green pepper, ham and garlic. Cook over medium heat for 5 minutes or until onions are tender. Stir in broth, tomatoes, parsley and seasonings. Cover. Bring to a boil. Add rice gradually, stirring with fork. Simmer, covered, for 20 minutes or until rice is tender. Mix in shrimp and ¼ cup green pepper. Cover. Simmer for 5 minutes longer. Yield: 6-8 servings.

*Mrs. Jewell T. Johnson*
*Albany, Georgia*

## Shrimp Louisiana

1 c. coarsely chopped onion
½ c. butter
2⅔ c. minute rice
2 to 3 tsp. salt
½ c. green pepper strips, ½-in. long
4 7-oz. cans shrimp
4 tbsp. finely chopped parsley

Brown onions in butter in saucepan. Add rice, salt and green pepper. Saute for 3 minutes, or until lightly brown, stirring constantly. Add shrimp and 3 cups water; mix lightly with fork. Cover. Simmer for 5 minutes. Add parsley Serve with Worcestershire sauce. Yield: 8 servings.

*Margaret E. White*
*Morrice, Michigan*

## Simplified Seafood a La King

1 can tuna, drained, flaked
1 can sm. shrimp drained
1 bottle olives, sliced
1 can peas
1 qt. white sauce
Patty shells, biscuits or rice

Combine tuna, shrimp, olives, peas and white sauce in top of double boiler. Blend with fork. Heat through. Pour over patty shells. Garnish with deviled eggs. Yield: 12 servings.

*Mrs. Barbara C. Sleeper*
*Dover, New Hampshire*

## Baked Shrimp En Casserole

1 lb. frozen shrimp
2 tbsp. lemon juice
½ c. melted butter
1 c. fine bread crumbs
1 clove of garlic
1 tsp. dried parsley
2 tbsp. Parmesan cheese
1 tsp. oregano

Separate shrimp under cold running water. Place in 8 × 8-inch baking dish; sprinkle with lemon juice. Combine butter, bread crumbs and remaining ingredients in bowl; mix well. Spread butter mixture over shrimp. Bake at 350 degrees for 15 minutes. Broil for 3 minutes. Yield: 4 servings.

*Mrs. Virginia Verrill*
*Rangeley, Maine*

## Scalloped Shrimp

2 tbsp. minced onion
1 tbsp. minced green pepper
4 tbsp. butter, melted
4 tbsp. flour
¼ tsp. dry mustard
2 c. milk
2 c. cooked shrimp
1 c. buttered crumbs

Saute onion and green pepper in butter in skillet until tender. Blend in flour and mustard; add milk. Cook until thick stirring constantly. Add shrimp. Pour into greased casserole; top with buttered crumbs. Bake at 350 degrees for 20 minutes. Yield: 6 servings.

*Mrs. Lana Giehl*
*Groveport, Ohio*

## Stuffed Fried Shrimp

1 c. minced onions
1 c. finely chopped celery
1 green pepper, finely chopped
3 tbsp. butter
1 c. crab meat
½ tsp. salt
1 clove of garlic, crushed
½ tsp. poultry seasoning
½ c. thick white sauce
2 egg yolks, beaten
1½ c. bread crumbs
Chopped parsley
12 jumbo shrimp, butterflied
1 c. flour
¼ tsp. salt
1¼ tsp. baking powder
⅔ c. milk
1 tbsp. salad oil
2 egg whites, stiffly beaten

Saute onions, celery and green pepper in butter in skillet until golden brown. Add next 4 ingredients; heat thoroughly. Remove from heat; blend in white sauce and egg yolks. Toss with bread crumbs and parsley. Fill shrimp with crab meat mixture. Refrigerate for 2 hours. Combine dry ingredients in bowl; stir in milk and oil. Fold in egg whites. Dip shrimp into batter. Fry until golden brown. Yield: 4 servings.

*Mrs. C. L. Hillis*
*Longview, Texas*

## Scampi a la Marinara

2 cloves of garlic, minced
5 tbsp. olive oil
1 No. 2½ can Italian tomatoes
2 tbsp. snipped parsley
½ tsp. dried basil
2½ tsp. salt
½ tsp. pepper
1 tsp. dried oregano
⅔ c. tomato paste
½ tsp. garlic salt
2 lb. cooked, shelled, deveined shrimp
Grated Parmesan cheese
Hot cooked spaghetti or rice (opt.)

Brown garlic in oil in large skillet. Add next 5 ingredients. Simmer, uncovered, for 30 minutes. Stir in oregano and tomato paste. Cook, uncovered, for 15 minutes. Add garlic salt and shrimp; heat through. Top with cheese. Serve over spaghetti.

Mrs. Marvel Wax
El Paso, Texas

## Spaghetti with Shrimp Sauce

2 cloves of garlic, finely chopped
¼ c. oil
1 14-oz. can tomatoes
2½ tsp. salt
½ tsp. dried basil
1 6-oz. can tomato paste
1 tsp. dried oregano
½ lb. cooked shrimp, deveined
½ tsp. garlic salt
1 tsp. prepared horseradish
8 oz. spaghetti, cooked
Grated Parmesan cheese

Saute garlic in oil in large skillet. Add tomatoes, salt and basil; mix well. Simmer, uncovered, for 30 minutes. Stir in tomato paste and oregano; simmer for 15 minutes longer. Stir in shrimp, garlic salt and horseradish; heat through. Serve over hot spaghetti; sprinkle with cheese.

Elizabeth Miller
Fulton, Mississippi

## Southern-Fried Shrimp

3 c. deveined shrimp
2¼ tsp. salt
¼ tsp. pepper
1 egg, well beaten
½ c. light cream
½ c. yellow cornmeal
½ c. flour
½ tsp. baking powder
Oil for frying

Season shrimp with 2 teaspoons salt and pepper. Let stand at room temperature for 15 minutes. Combine remaining ingredients in small bowl; mix until smooth. Combine batter and shrimp; stir until shrimp are well coated with batter. Drop shrimp into hot fat in clusters of 2 or 3 shrimp. Fry until light brown.

Mrs. Valerie S. Trahan
Abbeville, Louisiana

## Seafood Newburg

Margarine
1 tbsp. cornstarch
1 tsp. salt
1 tsp. paprika
Dash of cayenne pepper
2 c. light cream
½ c. dry Sherry
2 egg yolks, slightly beaten
2 c. cut up cooked lobster, crab or shrimp
8 slices fresh bread

Melt ¼ cup margarine in saucepan; blend in next 4 ingredients. Remove from heat; blend in cream gradually. Cook over medium heat, stirring constantly, until mixture comes to a boil. Boil for 1 minute. Reduce heat; stir in Sherry gradually. Blend a small amount of hot mixture into egg yolks; stir egg yolks into hot mixture. Add seafood; heat. Do not boil. Trim crusts from bread. Brush one side with margarine. Press into muffin cups, buttered-side up. Bake at 450 degrees for 10 minutes or until edges are well browned. Fill with seafood mixture. Yield: 6-8 servings.

Isabel Howard Gist
Sumter, South Carolina

# Soups and Stews

## Meatballs in Chicken Soup

Milk
1 lb. hamburger
1 c. prepared dry dressing mix
1 tsp. ground sage
Salt and pepper to taste
2 eggs, beaten
Oil
1 can cream of chicken soup

Combine ¾ cup milk and next 5 ingredients in bowl; mix well. Shape into meatballs. Brown meatballs in oil in skillet. Mix soup with 1 soup can milk. Pour over meatballs. Simmer for ½ hour. Yield: 5-6 servings.

Mrs. Erleen Johnson
Oregon, Ohio

## Rivels Cream of Potato Soup

2 to 3 c. flour
1 egg, beaten
1 lg. potato, cubed
Milk
Salt to taste
Butter to taste

Place flour in bowl. Add egg; work mixture with fingers form small balls. Remove excess flour. Let rivels stand until dry. Cook potato in a small amount of water in large saucepan until tender. Add 1 quart milk, salt and butter. Heat slowly. Do not boil. Add rivels; cook until tender, stirring occasionally. Add additional milk to desired thickness. Yield: 4 servings.

Mrs. Rosemary K. Harwood
New London, North Carolina

## Mexicali Soup

¼ lb. ground beef
¾ tsp. chili powder
¼ tsp. salt
Dash of pepper
2 tbsp. minced onion
1 tbsp. margarine
1 can tomato soup

Combine ground beef, ½ teaspoon chili powder, salt and pepper in bowl. Shape into 12 meatballs. Brown meatballs and onion in margarine in saucepan. Add soup, remaining chili powder and 1 soup can water. Simmer for about 5 minutes. Yield: 2-3 servings.

Mrs. Luella John
Amery, Wisconsin

## Russian Cabbage Soup

1 1½-lb flank steak
1 tbsp. salt
Pepper to taste
1 No. 2 can tomatoes
1 lg. onion
1 bay leaf (opt.)
½ clove of garlic, finely chopped (opt.)
1 med. head cabbage, coarsely shredded
2 tbsp. sugar
1 tbsp. vinegar

Place steak and 2½ quarts water in 5-quart saucepan. Add next 6 ingredients. Bring to a boil. Reduce heat. Simmer for 1½ hours. Add cabbage, sugar and vinegar. Simmer for 1½ hours longer. Serve hot. Top each serving with 1 heaping tablespoon sour cream. Yield: 4-6 servings.

Sister Mary Benedict Beehler
Crookston, Minnesota

## Brazilian Chicken Soup

1 tbsp. chopped onion
1 tbsp. butter
1 lg. chicken, cut into pieces
½ tsp. salt
1 sprig of parsley
2 carrots
1 leek (opt.)
1 c. rice
1 lg. tomato

Saute onion in butter in saucepan. Add chicken. Cook until golden brown. Add water to cover chicken. Add next 4 ingredients. Cook until chicken is tender. Remove chicken. Strain, reserving broth. Bone chicken; cut into 2-inch pieces. Add enough water to reserve broth in saucepan to measure 3½ pints. Add rice. Cook until nearly tender. Add chicken pieces. Adjust seasoning. Add tomato. Yield: 4 servings.

Mrs. Erma Winks
Noblesville, Indiana

## Chicken Gumbo

1 4-lb. frying chicken, disjointed
4 tbsp. bacon drippings
5 tbsp. flour
1 lg. onion, chopped
2 cloves of garlic, minced
Salt and pepper to taste

¼ tsp. cayenne pepper
1 lb. fresh link pork sausage
5 shallots, chopped
¼ c. chopped fresh parsley
1 tbsp. file
Hot steamed rice

Brown chicken lightly in 2 tablespoons bacon drippings in Dutch oven; drain. Add 3 quarts hot salted water. Simmer chicken until just tender. Pour remaining bacon drippings into skillet; add flour. Cook over low heat, stirring constantly until golden brown. Add onion and garlic to roux. Cook 5 minutes longer or until onion is wilted. Add salt, pepper and cayenne pepper. Cook for 45 minutes. Brown sausage lightly in skillet; drain. Add shallots and parsley; stir into gumbo. Remove from heat; add file, stirring well. Cover; let stand for 10 minutes. Serve over hot steamed rice. Yield: 8 servings.

*Mrs. Odessa N. Smith*
*Baton Rouge, Louisiana*

## Chicken-Noodle Soup with Butter Balls

3 c. grated bread crumbs
½ tsp. allspice
2 tsp. salt
1 egg
1 c. cream
Chicken broth
1 cooked diced chicken
1 pkg. noodles

Toast 1 cup bread crumbs slowly in oven. Combine all bread crumbs, seasonings, and egg in bowl. Add enough cream to make desired consistency. Mix with hands until smooth. Shape into balls the size of an egg yolk. Bring chicken broth to a boil in stockpot. Drop butter balls into broth. Stir in chicken. Boil for 5 minutes or until butter balls rise to the top of broth. Add noodles. Boil for 3 minutes. Serve. Yield: 10-12 servings.

*Mrs. Jolene Corcoran*
*Follett, Texas*

## Palatinate Chicken-Corn Soup

1 4-lb. chicken
2 tsp. salt
¼ tsp. saffron
2 c. noodles
2 c. corn
1 tsp. chopped parsley
⅛ tsp. pepper
2 hard-boiled eggs, chopped

Place chicken, salt and saffron in large saucepan with water to cover. Simmer until chicken is tender. Remove chicken. Cool. Bone chicken; cut into small pieces. Return chicken to stock. Add noodles and corn. Bring to a boil. Simmer until noodles are tender. Stir in parsley, pepper and eggs. Serve immediately. Yield: 6 servings.

*Lucy M. Bamberger*
*Schaefferstown, Pennsylvania*

## Ham-Pea Soup

1 lg. ham bone
1 c. split peas
½ to 1 c. chopped onions
1 c. each chopped celery, diced carrots
2 tbsp. finely cut parsley
Salt and pepper to taste

Place ham bone in 4-quart stock pot. Cover with 2 quarts water. Bring to a boil. Simmer for 1 to 2 hours. Remove bone; cut meat into pieces. Return meat to soup stock. Add split peas. Cook over low heat for 20 minutes. Add remaining ingredients. Simmer over low heat until vegetables are tender. Season to taste; serve. Vary amount of peas and liquid for thinner or thicker soup. Yield: 12 servings.

*Mrs. Marguerite S. Drechsel Darnall*
*Campo, California*

## Korean Egg Broth

⅓ c. diced celery
2 chicken bouillon cubes
½ lb. pork, thinly sliced
½ tsp. each salt, monosodium glutamate
Dash of pepper
2 eggs, well beaten

Place celery in 2 quarts water in large saucepan. Bring to a boil. Add bouillon cubes; dissove completely. Add pork. Cook until tender. Add seasonings. Simmer for ½ hour. Bring to a boil quickly. Pour eggs in gradually. Remove from heat immediately. Yield: 8 servings.

*Leanne Luke*
*Honolulu, Hawaii*

### New Hampshire Meat Soup

½ lb. each lamb, pork
1 lg. onion, minced
½ tsp. salt
Dash each of pepper, red pepper
Pinch of nutmeg
2 eggs, beaten
Flour
Butter, melted
6 c. beef broth
½ c. toasted bread crumbs
2 tbsp. tomato sauce
2 tbsp. chopped parsley

Force lamb and pork through food grinder. Combine meat mixture with next 6 ingredients in large bowl. Shape into small balls. Roll meatballs in flour. Brown meatballs in butter in skillet. Heat beef broth in saucepan. Add crumbs, tomato sauce, parsley, meatballs and pan drippings. Simmer for 15 minutes. Yield: 6 servings

*Mrs. Esther M. Hight*
*Weare, New Hampshire*

### Scotch Barley Broth

2 lb. lamb neck
½ c. pearl barley
Salt to taste
6 whole peppercorns
¾ c. each chopped onion, celery
¾ c. each diced turnip, carrot
1 carrot, grated
1 c. cooked peas
2 tbsp. minced parsley

Combine lamb, with next 3 ingredients and 2 quarts water in large saucepan. Simmer for 1½ hours. Cool. Skim. Remove lamb. Trim meat from bones; dice. Return lamb to stew; add next 4 ingredients. Simmer for ½ hour or until vegetables are tender. Add remaining ingredients just before serving.

*Valorie S. Jensen*
*Elko, Nevada*

### Clam Chowder

2 med. onions, minced
2 tbsp. butter
2 med. potatoes, diced
2 tsp. salt
⅛ tsp. pepper
2 7-oz. cans minced clams
3 c. milk

Saute onion in butter in saucepan until yellow. Add 2 cups water, potatoes, salt and pepper. Bring to a boil. Add clams. Simmer for 25 minutes. Add milk. Heat through, stirring occasionally. Yield: 8-10 servings.

*Mrs. Martha Swingle*
*Ashland, Ohio*

### Fish Soup

2 med. onions, diced
6 med. carrots, diced
1 bay leaf
8 boned perch, cut into 2-inch lengths
1 tsp. salt
⅛ tsp. pepper

Place vegetables and bay leaf in 2 quarts cold water in large saucepan. Bring to a boil. Place fish on top of mixture. Simmer until vegetables are tender. Add salt and pepper; mix well. Serve hot with crackers. Yield: 3-4 servings.

*Mrs. Eva J. Hill*
*Reese, Michigan*

### Lobster Bisque

2 tbsp. quick-cooking tapioca
1¼ tsp. salt
⅛ tsp. each pepper, paprika
1 tbsp. minced onion
3 c. milk
1 c. light cream
1 c. lobster, cut up
2 tbsp. butter

Combine first 7 ingredients in top of double boiler. Cook for 10 to 15 minutes over rapidly boiling water, stirring frequently. Add lobster and butter to cream mixture; mix well. Let stand over hot water for 15 to 20 minutes until heated thoroughly. Pour into soup bowls. Garnish with thin slice of tomato sprinkled with chives or grated lemon rind. Yield: 4 servings.

*Edith J. Anderson*
*Claymont, Delaware*

### Oyster Stew

4 c. milk
½ c. margarine
½ tsp. each salt, celery salt

12 saltine crackers, crushed
1 pt. oysters

Scald milk in heavy saucepan. Add margarine and seasoning. Stir until margarine is melted. Stir crackers into hot milk mixture. Add oysters. Cook until edges of oysters curl.

*Mrs. Frances Blount*
*Birmingham, Alabama*

## Seafood Chowder

¼ c. finely chopped bacon
¼ c. finely chopped onion
2 7-oz. cans minced clams
2 c. cooked diced potatoes
2 c. milk
1 tsp. salt
⅛ tsp. pepper

Saute bacon in large frypan for 1 to 2 minutes. Add onion. Cook until golden, stirring occasionally. Drain clams, reserving liquid. Add clam liquid and potatoes to bacon mixture. Cover. Cook until potatoes are thoroughly heated. Add clams, milk and seasonings to bacon mixture. Heat slowly to serving temperature. Yield: 4 servings.

*Mrs. Buena B. Hedden*
*Hayesville, North Carolina*

## Seafood Gumbo

6 tbsp. flour
6 tbsp. bacon drippings
3 onions, minced
3 cloves of garlic, minced
3 tsp. salt
Pepper to taste
2 tbsp. tomato paste
1 lb. shrimp
1 pt. oysters
1 can dark crab meat
2 tsp. file (opt.)

Brown flour in bacon drippings in large saucepan, stirring constantly. Add onions and garlic. Cook until transparent. Add 6 cups water gradually, stirring constantly. Stir in seasonings and tomato paste; mix well. Add shrimp. Simmer for ½ hour. Add oysters and crab meat. Simmer for 5 minutes longer.

Remove from heat, Add file; mix well. Serve over rice. Garnish with finely minced green onion. Yield: 8 servings.

*Nell Wall Papizan*
*Central, Georgia*

## Beef Stew Bourbonnaise

1½ lb. chuck, cut into 1-in. pieces
1 tbsp. shortening
1 clove garlic, minced
1 med. onion, chopped
½ tsp. each salt, pepper, basil
1 can tomato soup
¾ c. red wine
¼ tsp. thyme
½ c. catsup
4 med. carrots, cut into 1-in. pieces
1½ c. chopped celery
5 med. potatoes, peeled, quartered

Brown chuck lightly in shortening in stockpot. Add garlic and onion. Saute until onion is transparent. Season with salt, pepper and basil. Stir in soup, wine and ¼ cup water. Cover. Simmer for ½ hour. Add thyme and catsup. Arrange vegetables over chuck; cover. Simmer for 1½ hours. Add water to desired consistency. Yield: 6 servings.

*Mrs. Alice Blakeney*
*Runge, Texas*

## Easy Beef Stew

2 beef bouillon cubes
1 tsp. salt
½ tsp. each pepper, thyme, monosodium
    glutamate
3 med. potatoes, peeled, cut up
1 lg. onion, diced
3 med. carrots, diced
1 No. 2½ can beef
1 No. 2½ can tomatoes, cut up

Dissolve bouillon in 2 cups boiling water in large saucepan. Stir in seasonings. Add next 3 ingredients. Simmer until tender. Stir in beef and tomatoes. Simmer until thoroughly heated. Yield: 4 servings.

*Rudene Wilhanks*
*Powder Springs, Georgia*

## Hungarian Goulash

*2 lb. steak, cubed*
*1 lb. onions, sliced*
*Butter*
*2 tsp. paprika*
*1 c. stewed tomatoes*
*1 c. beef broth*
*1 clove of garlic, chopped*
*1 slice lemon rind, chopped*
*½ tsp. caraway seed*
*2 tbsp. flour*
*1 lb. noodles, cooked*

Cook steak and onions in ¼ cup butter in heavy skillet until onions are transparent. Add next 6 ingredients; mix well. Simmer for 45 minutes to 1 hour. Blend flour into 2 tablespoons butter in small bowl. Stir into broth mixture. Cook until thick, stirring constantly. Serve over noodles. Yield: 4-6 servings.

*Mrs. Richard Haas*
*Millville, New Jersey*

## Minute Steak Stew

*4 minute steaks, cut into 1-inch strips*
*2 tbsp. flour*
*Salt and pepper to taste*
*2 tbsp. butter*
*1 tbsp. finely chopped onion*
*1 c. cooked English peas and carrots*
*½ c. vegetable liquid*
*6 or 8 med. potatoes, cooked, cubed*
*1 8-oz. can tomato sauce*

Coat steak strips with flour seasoned with salt and pepper. Brown on all sides in butter in large skillet. Stir in remaining ingredients; mix well. Cover. Simmer for 10 to 12 minutes. Yield: 4 servings.

*Mrs. Fannye M. Franks*
*Columbus, Mississippi*

## Old-Fashioned Stew

*1 lb. beef stew meat*
*2 c. chopped carrots*
*2 c. chopped potatoes*
*1 sm. chopped onion*
*1 bay leaf*
*⅛ tsp. pepper*
*1 tsp. salt*

Brown stew beef in shortening in skillet. Add 2 cups water. Simmer for 2 hours. Add remaining ingredients. Simmer for 1 hour longer. Thicken liquid for gravy if desired.

*Mrs. Hazel Johnson*
*Pavillion, Wyoming*

## Oven Beef Stew

*1½ lb. beef chuck, cubed*
*3 tbsp. shortening, melted*
*12 to 16 sm. white onions*
*3 med. carrots, sliced ¼ in. thick*
*1 10-oz. package frozen green peas, thawed*
*1 tbsp. flour*
*2 tbsp. tomato sauce*
*1 bay leaf*
*1 tbsp. red wine vinegar*
*⅛ tsp. each thyme, pepper*
*1½ tsp. salt*
*1 clove of garlic*

Brown chuck in shortening in frypan. Drain; reserve pan drippings. Layer chuck with onions, carrots and peas in 2-quart casserole. Mix reserved pan drippings, 1½ cups water and remaining ingredients in skillet. Pour over casserole; cover. Bake at 350 degrees for 1 hour and 45 minutes or until beef and vegetables are tender. Yield: 8 servings.

*June Fletcher*
*Litchfield, Illinois*

## Southern-Style Brown Stew

*2 lb. boneless beef chuck, cut into 1½-in.*
*   cubes*
*Flour*
*2 tbsp. shortening*
*1 tsp. lemon juice*
*1 tsp. Worcestershire sauce*
*2 sm. bay leaves*
*2 tsp. salt*
*½ tsp. pepper*
*1 clove of garlic, minced*
*6 carrots, quartered*
*8 sm. onions*
*3 potatoes, quartered*

Dip beef into flour. Brown on all sides in shortening in skillet. Add 4 cup boiling water and next 6 ingredients. Simmer for 2 hours, stirring frequently. Add vegetables. Cook for 30 minutes longer or until vegetables are tender. Thicken stew with flour if desired.

*Mrs. Frydis M. Hansbrough*
*Magee, Mississippi*

## Spicy Beef Stew

3 lb. lean beef stew meat, cut into 1½-in.
  cubes
Salt and pepper to taste
½ c. butter
2½ lb. small onions, peeled
1 6-oz. can tomato paste
⅓ c. red wine (opt.)
2 tbs. red wine vinegar
1 tbsp. brown sugar
1 clove of garlic, minced
1 bay leaf
1 sm. cinnamon stick
½ tsp. whole cloves
¼ tsp. ground cuminseed
2 tbsp. currants

Season stew beef with salt and pepper. Melt
butter in Dutch oven. Add stew beef, stirring
until coated with butter but not brown.
Arrange onions over meat. Mix next 5 ingredients in bowl. Pour over onions. Add remaining ingredients. Cover onions with plate. Cover
with lid. Simmer for 3 hours or until stew beef
is very tender. Stir sauce to blend just before
serving. Yield: 6 servings.

Sonja Crummy
Wyoming, Illinois

## Stew and Dumplings

1  1½-lb. can beef stew
1 pkg. refrigerator biscuits

Place stew in 3-quart saucepan. Stir in ¼ cup
water. Bring to a boil over medium heat. Place
biscuits on stew. Cover. Reduce heat. Simmer
for 10 to 12 minutes. Serve immediately. Yield:
4 servings.

Marie B. King
Ligonier, Pennsylvania

## Ground Beef Stew

3 c. sliced potatoes
1 lb. ground beef
Cooked vegetables (opt.)
1 10¾-oz. can vegetable-beef soup

Place potatoes in bottom of 1-quart casserole.
Crumble ground beef over potatoes. Add
vegetables. Pour soup over top. Bake in 350
degree oven for 1 hour. Yield: 4-6 servings.

Betty Jo Keppen
Webster, Wisconsin

## Leftover Goulash

½ lb. hamburger
2 tbsp. chopped onion
Chopped green pepper (opt.)
½ tsp. salt
½ No. 202 can whole kernel corn
Leftover vegetables
1 10½-oz. can tomato soup
1 c. noodles
1 tbsp. chili powder (opt.)
½ c. cheese, sliced

Saute hamburger, onion and green pepper in
skillet. Add salt, vegetables and soup. Bring to
a boil. Add noodles. Cover. Reduce heat. Cook
for about 10 minutes or until noodles are
tender. Stir in chili powder. Top with cheese
slices. Cover. Heat until cheese melts.

Mrs. Eleanor R. Haner
Moses Lake, Washington

## Quick and Easy Stew

1 lb. ground beef
Salt and pepper
1 pkg. frozen mixed vegetables, thawed
1 tsp. parsley flakes
2 No. 2 cans tomato sauce
1 tsp. Worcestershire sauce
1 bottle catsup

Season ground beef with salt and pepper.
Brown in large Dutch oven, stirring until
crumbly. Add next 4 ingredients; mix well. Add
catsup until of desired consistency.

Jeanette Hulsey
Monticello, Arkansas

## Mexican Stew

1 sm. onion, finely chopped
2 tbsp. shortening
1 lb. lean hamburger
½ tsp. salt
Dash of pepper
1 c. cooked elbow macaroni
1 c. tomato sauce

Saute onion in shortening in skillet. Add
ground beef. Brown, stirring until crumbly.
Drain. Add salt, pepper and macaroni; mix
well. Pour tomato sauce over top. Cook until
heated through. Yield: 6 servings.

Mrs. Irene Demchak
Kingsley, Pennsylvania

## All-American Irish Stew

*2 lb. mutton, cut in 1-inch cubes*
*6 med. potatoes, peeled, quartered*
*6 sm. carrots, sliced 2-inches thick*
*6 sm. onions, peeled, quartered*
*1 sm. yellow turnip, diced*
*3 sprigs parsley*
*2 tsp. salt*
*¼ tsp. pepper*
*3 tsp. sugar*
*2 tbsp. flour*

Place mutton in large saucepan with enough water to cover. Bring to a boil. Add vegetables, parsley and seasonings. Cover. Simmer for about 2½ hours. Blend flour and ½ cup water in small bowl until smooth. Stir flour mixture into stew. Cook until thick, stirring constantly. Cook for 15 minutes longer, stirring frequently. Yield: 8 servings.

*Mrs. Helen Godwin*
*Greensboro, North Carolina*

## Baked Lamb Stew with Cornmeal Biscuits

*1½ lb. lamb shoulder, cubed*
*1 c. sliced onions*
*1½ c. sliced beets*
*1½ c. cut green beans*
*2 c. diced tomatoes*
*1 c. sliced mushrooms*
*3 c. stock*
*Salt and pepper to taste*
*1½ c. biscuit mix*
*½ c. yellow cornmeal*
*½ c. milk*

Combine lamb and onion in Dutch oven. Cook over low heat until lamb is brown on all sides. Combine next 5 ingredients with seasonings; mix well. Add to lamb. Cover. Bake at 350 degrees for 1 hour. Combine biscuit mix and cornmeal in bowl. Add milk; mix lightly. Turn onto lightly floured surface. Knead gently 10 times. Roll out ½ inch thick. Cut into 2½-inch rounds with floured cutter. Arrange biscuits over stew. Bake at 400 degrees for 15 minutes or until browned. Yield: 6 servings.

*Mrs. Lou Massey*
*Camden, Arkansas*

## Chicken and Vegetable Stew

*1 3½-lb. fryer, disjointed*
*2 tbsp. olive oil*
*2 tbsp. butter*
*1 c. diced onion*
*2 cloves of garlic, minced*
*2 tbsp. chopped parlsey*
*1 c. grated carrots*
*1 lb. cabbage, shredded*
*2 tsp. salt*
*½ tsp. pepper*
*⅔ c. chicken broth*
*½ c. pitted green olives*

Brown chicken in oil and butter in Dutch oven. Remove chicken. Add onion, garlic and parsley to pan drippings. Saute for 10 minutes. Return chicken to Dutch oven. Add carrots, cabbage and seasonings. Cook over low heat for 10 minutes. Add broth and olives. Cook over low heat for 45 minutes longer or until chicken is tender. Yield: 4 servings.

*Mrs. Jay Holliday*
*Plummer, Idaho*

## Savory Chicken Stew

*1 5-lb. chicken*
*3 No. 2 cans tomatoes*
*1 8-oz. can tomato paste*
*2 No. 2 cans okra*
*2 No. 2 cans corn*
*3 lg. onions, diced*
*Salt to taste*
*Crushed red pepper to taste*
*3 lb. potatoes, peeled, chopped*
*½ c. margarine*

Place chicken in large saucepan; add 3 quarts water. Cook until tender. Remove from broth; set both aside. Bone chicken; return to broth. Add next 7 ingredients; mix well. Simmer for 2 hours, stirring frequently. Place potatoes in saucepan; add water to cover. Cook until potatoes are tender. Mash potatoes; do not drain. Stir in margarine. Stir into stew; adding water if needed. Cook for 15 minutes longer, stirring constantly.

*Mrs. E. C. Henry*
*Canton, Mississippi*

# Salads

## Corned Beef Salad Mold

1 env. unflavored gelatin
1½ c. tomato juice
2 tsp. lemon juice
½ tsp. salt
1 12-oz. can corned beef, crumbled
½ c. chopped celery
½ c. chopped cucumber
1 tbsp. chopped onion
1 c. mayonnaise

Soften gelatin in ¼ cup cold water. Add boiling tomato juice; stir until gelatin dissolves. Add lemon juice and salt; mix well. Chill until partially set. Fold in remaining ingredients. Pour into 8½ × 4½ × 2½-inch loaf pan. Chill until firm. Unmold. Serve with deviled eggs. Yield: 8 servings.

Mary Sullivan Debevec
Chisholm, Minnesota

## Hearty Corned Beef Salad

1 7-oz. package macaroni, cooked,
    drained
2 c. canned corned beef
1 c. diced celery
¼ c. diced onion
½ c. tart pickle relish
½ c. mayonnaise
1 tsp. each, prepared mustard, salt

Separate corned beef in large salad bowl. Add next 4 ingredients. Mix well. Combine remaining ingredients in small bowl; mix well. Add to beef mixture; blend thoroughly. Garnish with sliced olives.

Carolyn Rose
Amherst, Ohio

## Mandarin Salad

¼ c. French dressing
1 tsp. soy sauce
2 c. diced cooked veal
1 can bean sprouts, drained
¼ c. chopped onion
½ c. chopped sweet pickle
1 tsp. salt
Dash of pepper
¾ c. mayonnaise

Combine French dressing and soy sauce in bowl; mix well. Add veal to mixture; marinate for ½ hour. Chill. Add remaining ingredients to veal mixture. Mix lightly. Serve on crisp salad greens. Yield: 6-8 servings.

Pauline Faerber
Adrian, Minnesota

## Mexican Salad

1 lb. ground beef
½ c. chopped onion
2 c. kidney beans, drained
½ c. French dressing
1 tbsp. chili powder
4 c. shredded lettuce
½ c. sliced green onions
2 c. sharp Cheddar cheese

Brown ground beef and onion in skillet, stirring until crumbly. Stir in next 3 ingredients with ½ cup water. Simmer for 15 minutes. Add lettuce, green onions and 1½ cups cheese; toss lightly. Sprinkle with remaining cheese; serve with crisp tortillas. Yield: 4-6 servings.

Mrs. John E. Hillhouse
Mathison, Mississippi

## Taco Salad

1 lb. ground beef
½ env. onion soup mix
1 med. head lettuce, torn in bite-sized
    pieces
1 lg. tomato, cut into wedges
1 sm. onion, thinly sliced, separated into
    rings
¼ c. chopped green pepper
½ c. sliced ripe olives
1 4-oz. package sharp natural Cheddar
    cheese, shredded
1 6-oz. package corn chips

Brown ground beef in skillet. Sprinkle soup mix over top. Stir in ¾ cup water; mix well. Simmer for 10 minutes. Combine next 6 ingredients in large bowl; toss well. Place lettuce mixture on individual salad plates. Spoon ground beef mixture on top. Sprinkle corn chips on top. Yield: 4-6 servings.

Mrs. Mary E. Jones
Detroit, Michigan

## Roast Beef Salad

1 c. diced cooked beef
2 hard-boiled eggs, sliced
2 tomatoes, quartered

1 sm. head lettuce
French dressing

Toss first 3 ingredients together in bowl. Place on bed of lettuce on serving plate. Add French dressing to taste. Yield: 6 servings.

*Mrs. Johnnie Mae Proctor*
*Dilley, Texas*

## Chick-Pea Salad

6 oz. Spanish sausage
1 1-lb. 4-oz. can chick-peas, drained
1 sm. onion, chopped
¼ c. sliced sweet gherkins
¼ c. sweet pickle liquid
½ tsp. salt
Dash of pepper
1 tbsp. wine vinegar
Pimento

Place sausage in skillet with water to cover. Bring to a boil. Simmer for 5 minutes. Drain. Slice sausage; fry in skillet until browned. Drain on paper towels. Combine sausage and next 7 ingredients in salad bowl; mix lightly. Garnish with pimento; chill until ready to serve. Yield: 4 servings.

*Eunice Walters*
*Omaha, Nebraska*

## Apple-Potato Salad with Ham

¾ c. each mayonnaise, sour cream
1 4-oz. package blue cheese, crumbled
1 tsp. salt
½ tsp. dillweed
⅛ tsp. pepper
2 tbsp. lemon juice
2 tart apples, chopped
6 c. cubed cooked potatoes
3 c. cooked ham, cut in narrow strips

Combine first 6 ingredients in large bowl; mix well. Sprinkle lemon juice over apples. Add to dressing. Add potatoes and ham; mix well. Chill until serving time. Yield: 6 servings.

*Alice Cummings*
*Albuquerque, New Mexico*

## Ham and Three-Bean Salad

1 lb. cooked ham, cut in bite-sized pieces
1 11-oz. can kidney beans, drained
1 8-oz. can cut green beans, drained
1 8-oz. can cut yellow beans, drained
½ c. chopped green pepper
¼ c. sliced onion
¾ tsp. salt
¾ c. salad oil
½ c. vinegar
¼ tsp. pepper

Combine ham and vegetables in large bowl; mix well. Combine remaining ingredients in small bowl; blend well. Pour over ham mixture. Toss thoroughly. Refrigerate until chilled, stirring occasionally. Yield: 4 servings.

*Mrs. James Stratico*
*Yonkers, New York*

## Luncheon Ham Salad

3 c. cooked rice
1 c. chopped ham
2 tbsp. minced onion
¼ c. each chopped dill pickle, tomato
½ c. oil
¼ c. white vinegar

Combine first 5 ingredients in mixing bowl. Mix oil and vinegar together. Pour over rice mixture; mix well. Refrigerate until serving time. Yield: 6 servings.

*Mrs. Zella Weidenbach*
*Parkston, South Dakota*

## Molded Chef's Salad

2 3-oz. packages lemon or lime gelatin
1 tsp. salt
3 tbsp. vinegar
¾ c. diced ham
½ c. cheese strips
⅓ c. chopped onion
¼ c. each diced green pepper, celery
3 tbsp. pimento

Dissolve gelatin and salt in 2 cups boiling water in bowl. Add 1 cup cold water and vinegar; blend well. Chill until thick. Fold in remaining ingredients. Pour into mold; chill until firm. Unmold onto bed of lettuce on serving plate. Garnish with salad dressing and green pepper rings.

*Clara Blakney*
*Moscow, Kansas*

## Spicy Ham Salad Ring

1 med. onion, minced
1 c. mayonnaise
1½ c. diced cooked ham
½ c. chili sauce
1 tsp. horseradish
2 tsp. prepared mustard
¼ tsp. hot sauce
2 env. unflavored gelatin
2 c. diced cooked potatoes
1 c. diced celery
2 tbsp. finely chopped green pepper
1 tbsp. vinegar
1¼ tsp. salt
⅛ tsp. pepper
Salad greens

Combine 2 tablespoons minced onion, ½ cup mayonnaise and next 5 ingredients in bowl; mix well. Soften 1 envelope gelatin in 1 cup water in saucepan. Cook over low heat until gelatin dissolves. Add to ham mixture; blend well. Turn into 6-cup ring mold. Chill until nearly firm. Combine ½ cup mayonnaise, and remaining ingredients except gelatin in bowl. Soften gelatin in ½ cup water. Cook over low heat until gelatin dissolves. Blend into potato mixture. Spoon potato salad over ham in mold. Chill until firm. Unmold onto serving plate lined with salad greens. Garnish with tomato wedges. Yield: 8 servings.

Mrs. Alice Hansberger
Canton, Illinois

## Lamb Salad

2 c. diced cooked lamb
1 head lettuce, broken into pieces
1 c. sliced celery
2 c. diced cooked potatoes
1 c. chopped fresh dill
¼ c. each French dressing, mayonnaise
⅓ c. chopped stuffed olives
2 tbsp. vinegar
Salt and pepper to taste

Combine first 5 ingredients in bowl; toss lightly. Chill. Combine remaining ingredients. Blend; add to lamb mixture. Toss lightly, but thoroughly. Yield: 6 servings.

Mrs. Delia McClurg
Merino, Colorado

## Meal-In-One Salad

6 slices luncheon meat, slivered
¼ lb. Swiss cheese, slivered
2 hard-boiled eggs, sliced
1 each, cucumber, green pepper, carrot, chopped
2 tomatoes, chopped
1 tsp. minced onion
1 tsp. vinegar
4 tbsp. mayonnaise
3 tbsp. milk

Combine all ingredients in large serving bowl. Mix lightly. Serve with Sharp Cream Dressing. Yield: 6 servings.

Pearle Peterson
Perth Amboy, New Jersey

## Spanish Salad

½ head romaine lettuce
2 slices crisp-cooked bacon, crumbled
2 green onions, sliced
¼ c. chopped celery
1 tbsp. chopped green pepper
⅛ c. sliced cheese
¼ c. each cucumber, salami, sliced into 1-inch strips
1 med. tomato, quartered
½ c. hot bacon drippings
¼ c. hot wine vinegar
1 tsp. garlic salt
¼ tsp. pepper
¼ c. black olives
1 hard-boiled egg, sliced

Tear romaine lettuce into bite-sized pieces in large bowl. Add next 8 ingredients; toss well. Combine next 4 ingredients in bowl; blend well. Pour over salad. Garnish with olives and egg slices. Yield: 4 servings.

Mrs. Elvira Schmidt
Frederic, Wisconsin

## Vienna-Macaroni Salad

1 8-oz. package elbow macaroni, cooked, drained
1 c. each chopped celery, sweet pickles
1 can Vienna sausage, thinly sliced
2 tbsp. grated onion
1 c. mayonnaise
2 tbsp. pickle juice

1 tsp. salt
¼ tsp. pepper

Combine first 5 ingredients in large bowl, reserving several Vienna sausage slices. Mix well. Blend remaining ingredients in small bowl. Stir into macaroni mixture; mixing well. Arrange on salad plate. Top with reserved Vienna sausage. Garnish with deviled eggs.

*Ernestine Gresham*
*Bullard, Texas*

## Winter Salad Bowl

½ sweet onion, finely chopped
2 tomatoes
1 lg. carrot, cubed
2 c. peas, cooked (opt.)
2-3 Jerusalem artichokes, scraped, thinly
    sliced
½ sm. green pepper, thinly sliced
⅔ c. cubed tongue
Low-calorie salad dressing

Toss first 7 ingredients together in large bowl. Refrigerate until crisp. Combine with salad dressing; toss lightly. Serve on bed of lettuce. Yield: 6 servings.

*Berniece M. Cobb*
*Westminster, Colorado*

## California Chicken Salad

1 c. diced cooked chicken
½ c. chopped ripe olives
Juice of 1 lemon
2 tbsp. each mayonnaise, cream
½ c. each diced apples, chopped celery

Combine first 3 ingredients in bowl; mix lightly. Refrigerate until chilled. Combine remaining ingredients in bowl. Add to chicken mixture; toss gently. Serve on lettuce leaves.

*Mrs. Mae Van Citters*
*Sault Ste. Marie, Michigan*

## Chicken Salad in Cheese Shell

½ c. shredded American cheese
½ c. shortening
½ tsp. salt
1½ c. sifted flour
1 9-oz. can pineapple tidbits, drained
1½ c. chopped cooked chicken
1 c. chopped walnuts

½ c. chopped celery
1 c. sour cream
⅔ c. salad dressing

Blend ⅓ cup cheese and shortening in bowl. Stir in salt, flour and 4 to 5 tablespoons water. Roll out on lightly floured surface. Fit into 8-inch pie plate; flute edges. Bake at 450 degrees for 12 minutes. Cool. Combine next 4 ingredients in large bowl. Blend sour cream and salad dressing in small bowl. Stir ⅔ cup sour-cream mxture into chicken mixture. Spoon into pie shell; top with remaining sour-cream mixture. Sprinkle with remaining cheese. Refrigerate until chilled.

*Mrs. Blanche Ivanish*
*Malta, Montana*

## Curried Chicken and Grape Salad

3 c. diced cooked chicken
1½ c. thinly sliced celery
1 c. green seedless grapes
1 tbsp. lemon juice
1¼ tsp. salt
¼ tsp. pepper
1½ tsp. curry powder
6 tbsp. mayonnaise
3 tbsp. roasted slivered almonds

Combine first 8 ingredients in salad bowl; toss lightly. Refrigerate for several hours. Garnish with almonds. Serve on lettuce.

*Lois Pullen*
*Baton Rouge, Louisiana*

## Hawaiian Chicken Salad

1 pineapple, cored
1½ c. cubed cooked chicken
1 c. chopped celery
1 c. green grapes, cut into halves
½ c. chopped walnuts
¾ c. mayonnaise
¾ tsp. salt

Cut pineapple into quarters lengthwise. Remove core; discard. Scoop out fruit; cube. Combine pineapple cubes with remaining ingredients in large bowl; mix well. Spoon into pineapple wedges. Garnish with maraschino cherries.

*Rhuie Hollens*
*Lake Orion, Michigan*

### Cranberry-Turkey Mold

2 tbsp. unflavored gelatin
2 c. turkey broth
1 tsp. grated onion
Salt and pepper to taste
1 c. finely diced celery
2 c. diced turkey
2 pimentos, chopped
1½ c. sugar
4 c. cranberries
1 stick cinnamon
6 cloves
Grated rind of 1 orange
½ c. each finely diced apple, chopped
   nuts

Soften 1 tablespoon gelatin in 2 tablespoons cold water. Add to hot turkey broth in bowl; stir until gelatin dissolves. Add onion and seasonings. Cool until partially congealed. Fold in celery, turkey and pimentos. Pour into fancy mold. Chill until almost firm. Boil sugar and ¾ cup water in saucepan. Add cranberries, spices and orange rind. Cook until cranberry skins pop. Press through fine sieve into bowl. Soften remaining gelatin in 2 tablespoons cold water. Add to hot cranberry mixture, stirring to dissolve. Cool until thick. Add apple and nuts. Pour over gelatin in mold. Chill until firm. Unmold onto lettuce-lined platter. Garnish with mayonnaise. Yield: 6-8 servings.

Mrs.Ethel S. Nash
Ridgefield, Connecticut

### Isley's Salad Supreme

Lettuce
¼ head purple cabbage, shredded
4 or 5 carrots, shredded
2 to 4 slices each turkey, ham, cheese
3 tomato wedges
1 hard-boiled egg, cut into wedges
Olives
1 c. mayonnaise
1 c. catsup
2 c. buttermilk
Salt and pepper to taste
1 tsp. garlic oil

Slice 1 medium head lettuce. Mix with cabbage and carrots in bowl. Spoon into lettuce-lined salad bowl. Add turkey, ham, cheese, tomato and egg wedges. Garnish with olives. Combine remaining ingredients in bowl; mix well. Chill until serving time. Serve over salad. Yield: 6-8 servings.

Mrs. Joy Isley
Phoenix, Arizona

### Crab Louis

1 head lettuce, shredded
½ tsp. salt
1 lb. crab meat
1 cucumber, sliced
4 tomatoes, sliced
3 hard-boiled eggs, sliced
1 c. mayonnaise
3 tbsp. catsup
2 tbsp. chopped sweet pickle
1 tbsp. lemon juice

Arrange lettuce in large shallow salad bowl; sprinkle with salt. Arrange crab meat over lettuce. Place alternate slices of cucumber, tomatoes, and eggs around edge. Combine remaining ingredients; mix well. Spread over crab meat. Chill until serving time. Yield: 6 servings.

Mrs. Viola Gracey
Snyder, Texas

### Calico Clam Rings

1  7-oz. can minced clams
1 c. dry cottage cheese
1 tsp. garlic salt
1 tsp. Worcestershire sauce
1 med. sweet red pepper
1 med. sweet green pepper
Romaine

Drain clams; reserving liquid. Press cottage cheese through sieve into medium bowl. Stir in clams, ¼ cup clam liquid, garlic salt and Worcestershire sauce; mix well. Chill for 1 hour. Cut each pepper into 4 rings; remove seeds. Place 1 red and 1 green ring on each of 4 romaine-lined salad plates. Spoon clam mixture into each ring, dividing evenly.

Mrs. Barbara Elledge
Grand Prairie, Texas

### Lobster in Cucumber

½ sm. onion, finely minced
Juice of 1 lime
2¼ c. mayonnaise
¾ c. chili sauce

Salt and pepper to taste
Cayenne pepper
10 7 to 8-in. cucumbers
1½ lb. lobster, cooked, diced
¾ c. minced celery
3 tbsp. each minced parsley, dill

Mince onion in bowl until almost pureed. Turn into cloth dampened with cold water. Press out all juice into larger bowl. Add lime juice, mayonnaise and chili sauce; mix well. Season with salt, pepper and cayenne pepper. Peel cucumbers. Cut into halves lengthwise. Scoop out pulp to make 20 shallow boats. Mix lobster, celery and 2 cups of mayonnaise mixture. Fill cucumbers with lobster mixture. Sprinkle each with parsley and dill. Chill until serving time. Serve on lettuce with remaining dressing.

Anne C. Chiungos
Dracut, Massachusetts

## Shrimp Salad New Orleans

1 c. cooked rice
1 c. diced cooked shrimp
¾ tsp. salt
1 tbsp. lemon juice
¼ c. slivered green pepper
1 tbsp. minced onion
1 tbsp. chopped olives
¾ c. diced fresh cauliflower
2 tbsp. French dressing
Dash of pepper
⅓ c. mayonnaise

Combine first 8 ingredients in salad bowl; toss well. Combine next 3 ingredients in small bowl; mix well. Spoon dressing over salad; toss lightly. Chill thoroughly. Serve on lettuce.

Mrs. Richard A. Dearing
Christiansburg, Virginia

## Macaroni Salad with Shrimp

3 c. elbow macaroni
Vinegar
1 c. mayonnaise
1 sm. white onion, finely chopped
1 6-oz. can shrimp
1 sm. green pepper, finely chopped
4 stalks celery, coarsely chopped

Cook macaroni according to package directions; cool. Combine a small amount of vinegar with mayonnaise in bowl; mix well. Combine all ingredients in salad bowl; mix well. Chill until serving time. Yield: 6-8 servings.

Brenda Seger
Suffield, Connecticut

## Salmon Salad

2 c. salmon
3 hard-boiled eggs
½ c. diced cheese
3 med. tomatoes, diced
1½ c. macaroni, cooked
¼ c. diced sweet pickles
2 tbsp. sweet pickle juice
½ c. diced celery
Salt to taste
¾ c. mayonnaise

Combine all ingredients in large salad bowl; mix thoroughly. Chill until serving time.

Frances M. Watson
Millbury, Ohio

## Bowl 'Em Over Salad

¼ c. butter
½ c. flour
Salt
1 tsp. caraway seed
2 eggs
1 c. tuna
1 c. diced celery
1 c. chopped lettuce hearts
1 tsp. lemon juice
1 tsp. minced onion
Paprika to taste
Mayonnaise

Combine ½ cup water and butter in saucepan. Bring to a boil. Add flour, dash of salt and caraway seed. Stir vigorously over low heat for about 1 minute or until mixture leaves side of pan and forms ball. Remove from heat. Cool for 10 minutes. Add eggs one at a time, beating until smooth after each addition. Spread batter evenly in bottom of greased 9-inch glass pie plate. Bake in preheated 400-degree oven for 45 to 50 minutes. Puff will form bowl, high on side and flat in center. Remove from pie plate; cool on wire rack. Combine next 7 ingredients in mixing bowl. Add mayonnaise to moisten. Spoon into center of puff just before serving. Yield: 6-8 servings.

Mrs. Abbie Kehl
Waco, Texas

# Photograph Recipes

## Rump Roast of Beef in Blanket

1 4 to 5-lb. boneless rump roast of beef, trimmed
Salt and pepper to taste
1 8-oz. package refrigerator crescent dinner rolls
¼ c. chopped onion
2 tbsp. butter
1 10½-oz. can mushroom gravy
2 tbsp. Burgundy
1 tbsp. chopped parsley

Season roast with salt and pepper. Bake in 325-degree oven for 20 to 25 minutes per pound for rare, 25 to 50 minutes per pound for medium. Separate crescent rolls. Place dough crosswise over top and down sides of roast, overlapping slightly so top of entire roast is covered. Increase oven temperature to 375 degrees. Bake for 10 to 15 minutes longer. Cook onion in butter in saucepan until tender. Stir in remaining ingredients. Cook over low heat, stirring occasionally. Serve with roast.

*Photograph for recipe on page 4*

## Barbecued Meatballs

1½ c. soft bread crumbs
1 lb. ground beef
½ lb. ground pork
1 c. instant dry milk
¼ c. chopped onions
1 egg, slightly beaten
1 tsp. salt
¼ tsp. pepper
Barbecue Sauce

Soak bread crumbs in ½ cup water. Combine with next 7 ingredients in large bowl; mix well. Shape into 12 medium-sized balls. Place in baking dish; cover with Barbecue Sauce. Bake at 350 degrees for 1 hour. Turn once during baking. Add additional water to prevent sticking. Serve with rice. Yield: 6 servings.

Barbecue Sauce
1 sm. onion, chopped
2 tbsp. butter, melted
1 slice lemon
½ tsp. chili powder
1 tbsp. celery seed
2 tbsp. brown sugar
¼ c. vinegar
1 tsp. Worcestershire sauce
1 c. catsup
Dash of Tabasco sauce

Saute onion in skillet in butter. Add remaining ingredients and 1 cup water; mix well. Bring to a boil.

*Photograph for recipe on page 9*

## Vegetable-Stuffed Flank Steak

1 2-lb. flank steak
½ c. each, finely chopped onion, carrot, celery
¼ c. butter
1 c. peeled, chopped apple
2 tbsp. chopped parsley
1 tsp. salt
½ tsp. each, ground sage, marjoram
1 c. cubed bread
2 tsp. cornstarch

Score one side of steak with knife. Saute vegetables in 3 tablespoons butter in Dutch oven for about 5 minutes or until tender. Add apple, parsley and seasonings. Saute for 3 minutes longer. Add cubed bread; mix well. Spread stuffing on unscored side of steak to within 1 inch of edges. Roll as for jelly roll from long end. Tie with string. Brown rolled steak on all sides in remaining butter in Dutch oven. Add 1½ cups water. Bake, covered, in 350-degree oven for 1½ hours or until steak is tender. Place on serving platter; remove string. Blend cornstarch and ¼ cup water. Add to pan drippings. Cook until gravy is thick, stirring constantly.

*Photograph for recipe on page 29*

## Buffet Ham Balls

1⅔ c. milk
¾ c. dry bread crumbs
½ tsp. dry mustard
1 egg, beaten
2 c. ground cooked ham
3 tbsp. butter, melted
2 tbsp. flour
1 c. sour cream
1 tbsp. sugar
1 tsp. dillweed
½ tsp. salt

Combine milk and crumbs in bowl. Let stand until milk is absorbed. Add next 3 ingredients; mix well. Shape into 1½-inch balls. Brown ham balls in butter in heavy skillet. Add ¼ cup water; cover. Cook over low heat for 15 minutes. Remove ham balls to heated platter. Blend flour into 2 tablespoons pan drippings in skillet. Add sour cream and sugar; mix well. Heat through, stirring constantly. Add dill-weed and salt. Pour sour cream sauce over ham balls.

*Photograph for recipe on page 39*

## Turkey Shish Kabobs

*½ c. each pineapple juice, catsup*
*2 tbsp. each wine vinegar, honey*
*½ tbsp. prepared mustard*
*2 tsp. Kitchen Bouquet*
*Dash of Tabasco sauce*
*2 lb. fresh turkey breast, cut into 1½-inch*
  *cubes*
*1 fresh pineapple, cut into 1½-inch cubes*

Combine first 5 ingredients in bowl; mix well. Add turkey; marinate for several hours. Thread turkey and pineapple alternately onto skewers. Broil over hot coals, turning and basting with marinade regularly, until turkey is tender and pineapple is heated through. Yield: 8 servings.

*Photograph for recipe on page 57*

## American Leg of Lamb

*1 leg of lamb*
*Salt and pepper to taste*
*¼ c. butter*
*1 tsp. fines herbes*
*1 clove of garlic, cut in half*

Sprinkle lamb with salt and pepper. Place on rack in shallow roasting pan. Roast at 325 degrees for 30 to 35 minutes per pound or to 175 degrees on meat thermometer. Melt butter in saucepan. Add fines herbes and garlic. Simmer for 1 minute. Brush lamb with butter mixture frequently during last 1½ hours roasting time. Yield: 6-8 servings.

*Photograph for recipe on page 78*

## Spinach-Stuffed Fish Rolls

*1 10-oz. package frozen chopped*
  *spinach, thawed*
*¼ c. grated Parmesan cheese*
*2 tbsp. grated onion*
*¼ tsp. Tabasco sauce*

*4 ¼-lb. fish fillets*
*2 tbsp. butter, melted*
*1 clove of garlic, minced*
*Paprika*

Drain spinach; squeeze dry. Combine first 4 ingredients in bowl. Wash fish; pat dry. Spoon spinach mixture onto each fillet. Roll as for jelly roll from short end. Combine butter and garlic. Brush fish rolls with garlic-butter. Place in shallow baking pan. Sprinkle with paprika. Bake at 350 degrees for 20 minutes or until fish flakes easily. Serve over brown rice. Yield: 4 servings.

*Photograph for recipe on page 87*

## Tomato–Stuffed with Pineapple–Chicken Salad

*8 med. tomatoes*
*3 tbsp. sugar*
*¼ c. flour*
*½ tsp. salt*
*¾ c. pineapple juice*
*2 egg yolks, beaten*
*¼ c. lemon juice*
*⅓ c. instant nonfat dry milk*
*4 c. cubed cooked chicken*
*2 c. pineapple chunks*
*1 c. chopped celery*
*½ c. slivered almonds*
*½ c. chopped green pepper*

Cut tomatoes into quarters to within ½ inch of bottom. Set aside. Combine sugar, flour and salt in saucepan. Add pineapple juice gradually, mixing well. Cook over low heat until mixture thickens, stirring constantly. Stir a small amount of hot mixture into egg yolks; stir egg yolks into hot mixture. Cook for 3 minutes, stirring constantly. Remove from heat. Add lemon juice; mix well. Chill until thick. Combine ⅓ cup ice water with dry milk in bowl; beat on high speed of electric mixer until stiff. Fold into cooked dressing. Combine remaining ingredients in large bowl; mix well. Fold in 1 cup cooked dressing. Spoon into tomatoes. Place on lettuce-lined serving platter. Garnish with strips of pimento and olives. Serve with remaining dressing.

*Photograph for recipe on page 113*

## Cockaleekie Soup

2 broiler-fryer chickens, cut up
3 tsp. salt
¼ tsp. pepper
2 celery tops
2 bay leaves
12 leeks, sliced
1 c. rice

Place chickens in stockpot. Add 2 teaspoons salt, pepper, celery tops, bay leaves and 2 quarts water. Bring to a boil. Cover. Reduce heat. Simmer for 50 minutes. Remove chicken; strain broth. Return broth to stockpot. Add remaining salt, leeks and rice. Bring to a boil. Cover. Simmer for 25 to 30 minutes. Remove chicken from bones; cut into large pieces. Return to soup. Heat to serving temperature. Yield: 6-8 servings.

*Photograph for recipe on page 105*

Photography Credits:

Cover Design: Tal Howel; Florida Department of Citrus; Campbell Soup Company; American Dry Milk Institute; Spanish Green Olive Commission; Pickle Packers International, Inc.,; National Diary Council; National Live Stock and Meat Board; American Lamb Council; Turkey Information Service; Ruth Lundgren, LTD; The McIlhenny Company (Tobasco) and National Broiler Council.

# ABBREVIATIONS USED IN THIS BOOK

| | | | |
|---|---|---|---|
| Cup..................................c. | | Large.............................. lg. | |
| Tablespoon......................tbsp. | | Package..........................pkg. | |
| Teaspoon.........................tsp. | | Square............................. sq. | |
| Pound............................. lb. | | Dozen............................ doz. | |
| Ounce............................ oz. | | Pint............................... pt. | |
| Gallon............................gal. | | Quart..............................qt. | |

## MEASUREMENTS

3 tsp. = 1 tbsp.
2 tbsp. = ⅛ c.
4 tbsp. = ¼ c.
8 tbsp. = ½ c.
16 tbsp. = 1 c.
5 tbsp. + 1 tsp. = ⅓ c.
12 tbsp. = ¾ c.
4 oz. = ½ c.
8 oz. = 1 c.
16 oz. = 1 lb.
1 oz. = 2 tbsp. fat or liquid
2 c. fat = 1 lb.

2 c. = 1 pt.
2 c. sugar = 1 lb.
1 lb. butter = 2 c. or 4 sticks
⅝ c. = ½ c. + 2 tbsp.
⅞ c. = ¾ c. + 2 tbsp.
2 pts. = 1 qt.
1 qt. = 4 c.
A few grains = less than ⅛ tsp.
Pinch = as much as can be taken
        between tip of finger and thumb
Speck = less than ⅛ tsp.

## OVEN TEMPERATURES

| Temperature (°F.) | Term |
|---|---|
| 250-300 | Slow |
| 325 | Moderately slow |
| 350 | Moderate |
| 375 | Moderately quick |
| 400 | Moderately hot |
| 425-450 | Hot |
| 475-500 | Extremely hot |

## CAN SIZE CHART

8 oz. can or jar...........................1 c.
10½ oz. can (picnic can).........................1¼ c.
12 oz. can (vacuum)...............................1½ c.
14-16 oz. or No. 300 can.........................1¾ c.
16-17 oz. can or jar
    or No. 303 can or jar.............................2 c.
1 lb. 4 oz. or 1 pt. 2 fl. oz.
    or No. 2 can or jar..............................2½ c.

1 lb. 13 oz. can or jar
    or No. 2½ can or jar..........................3½ c.
1 qt. 14 fl oz. or 3 lb 3 oz.
    or 46 oz. can....................................5¾ c.
6½ or 7½ lb.
    or No. 10 can..................................12-13 c.

# INDEX

## *Favorite Recipes®*
## *of Home Economics Teachers*
# COOKBOOKS

# Add to
# Your Cookbook Collection
# Select from These ALL-TIME
# Favorites

| BOOK TITLE | ITEM NUMBER |
|---|---|
| *Holiday Season Cookbook* (1981) 160 Pages | 14621 |
| *Breads* (1981) 128 Pages | 14656 |
| *Meats* (1981) 128 Pages | 14648 |
| *Salads * Vegetables* (1979) 200 Pages | 05576 |
| *Desserts—Revised Edition* (1962) 304 Pages | 01422 |
| *Quick and Easy Dishes—Revised Edition* (1968) 256 Pages | 00043 |
| *Dieting To Stay Fit* (1978) 200 Pages | 01449 |
| *Foods From Foreign Nations* (1977) 200 Pages | 01279 |
| *Life-Saver Cookbook* (1976) 200 Pages | 70335 |
| *Canning, Preserving and Freezing* (1975) 200 Pages | 70084 |
| *New Holiday* (1974) 200 Pages | 70343 |
| *Americana Cooking* (1972) 192 Pages | 70351 |

# FOR ORDERING INFORMATION

# Write to:
Favorite Recipes Press
P. O. Box 77
Nashville, Tennessee 37202

## BOOKS OFFERED SUBJECT TO AVAILABILITY.